Teaching technology

Books are to be returned on or before
the last date below.

**7-DAY
LOAN**

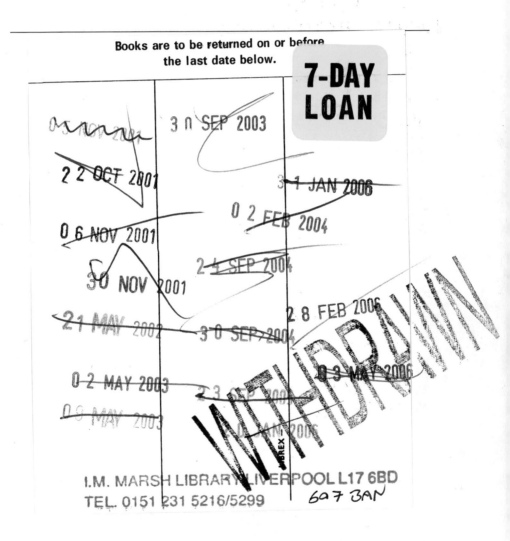

The Open University Postgraduate Certificate of Education

The readers in the PGCE series are:

Thinking Through Primary Practice
Teaching and Learning in the Primary School
Teaching and Learning in the Secondary School
Teaching English
Teaching Mathematics
Teaching Science
Teaching Technology
Teaching Modern Languages
Teaching History
Teaching Music

All of these readers are part of an integrated teaching system; the selection is therefore related to other material available to students and is designed to evoke critical understanding. Opinions expressed are not necessarily those of the course team or of the University.

If you would like to study this course and receive a PGCE prospectus and other information about programmes of professional development in education, please write to the Central Enquiry Service, PO Box 200, The Open University, Walton Hall, Milton Keynes, MK7 6YZ. A copy of *Studying with the Open University* is available from the same address.

Teaching technology

Edited by Frank Banks
at The Open University

London and New York
in association with
The Open University

First published 1994
by Routledge
11 New Fetter Lane, London EC4P 4EE

Simultaneously published in the USA and Canada
by Routledge
29 West 35th Street, New York, NY 10001

Reprinted 1995

Typeset in Garamond by Florencetype Ltd, Stoodleigh, Devon
Printed and bound in Great Britain by
Biddles Ltd, Guildford and King's Lynn

British Library Cataloguing in Publication Data
A catalogue record for this book is available from the British Library

Library of Congress Cataloguing in Publication Data
A catalogue record for this book is available from the Library of Congress

ISBN 0-415-10254-5

Contents

Foreword

The form of teacher education is one of the most debated educational issues of the day. How is the curriculum of teacher education, particularly initial, pre-service education, to be defined? What is the appropriate balance between practical school experience and the academic study to support such practice? What skills and competence can be expected of a newly qualified teacher? How are these skills formulated and assessed and in what ways are they integrated into an ongoing programme of professional development?

These issues have been at the heart of the development and planning of the Open University's programme of initial teacher training and education – the Postgraduate Certificate of Education (PGCE). Each course within the programme uses a combination of technologies, some of which are well tried and tested, while others, on information technology for example, may represent new and innovatory approaches to teaching. All, however, contribute in an integrated way towards fulfilling the aims and purposes of the course and programme.

All of the PGCE cources have readers which bring together a range of articles, extracts from books, and reports that discuss key ideas and issues, including specially commissioned chapters. The readers also provide a resource that can be used to support a range of teaching and learning in other types and structures of course.

This series from Routledge, in supporting the Open University PGCE programme, provides a contemporary view of developments in primary and secondary education and across a range of specialist subject areas. Its primary aim is to provide insights and analysis for those participating in initial education and training. Much of its content, however, will also be relevant to ongoing programmes of personal and institutional professional development. Each book is designed to provide an integral part of that basis of knowledge that we would expect of both new and experienced teachers.

Bob Moon
Professor of Education, The Open University

Introduction

Frank Banks

Technology is a new subject. Many people who have an interest in teaching this new area of the curriculum did not study it at secondary school. For many years children have learnt subjects which have contributed to their technological understanding, such as craft, science, design and aspects of home economics, but nothing specifically called 'technology'. The national curriculum has now made 'design and technology' (called 'technology and design' in Northern Ireland) and information technology compulsory for all pupils up to the age of 16 years. Britain is the first country to do this which, considering technological activity was one of the earliest of human achievements, is very surprising!

What is school technology and why did it take so long for it to arrive? What do pupils learn when they study it? How do teachers teach it? If all pupils are to learn technology what are the implications of this for them, for teachers and for society in general? It is in an attempt to answer these questions that the articles in this reader have been selected and organised.

Defining technology as a school subject has not been easy as technological activity is so all-embracing. During teacher in-service courses in the early 1980s, the organiser would invariably encourage a discussion aiming to define what was technology. It happened so frequently that it became almost a cliché, yet the debate over what pupils should learn in schools, what they should know and be able to do, and how the subject relates to technology outside schools still continues fifteen years later. Part 1 contains chapters which set the context within which the current discussion is conducted. Every subject has a 'curriculum history' and none has been as diverse as that of technology. Real-world problems do not respect traditional subject boundaries and in responding to an 'identified need' a pupil will need a range of skills and a variety of concepts drawn from many curriculum areas. Eggleston's chapter considers the idea that the unifying theme that identifies the new subject is a common way of working. It is suggested that different technological activities, such as building bridges or designing and making a fashion bag, use a common process and that it is this 'process' that should be taught. Others have complained that such a view is too general and leads to a lack of clarity in teaching (see Smithers and Robinson). There are not simply two sides to this controversy. Many teachers who contribute to the technology curriculum come from a variety of specialist areas and their opinions are coloured by their personal history. The debate is not just academic. It is real, live and conducted in schools across the country with varying degrees of passion.

Technological capability as an entitlement to all pupils is enshrined in the national curricula of England and Wales and Northern Ireland. The revised order which was proposed in 1992 continues a move towards designing and making. A practical curriculum for all ensures balance across the whole school experience of the learner, for pupils should not only be taught to 'know and understand' but also to 'create and do'. But if knowledge is to cross subject boundaries and be used in new contexts for solving 'real' problems then we as teachers need to be aware first that pupils find this transference difficult and, second, of the possible teaching strategies we can employ to help them. Parts II and III address learning and teaching technology respectively. There is a need for a synthesis between what we know from educational research about how learners respond to both non-school and in-school practical activities, and how teachers organise technology teaching. The links are explicit. For example, Hennessy and McCormick discuss their research findings on pupils' learning and the implications this has for teachers and Denton's chapter on teaching in groups considers the possible benefits such strategies have for the learner.

Being close to the problem of teaching and learning about technology and concerned about the minutiae of statements of attainment and the programmes of study, it is easy for teachers to lose sight of the wider reasons for a policy of technology education for all and the effect that will have on future generations. What created the political will to make technology a foundation subject? Technology may be viewed by politicians as a preparation for the 'world of work' and, as is the case in any subject, this will indeed be one aim. However, a broader curriculum which addresses the values implicit in technological decision-making, for example exploring the question of 'who wins, who loses' when a new product is developed, is very important. A consideration of purpose wider than vocationalism and of a curriculum equally accessible to all is taken up in the final section. Technological capability is extremely valuable but people's attitude to technology is also important to our society. A more technologically literate society may help the economic well-being of the country but it will also have an impact on forming more widespread views about what are appropriate technical solutions.

The changes in schools regarding the purposes, scope and teaching in this practical area of the curriculum have been rapid and profound. Within the professional life of teachers now in school an acceptance of a skills-based apprentice model has been overturned in favour of an intellectually demanding problem-based model requiring many different sorts of skills and knowledge. Both novice teachers and those with more experience will be updating their own understanding of the subject-specific knowledge necessary for the content of the new national curricula, but that alone will not improve the learning of young people. The diverse team of people who teach technology need to share a sense of purpose, to understand the ways the subject is learnt and to appreciate the implications of a technology curriculum for all. It is with these aims in mind that the articles in this book have been collected.

Part I

The development of technology education

Chapter 1

What is 'technology'?

John Naughton

This is taken from the 'Introduction' of the OU course Living with Technology, *written by John Naughton. It sets the scene for that course by discussing the different definitions which exist about what is technology.*

TECHNOLOGY AS 'THINGS'

Equating technology with machinery (sometimes spoken of as 'hardware') is very common. For example, I remember an advertisement for an expensive hi-fi system. Over a photograph of this magnificent piece of equipment was the caption: 'Isn't Technology Beautiful?'

This definition of technology as machinery clearly has its uses, and not just in advertisements. For example, in Block 1 of *Living with Technology* (Open University 1988), the author talks about the 'technology of the home', and refers to a house as a piece of technology, 'a machine for living in', as a famous architect (Le Corbusier) once put it.

The equation of technology with machinery is clearly valid in the sense that it represents common usage, but it also has severe limitations. Consider, for example, the American moon programme of the 1960s (the Apollo Project, as it was named). The success of the programme was hailed as a 'major feat of modern technology'. This claim makes little sense if technology is defined solely in terms of machinery. For although the programme made use of sophisticated machines, the machinery by itself was not sufficient to account for the achievement of putting men on the moon and returning them safely to earth. Clearly, something more than machinery was involved.

What were the extra ingredients? Well, first of all there was a *goal*. This was set by President John F. Kennedy as getting a man onto the moon by the end of the 1960s. This goal was then broken down into a series of *practical tasks* – building rockets, sending astronauts into orbit, designing and testing lunar vehicles, etc. Second, there were *people*, namely scientists, engineers, technicians and computer experts, who were often very specialised and highly skilled. This implies that a third ingredient was *knowledge* of certain kinds.

As individuals, however, none of these people (and there were more than 40,000 of them at the height of the project) could have achieved the task, no matter how individually skilled they were. So the fourth ingredient was some form of *social organisation* to manage and direct the combined effort of all the people involved; in this case it was the managerial structure of the National Aeronautics and Space Administration (NASA).

How might we combine these ingredients to form a definition of technology that is wider than just machinery?

TECHNOLOGY AS A HUMAN ACTIVITY

Here is a first shot at a definition that meets the above requirements: Technology is the application of *scientific knowledge* to *practical tasks* by *organisations* that involve *people* and *machines*. In fact this is almost good enough, but not quite. A brief critical examination will show why.

Looking at the definition, you will notice that I have cheated a bit. Having originally identified just 'knowledge' as an essential ingredient of technology, I have now specified a *special* kind of knowledge, namely the kind called 'scientific'. This may be a reasonable way of tightening up the definition, but you should not take it on trust. So let me ask the question: 'Is technology necessarily the application of only one type of knowledge – the scientific kind?' But that only begs another question: what is scientific knowledge?

What is scientific knowledge?

Imagine you are listening to a conversation between two 10-year-old children. One of them is trying to pump up his bicycle tyre – with some difficulty, it would seem. (There's probably something wrong with the valve.)

> 'Ouch,' he says, 'this pump is getting hot.'
> 'Pumps always do,' replies his companion, 'I've noticed that.'
> 'But why do they get hot?' asks the first child.
> 'Dunno,' says his friend, 'they just do.'

The second child clearly possesses knowledge of some kind about the behaviour of bicycle pumps under pressure. But is it scientific?

The answer is 'no', and the clue to why it is not scientific is contained in the friend's answer to the boy's question – as we shall see in a moment.

Now imagine that an older sister arrives on the scene and is asked why the pump gets hot. Fresh from a school physics class, she has the answer pat: 'Because when you pump you're really compressing the air in the pump, and the Universal Gas Law says that the temperature of a gas is related to its volume and pressure.'

The answer might not have enlightened the 10-year-olds, but from our point of view it is sufficient to indicate that the older girl possesses *scientific* knowledge about this particular matter. The clue which indicates this is that she explains a particular phenomenon (the heating of a bicycle pump) in terms of a *general*, theoretical 'law'. This states that for any gas, its volume multiplied by the pressure under which it is kept is a quantity which is proportional to its temperature.

This law was proposed a long time ago as an explanation for the behaviour of gases under certain conditions and, having been tested over the years, has been found to be reasonably accurate for low pressures. It is a *scientific* law because (1) it can be tested (e.g. by experiments) and (2) it explains a wide variety of different phenomena in one general abstract statement. It is not, in other words, just a law of bicycle pumps: it applies to motor-driven compressors, refrigerators and similar machinery as well.

I described the gas law as being 'theoretical'. By that I mean that it is expressed in terms of abstract *concepts* (pressure, volume, temperature) rather than in terms of concrete things. And if you were to ask *why* the law holds, a scientist would explain it in terms of another, more fundamental set of theoretical statements called the molecular theory of gases. And this theory, in its turn, can be explained by a still more fundamental one, the atomic theory of matter.

I mention all this not to try to impress you, but simply to highlight two important features of scientific knowledge. The *first* is its tendency to explain everyday events, problems or phenomena in abstract, theoretical terms. The *second* is the tendency, described above, for scientific theories to be linked to (supported by) other theories at deeper levels of abstraction (see Figure 1.1).

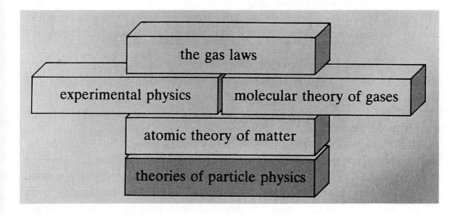

Figure 1.1 Scientific theories depend on other scientific theories

Not all technological knowledge is scientific

Having gone through all this rigmarole let's return to our original question: 'Is technology just the application of scientific knowledge?'

The answer is 'no', because there are many examples of activities that are clearly 'technological' and yet involve types of knowledge *other than* the scientific kind.

For example, the construction of Durham cathedral in the eleventh and twelfth centuries was a great technological achievement. The men who built it had to solve a very difficult practical problem, namely that of constructing a high, wide church with a stone ceiling or 'vault'. The problem arose in the first place because the physical properties of stone mean that it cannot be used over wide spans. The builders of the time had learnt about this deficiency by bitter experience (the collapse of earlier attempts at wide spans), but they did not know *why* stone had this property. They lacked, in other words, the scientific knowledge about the internal structure of materials that is provided by the modern specialism known as materials science.

Not only did the builders of Durham cathedral lack a scientific explanation of their problem, but they were also able to solve it without recourse to science. What they did was to divide the vault into small areas of 'shell' by means of stone ribs, that is, arches which crossed the church both traversely and diagonally, as shown in Figure 1.2. By doing this they simultaneously made the roof stronger and lighter.

However, this brilliant technical solution in turn gave rise to another serious structural problem, because the forces resulting from the weight of the vault could not simply be supported by the piers and walls of the building. This was because these forces exerted an *outward* rather than a downward vertical thrust, thereby threatening to push the walls apart. Nowadays this problem could be routinely analysed using standard techniques of the science of engineering mechanics. The Durham builders knew nothing of this; nevertheless, they solved the problem by supporting the piers of the building using what are called 'flying buttresses' (see Figure 1.2 again).

This is a simple example, but it illustrates the point that technology need not necessarily involve the application of formal *scientific* knowledge. The cathedral builders in fact applied another kind of knowledge, namely the 'craft' knowledge they picked up from experience and passed on through successive generations of master masons.

Talking about medieval cathedrals may seem to you to be going too far back into the past, so let's consider a more modern example. Take a typical technological problem – the design of a motor car. Clearly there is a good deal of scientific knowledge involved: the science of aerodynamics guides the way the shape of the vehicle is designed to reduce wind resistance; the theory of mechanics and fluids helps engineers to design the combustion

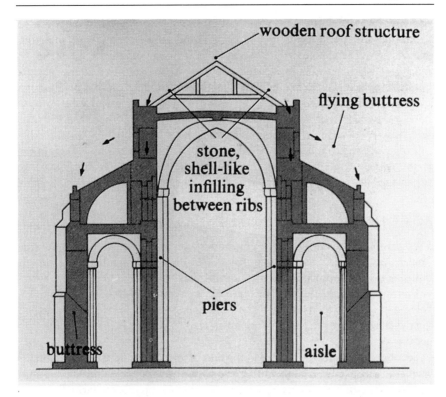

Figure 1.2 The structure of Durham cathedral. Arrows show how thrusts (forces) from the ribs are carried partly by the flying buttresses

chambers in which the fuel is burned; the same scientific theories guide the design of suspension elements such as shock absorbers; the sciences of chemistry and materials guide the selection of particular rubber compounds for the tyres. And so on.

But even though a lot of scientific knowledge goes into the design of a car, the task cannot be accomplished without the other kinds of knowledge too. For example, one of the most important and distinctive features of a car is how it 'feels' to the driver: is it responsive, lively, stable? Or sluggish and heavy? Does it look elegant, or ugly, or functional? Does the driving position 'feel' right to you? There are few *scientific* theories that designers can draw on to help them here: they have to look to other sources of knowledge such as experience, design and craft knowledge and to their own feelings for particular configurations. Science, in other words, though vital to the technologist, is not enough.

Nor is 'knowledge about things', such as craft knowledge, the only thing the technologist needs to supplement science. He or she also needs knowledge about how to make things happen in organisations. Consider our previous example, the US moon programme (the Apollo Project). Here again the same point holds. For although much of the knowledge applied to the design of the machinery necessary to land on the moon *was* scientific, the managerial skills and knowledge necessary to manage the whole gigantic enterprise effectively were definitely not scientific. For there is no 'management science' in the sense that there is, say, a 'science' of physics. So you have to concede that, once again, forms of knowledge other than scientific were also involved in this particular technology.

This leads me to amend my definition in the following way: 'Technology is the application of scientific *and other knowledge* to practical tasks by organisations that involve people and machines.'

SOME IMPLICATIONS OF THE DEFINITION

I would like to make sure that you understand the implications of defining 'technology' in the way I have just done. I want to stand back from the definition for a moment to see its significance.

First of all, I have defined 'technology' as a *practical* activity. Its goal is to solve a problem, to make something happen. In that sense, technology is very different from science, because the goal of science is *understanding* not action.

Second, my definition says that technology involves applying not just scientific knowledge but also other types of knowledge. Although the truth of this is recognised by every practising engineer, it tends to alarm university teachers, because it suggests that technology involves not just the respectable theoretical knowledge that you get from studying science, but also the more uncertain practical knowledge you get from experience, craft, apprenticeship and other sources. But because the knowledge in question is not theoretical it doesn't mean that it isn't important, or that we should somehow deny its existence in the practice of technology.

The third implication of my definition of 'technology' is that technology invariably involves people and organisations as well as machines. That means that it also *involves ways of doing things*. The whole thing is always a complex interaction between people and social structures on the one hand, and machines on the other. New technology, in this sense, does not just involve new machines: it also involves new ways of working, and perhaps new types of organisation too.

REFERENCE

Open University (1988) *T102 Living with Technology*, Milton Keynes, The Open University.

Chapter 2

Technological capability

Paul Black and Geoffrey Harrison

In this extract from their pamphlet, Black and Harrison make an attempt to disentangle the purposes of technology and science.

INTRODUCTION

If we want to know how we should educate children in and through technology, we must first answer two questions:

- What is technology?
- For what purposes should it play a part in children's education?

This chapter attempts to answer these questions. The argument is developed as follows:

- Section 1 attempts to define the essence of technology.
- Section 2 looks at human capability in more general terms.
- Section 3 sums up the argument with the concept of Task-Action-Capability.
- Section 4 gives examples of situations in which such capability can develop.

1 THE ESSENCE OF TECHNOLOGY

Technology is the practical method which has enabled us to raise ourselves above the animals and to create not only our habitats, our food supply, our comfort and our means of health, travel and communication, but also our arts – painting, sculpture, music and literature. These are the results of human capability for action. They do not come about by mere academic study, wishful thinking or speculation. Technology has always been called upon when practical solutions to problems have been called for. Technology is thus an essential part of human culture because it is concerned with the achievement of a wide range of human purposes.

In the mid-1960s, those wanting technology to play an important part in education asked, 'What is technology?' The question was answered in the following way. 'Technology is a disciplined process using resources of materials, energy and natural phenomena to achieve human purposes.' This definition led to three complementary sets of educational aims:

1 to give children an *awareness* of technology and its implications as a resource for the achievement of human purpose, and of its dependence on human involvement in judgmental issues;
2 to develop in children, through personal experience, the *practical capability* to engage in technological activities, and
3 to help children acquire the resources of knowledge and intellectual and physical skills which need to be called upon when carrying out technological activities.

However, the above definition and aims have not been totally accepted or understood. Some teachers have concentrated their effort on practical capability, to the neglect of other aspects. Others have emphasised the resources and given little attention to their use. Emphasis on its many harmful effects has called in question the value-free promotion of technology – thus exposing problems about aim 1. Such difficulties suggest that the definition and the aims need to be re-examined.

So, what are the questions which *should* be asked?

How do we describe, and educate our children for, those human activities which bring about change, enhance the environment, create wealth, produce food and entertainment, and generally get things done? What is the nature of capability in these activities, how can it be fostered and what kind of back-up knowledge and experience is needed? How can future citizens be better equipped to foresee consequences and make choices?

2 HUMAN CAPABILITY

First, let us consider a range of such activities which, although diverse, do perhaps have a common pattern. Then let us examine the implications for education and its opportunities and responsibilities for fostering such capability in young people.

Human capability lies at the heart of such diverse activities as:

- creating a self-propelled flying machine
- composing a symphony
- writing and directing a television show
- organising an office business system
- managing a mixed arable and livestock farm
- creating a three-dimensional mural for a public building.

The activities need not be on a grand scale. Capability is also called for in:

- designing and building a garden shed
- writing and producing a sketch in a school revue
- setting up a system of domestic accounts
- maintaining a car or bicycle
- putting up shelves
- carving a piece of sculpture
- hanging wallpaper.

Large or small, these activities call for a variety of competencies which the capable person knits together in order to achieve success. Maintaining a motor car requires competence in mechanical and electrical fault-finding, in correct and skilful use of tools, in treatment and preservation of materials susceptible to corrosion, in manipulating heavy equipment with safety.

Similarly, setting lyrics to music calls for imagination and intuitive flair. It also calls for perception of meaning in words and in music and an ability to match one to the other. In addition to these imaginative and creative processes, the composer needs to have at his or her fingertips an understanding of harmony, melody, rhythm and structure.

A similar analysis could be made for all of the examples. They have a common pattern. Each requires:

- application of personal driving qualities such as determination, enterprise, resourcefulness;
- personal innovative powers of imagination, intuition and invention;
- powers of observation and perception;
- willingness to make decisions based both on logic and on intuition;
- sensitivity to the needs being served, to the possible consequences, benign or harmful, of alternative solutions, to the values being pursued.

However, overlapping all these is the common necessity to possess a sound base of knowledge and both intellectual and physical skill appropriate to the job in hand. The shed builder must know about the treatment and processing of timber, about how to make effective connections between structural members and about principles of strength and weakness, rigidity and stability, weatherproofing and foundations. The composer needs to know the principles of harmony and rhythm and have the skill to perform on musical instruments. The office manager needs to know the principles of accounts and the techniques for management relevant to his or her business. The farmer needs to know about fertilisers, pesticides, basic medical treatment and the technical requirements of machinery, plant, equipment and building.

Thus the common pattern shows that full capability for personal action calls simultaneously for both action-based qualities and the resources of knowledge, skill and experience.

The first without the second may lead to frustrated, hyperactive, but ineffective individuals. The second without the first leads to individuals who are highly knowledgeable and skilled but who may be incapable of producing new solutions to problems.

This interaction between the *processes* of innovative activity and the *resources* being called upon is itself one of the key elements of successful human capability. It is a continuous engagement and negotiation between ideas and facts, guesswork and logic, judgments and concepts, determination and skill.

3 TASK-ACTION-CAPABILITY

If the nature of these personal human attributes which bring about a capability to engage in active tasks is becoming clearer, the second question remains to be answered. How do we educate our children with a view to maximising their individual potential for what might be called 'Task-Action-Capability' (TAC)?

There are three dimensions to TAC which are amenable to educational development. Each might be considered central from particular and different points of view, but, nevertheless, each represents a personal attribute of direct practical value in the real world:

1 *resources* of knowledge, skill and experience which can be drawn upon, consciously or subconsciously, when involved in active tasks;
2 *capability* to perform, to originate, to get things done, to make and stand by decisions;
3 *awareness*, perception and understanding needed for making balanced and effective value judgments.

These three clearly interact. To develop capability and awareness, experience of tackling tasks is essential. Through such tasks we learn how to use and apply resources of knowledge and skill, for the mere possession of such resources does not imply or confer the ability to apply them. The relationship is mutual, for the needs of real tasks can provide a motive for acquiring new knowledge and skills or for consolidating those already learnt.

This mutual interaction between Resources, and Tasks chosen to develop Capability and Awareness is represented in Figure 2.1.

4 TASKS FOR LEARNING

In the particular areas of engineering and design, where the concepts of science and technology play essential roles, the three dimensions of TAC become very obvious. Nevertheless, in order to be able to construct learning systems which will be effective in the overall development of TAC all three dimensions will need to be planned, interwoven and modulated to meet the needs which change with age, ability, interest and motivation. Three brief examples may help to illustrate this point.

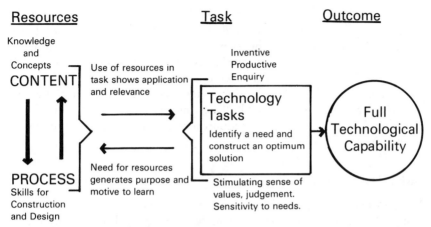

Figure 2.1 A model of technology education

Task 1 Moving loads up a long ramp

Children aged 13 years were given this task to help develop learning about technological concepts of energy (a *resource*).

They were given assorted motors, electricity supplies, gears, pulleys, wire and other raw material. By giving different briefs to different groups, recognising diverse abilities, the children were faced with appropriately challenging opportunities to engage in inventive problem-solving (and so develop their process skills as another *resource*).

Between them they were expected to identify, use and compare three choices in transport technologies: the use of a locomotive with a self-contained power unit; electrical power delivered to a vehicle along wires; and power delivered to a vehicle mechanically by string.

The need to compare these led to the idea of power/weight ratios which in turn led to structural design concepts for the vehicles themselves. At this age the concepts could not be quantified except in general comparative terms. It was the beginning, however, of the development of all three dimensions of TAC within the one project.

Children learned to develop *resources* – problem-solving, skills of observation, experiment, evaluation, designing and decision-making, and concepts of power and energy.

Children learned to develop *practical capability* in using these resources. The varied approach led to varied solutions bringing with them the understanding that there is no single correct solution; one had to be evaluated against another, for which criteria needed to be defined. Children learnt that, from the smallest detail (say, wheel bearings) to the overall concept, decisions have to be taken in order to achieve success.

This exercise also promoted wider discussion of examples from all over the world: the two common forms of electric train in this country; the diesel-electric locomotive, diesel multiple units; the cable cars of San Francisco; trams and trolley buses in continental cities. So children developed an *awareness* that the real world has no single optimum solution. The factors which influenced decisions were seen to be environmental; economic costs, energy resource implications, and relations between these and technological optimisation could all be touched on in order to awaken a concern for *value judgments*, including moral and aesthetic, in technological developments.

Task 2 The hybrid car

This task involved a class of 15-year-olds in an inner city school which, as a group, designed the complete system for a car propelled by a hybrid of petrol and electrical propulsion. The design process involved children in acquiring new *intellectual resources*, including detailed knowledge about high current electronic control circuitry, and about the mechanical, structural and dynamic principles essential in a road vehicle which has to conform to the Road Traffic Acts and win awards in the BP Buildacar competition.

The main purpose of this project was to motivate a group of children to become fully involved in a real task which would not only develop their inventive and design skills and their manufacturing capability but do two further things. It helped those children to become *aware* of the importance of learning some science in order to achieve something useful; it also brought about a vivid realisation of the *value judgments* involved when conservation of energy resources and the potential impact of the internal combustion engine on the environment had to be considered.

Task 3 Building the motorway

Both of the previous examples involved children in designing and making as a process. The tasks that might be set for such processes can be modulated to take account of the maturing minds and skills. They can be appropriately modelled for the youngest ages in the primary schools. However, studies may also be more investigative than design-based and these too can be adapted to all ages.

For instance, a group of primary school children were engaged in a topic that focused on the construction of a nearby motorway. They had to engage in various *processes* of enquiry: they visited the site and talked to construction workers, nearby residents and a farmer whose land was being used; the discussion of the advantages and disadvantages of the change raised the problems of choice and conflicting *values*. They went on to study methods of road construction and examined different soil samples so acquiring new *resources* of knowledge. They also built models of soil-moving machinery using electric motors, simple levers and gears. The theme also involved them in map reading, in studying transport past and present, in drawing and in writing poetry.

The list of possible examples is endless, but they should not be seen as isolated examples. Any successful example illustrates kinds of capability appropriate to particular stages in the development of the individuals involved. An essential condition for success is that the tasks be structured progressively, comprehensively and in close co-ordination between those areas of the curriculum which can contribute to resources of knowledge and skill and those which can help in making the judgments which the exercise of modern technology forces on society.

Indeed, it is only when the three dimensions of TAC have been properly developed that young people become able to take part in decisions, whether these be the complex decisions of any democratic society – such as those concerned with transport, land use and services – or the decisions which face individuals seeking to make a go of running their own homes and gardens.

Chapter 3

What is design and technology education?

John Eggleston

Eggleston takes as his starting point the national curriculum for technology (1990) in England and Wales. Although a revision was proposed in 1992, this remains an appropriate place from which to explore the question of what is design and technology education.

Technology is now a compulsory subject from the age of 5 for all children in state schools in England and Wales up to 16 years. Moreover, there is every sign that many independent schools are following suit. Yet the precise identity of this new subject is still unclear to many teachers – either through total or partial unfamiliarity with it in their professional training or in their experience to date. This chapter attempts to remedy this deficiency for teachers and, hopefully, to enable them to know and to explain the nature of their subject to even more bewildered parents, employers and pupils.

Design and technology is unique in the school curriculum. It is the one subject directly concerned with the individual's capacity to design and make, to solve problems with the use of materials and to understand the significance of technology.

It will be easiest to begin to define design and technology by reference to technology in the national curriculum (DES 1990). Essentially this is defined in the attainment targets. These are:

- *Attainment target 1: identifying needs and opportunities*
  Pupils should be able to identify and state clearly needs and opportunities for design and technological activities through investigation of the contexts of home, school, recreation, community, business and industry.
- *Attainment target 2: generating a design*
  Pupils should be able to generate a design specification, explore ideas to produce a design proposal and develop it into a realistic, appropriate and achievable design.
- *Attainment target 3: planning and making*
  Pupils should be able to make artefacts, systems and environments, preparing and working to a plan and identifying, managing and using appropriate resources, including knowledge and processes.

- *Attainment target 4: evaluating*
  Pupils should be able to develop, communicate and act upon an evaluation
  of the processes, products and effects of their design and technological
  activities and of those of others, including those from other times and
  cultures.

Some teachers have seen this as a 'design and make' process but it is much
more than that as the Final Working Group Report (DES 1989) and the
ensuing Regulations and exemplary material (DES 1990) make clear.

DEFINING DESIGN AND TECHNOLOGY

Although the national curriculum provides a useful working basis, it cannot,
and does not, attempt to be the authoritative and complete definition of
design and technology. Indeed, there is no doubt that the Working Group
would not have accepted this responsibility even if it had been asked to
exercise it. At the simplest level design and technology has two components
– 'design' and 'technology' in close relationship. It consists in using technology to achieve solutions that satisfy sound design criteria and using
design to achieve solutions that satisfy sound technological criteria. As we
have seen, most secondary schools have, for a very long time, offered a range
of technology and design activity in areas such as food, fashion, work with
wood and metal, applied science, business education and much else. The
importance of this relationship and integration is strongly emphasised in the
Working Group Report (DES 1989: sections 1.20, 1.21) which read:

1.20 The activities of design and of technology overlap considerably. As
     we said in the Interim Report, 'most, though not all, design activi-
     ties will generally include technology and most technology activities
     will include design'. However, we believe that the core of knowl-
     edge and skills as encompassed by our programmes of study, taken
     alongside the four attainment targets we detail, cover the significant
     aspects of design.

1.21 That is not to say that the knowledge, skills, values and processes of
     designing cannot be used and developed in other subjects. For
     example, in environmental design pupils will rarely be involved in
     creating a totally new environment, but will need to appraise what
     already exists, explore needs and devise ways of organising and
     achieving change. In pursuing their ideas, they will develop their
     sense of historical and cultural continuity and a recognition that the
     new has to grow out of the old. There are clear opportunities here
     for work in history, but also for other subjects such as geography,
     to build on and develop these ideas.

The close integration of design and technology is emphasised by statutory orders for national curriculum technology. They require that, at each key stage pupils' design and technological capability is to be developed through:

- A broad range of practical activities. In each key stage, pupils should design and make: *artefacts* (objects made by people); *systems* (sets of objects or activities which together perform a task); *environments* (surroundings made, or developed, by people) in response to needs and opportunities identified by them.
- Five broad contexts of work (situations in which design and technological activities take place): home, school, recreation, community, business and industry. Work should progress from familiar to unfamiliar contexts.
- Working with a broad range of materials including textiles, graphic media (such as paint, paper, photographs), construction materials (such as clay, wood, plastic, metal) and food.
- A breadth of knowledge, skills, understanding, attitudes and values required in the attainment targets and programmes of study. In addition, 'pupils should be taught to draw on their knowledge and skills in other subjects, particularly the foundation subjects of science, mathematics and art, to support their designing and making activities'.
- Personal development through activities in design and technology. 'Pupils should be taught to discuss their ideas, plans and progress with each other and should work individually and in groups. . . . They should be taught to take reasonable care at all times for the safety of themselves and others. . . . Activities should also reflect their growing understanding of the needs and beliefs of other people and cultures, now and in the past.'
- Progression of individual capability. 'As pupils progress, they should be given more opportunities to identify their own tasks for activity, and should use their knowledge and skills to make products which are more complex, or satisfy more demanding needs.'

The integration of design and technology is interestingly expressed in a course module at Middlesex University. Headed 'The Technology Dimension' it asserts:

The principal objective of this module is to enable students to develop their knowledge and understanding of the Technology dimension in the past, at the present and in the future and in a variety of cultural contexts. It will seek to challenge and develop students' critical awareness and understanding of the influence of designers/technologists in all sectors. The module has three key components.

Images of Progress – the history of style and fashion. Design alters the way people see artefacts, systems and environments. Capitalism depends on this capacity to innovate and sell products thus creating wealth. This component will explore how style and fashion have been and are being created and how they are exploited.

Engineering our Environment – the history of technology. Engineering, in all its guises, has been responsible for improving every aspect of our lives and will continue to do so in the future. Every innovation brings benefits for some and problems for others. This component will explore the impact and implications of technological innovation.

The Design Revolution – the impact of design on industrial strategy and performance. The impact of new technologies, the blossoming of international competition and global markets, the tension created between the creative function of design, goal orientated marketing and profit taking investment are all aspects which this component will explore. The theoretical analysis of issues such as product life cycle, technological maturity, globalisation, etc. will be set in the contexts of case studies drawn from a range of activities and scales. This will include contact with design professionals from all elements of the design spectrum.

But even though there is abundant evidence of integration, it remains true that few schools have presented the curriculum in a way that fully incorporates it or even identifies the true nature of design and technology. In very many schools technology and design are still seen as lesser areas of activity – taking place in workshops and studios, respectively, with a dominantly practical nature and largely unrelated to the other subjects in the curriculum.

The incidence of technology issues across the curriculum was interestingly displayed in an early Assessment of Performance Unit study undertaken at Trent Polytechnic (APU 1983). It divided technology into three components, value judgments, knowledge and skills and explored where they occurred in the curriculum. The results are indicated in Figure 3.1. The exercise threw up some interesting illumination – for instance the considerable attention being paid by religious education classes to the technology of warfare and its human and social consequences (the study was undertaken during the Falklands War and could almost certainly have been replicated during the Gulf War).

THE NATURE OF TECHNOLOGY

The problems of identity of both technology and design in the curriculum are exacerbated by the long and complex history of both areas in society at large. Technology has played a major role in the development of civilisation – in the long path from primitive, nomadic, minimal livelihood to the opportunities of sophisticated modern society. Yet until comparatively recent times the technologists who created the cathedrals and all other enduring buildings, the roads and highways, the canals, the coaches and other vehicles, the heating and lighting systems and much more, have been largely invisible. Usually only the patrons were identified. Only in the eighteenth and nineteenth centuries did things begin to change spectacularly

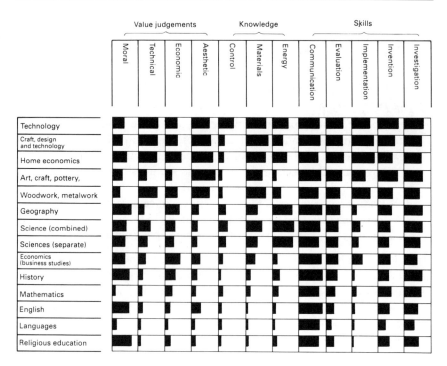

Figure 3.1 The contributions of subjects to technological understanding (*Trent Polytechnic Survey* for APU 1983)

with the achievements of some of the technologists – Wren, Brunel, Arkwright and others. It was only in the nineteenth and twentieth centuries that the great national institutions were founded: The Institution of Mechanical Engineers, The Institution of Chemical Engineers, The Royal Institute of British Architects, The Institute of Chartered Accountants – all these were nineteenth- or twentieth-century inventions. Indeed, it is only in very recent times that accountants and bankers have been recognised as technologists in any regular way. Only in the mid-twentieth century has the accreditation of technology and associated programmes of study been fully formulated for virtually all branches of technology.

Elsewhere technology was being delivered by craftsmen and women or people who, in the twentieth century, have become more generally known as 'technicians'. The immense social significance of the distinction between the terms technologist and technician cannot be overemphasised. The term 'technician' came to cover the full range of people who *did* technology – who made things work and continued to make them work. But their status was inferior; they worked to the orders of their patrons, clients, employers or managers who were not required to have any of the requisite practical technical knowledge or capability. The establishment of the role of professional technologist such as the engineers, architects, town planners and financiers reinforced rather than diminished this distinction. In their training and in their professional work there was no need for them to lay bricks or saw timber. No mechanical engineer needed to be able to machine metal or assemble machinery. Essentially, their role was cerebral rather than manual.

The segregation of technical education followed the segregation of the occupational structure. The most able children in the schools – selected by their achievements in academic subjects (notably science, literature and language) – proceeded to higher education and to follow professional and managerial courses. The less able left school at minimum leaving age and, unqualified, became apprentices or some form of on-the-job trainees, perhaps to achieve technician status. For some, training became available in technical schools and vocational classes. Essentially they were seen as avenues for less able pupils to become occupationally useful.

Technology education in the national curriculum marks an attempt to override such old distinctions and especially to break out of the low status of technical education and to bring technological education from higher education into the schools. It is also an attempt to demonstrate that technology is an appropriate and important subject for the education of all children including the most able. Furthermore, it is making the point that not only technicians but also technologists and indeed all citizens need to be able to understand, develop and handle technology in all its aspects. If it succeeds it may achieve a major goal – to break down the status barriers which have so long impeded the economic development of England and Wales and many other Western countries – the low status of actually making things in a system controlled by those who do not. The spectacular success of Japanese manufacturing industry where, culturally, these divisions do not exist, offers a justification of the need for such a change. But to achieve these goals it is vital that technology in schools does not suffer the same pitfalls and devalue sound practical capability. The danger of turning technology into a subject where realisation is only the making of drawings and models is considerable.

But of course, technology education is not only about occupation. Every citizen needs to be familiar with a wide range of technology in order to have sufficient understanding and capacity to live effectively in modern society: electrical, financial, child-rearing and architectural technology – these and many more technologies determine the quality of life and range of opportunity of every citizen. Individuals must not only be able to involve themselves in technology but also be able to enter into effective dialogue with the professional technologists who every day are making key decisions about their lives and welfare. Just as the technologists need to be able to think and make, so do the non-technologists need to be able to make and think about technology.

THE NATURE OF DESIGN

The nature and status of design is at least as complex as that of technology. Archer (1973) writes:

> Design is that area of human experience, skill and knowledge which is concerned with man's ability to mould his environment, to suit his material and spiritual needs. . . . There is a sufficient body of knowledge for this area called 'design' to be developed to a level which will merit scholarly regard for the future.

At the heart of the matter is the design process. This is the process of problem-solving which begins with a detailed preliminary identification of a problem and a diagnosis of needs that have to be met by a solution, and goes through a series of stages in which various solutions are conceived, explored and evaluated until an optimum answer is found that appears to satisfy the necessary criteria as fully as possible within the limits and opportunities available. The design process at its most complete is one that can be used to describe, to analyse and hopefully to improve every aspect of human activity and especially those human activities that lead to end products and services. Jones (1970) puts it effectively when he says 'the effect of designing is to initiate change in man-made things'. But of fundamental importance in the concept of design is rationality. The design process above all else is one of rational, logical analysis. Jones emphasises this strongly, commenting that the picture of the designer is

> very much that of a human computer, a person who operates only on the information that is fed to him and who follows through a planned sequence of analytical, synthetic and evaluative steps and cycles until he recognises the best of all possible solutions.

Defined in this way, the concept of design was given its most powerful impact in the work of the Bauhaus, an industrial arts school in pre-war Germany. Here, in close association with artists and thinkers such as Gropius, Kandinsky and Klee, there developed a new and powerful movement to explore fundamentally and rigorously the process of design as a human activity.

Until the time of the Bauhaus the form of hand and machine-made objects had normally been achieved by a combination of tradition, expediency and chance. Design was commonly a unilateral activity in which the requirements of one participant tended to predominate and often to monopolise the specifications. Thus, the craftsman alone could impose considerations of skill or availability of material; the engineer alone could impose technological requirements; the client alone could impose considerations of taste or finance. Not infrequently the result of such 'designing' was brilliantly successful – but only occasionally and incompletely was it rational. The

Bauhaus set out to change all this. Students were encouraged to study the process of design in a way that was both total and detailed. The results were of central importance; the new wave of industrial design that began in the inter-war years revolutionised the chaos of design in a multitude of manufactured products. To some extent, many of the most famous industrial products of the mid-twentieth century owe some debt to the influence of the Bauhaus – including the Braun food mixer, the Volkswagen 'Beetle' and the Olivetti typewriter.

In the art colleges of Europe and the United States, the Bauhaus influence was widespread. It did much to develop among students a concern for purity and simplicity of form and an appreciation of properties of materials, of colour and texture that, by comparison with what had gone before, appeared to be austere, even chaste. To a great extent it was responsible for the concept of the foundation course, still almost a mandatory part of most art school courses, in which students undertake fundamental explorations of the nature and the property of materials. But it is easy for any new movement to become obsessional, and the rationality and purity of the design movement was no exception. De Sausmarez (1964) wrote

> basic design is in danger of creating for itself a frighteningly consistent and entirely self-sufficient form, a deadly new academicism of general obstruction for young painters and young designers – a quick route to the slick sophistication of up to the minute graphic design.

Like any system of ideas, the design process was certainly guilty of over-sophistication, rigidity and abuse. A particular problem was that design came to be an exercise for designers. It was an exercise in which, by virtue of their knowledge of the rules, they came to hold power and control, and in which all other participants, often including the client, came to be imprisoned in the designer's ethic. More recently, we have come to realise yet again that there are many participants in the process of design and that not all of them act in a wholly rational way or even accept the 'rationale' of the designer.

In the closing years of the present century there has been a sharp reaction to the design movement, as individuals have sought to reimpose their feeling and individuality on designed products of all kinds led, in the UK, by Prince Charles in his commentary on modern architecture. At a personal level, this is perhaps most strikingly to be seen in the world of leisure where, for example, motor car owners have sought, with much energy, to make their mass-produced cars distinctive from those of other people, and thereby in some way to express their own self-image and lifestyle. It is only necessary to purchase a copy of a popular car magazine or to read the works of Tom Wolfe to see how widespread and effective such a movement is. It is a movement that will sometimes lead individuals to apparently extreme lengths to satisfy its aims. Fashions in leisure equipment such as motor cycles, clothing and music systems may be adopted not so much on technological criteria but on their potential for self-image, style and personal expression – as any parent of adolescents or even young children knows well.

THE DESIGN AND TECHNOLOGICAL PROCESS IN THE SCHOOLS

The preceding sections alert us to a realisation that design and technology is a shared activity between those who make things and those who use them – an activity in which very many people participate, ranging from those who plan and execute manufactured products to those who acquire an object at second- or even third-hand. It is an understanding that is now widely appreciated by all who design, whether they be product managers, artists, architects, landscape specialists or consumers. It is this socially-sensitive concept of technology and design that is at the heart of design and technology education as it is developing in the schools. Below there are reproduced diagrams of the design process and the technology process adopted respectively by the Schools Council Project on Design and Craft Education (Figure 3.2) and Project Technology (Figure 3.3). Both diagrams illustrate clearly the similar detailed and analytical process of enquiry that leads to the achievement of design and technology and the meaningful social context and range of participation within which the process is undertaken.

THE EXPERIENCE OF DESIGN AND TECHNOLOGY EDUCATION

What are the practical consequences of the above activities within the school? Let us consider how the design and technology process might be experienced by a group of students in key stage 4 of a local secondary school. Let us suppose that the school has a project that aims to involve its students more fully in the community in which they live, to give them the experience of responsibility, decision-making and participation in local affairs. Let us assume that the school is serving a large and somewhat underprivileged housing estate in an industrial city. As in many similar situations, the school is attempting to improve the facilities of the neighbourhood as part of the project. An often needed facility is equipment for younger children to play with in their leisure time. The designing of such equipment would almost certainly be seen to be a major responsibility of the design and technology department of the school. How would this be done? The teachers and their students would already have a preliminary knowledge of the problem and an understanding of the human purposes at issue. These would, however, require some further exploration. How large is the relevant child population of the area? What is its age distribution? Is the birth rate

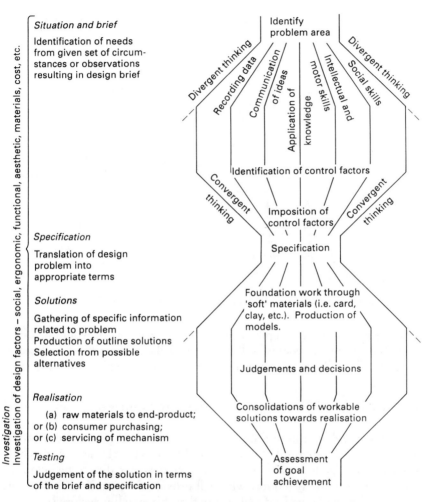

Figure 3.2 Design process (Design and Craft Education Project 1971)

rising, falling or remaining steady? Information of this kind, which could be sought from the Education and Social Services Departments of the local authority, would give some indication of the demand for facilities and the existence of any play facilities in the neighbourhood which, unknown to the school, were in fact being used. Are there special reasons, such as traffic hazard or violence, that would make mothers of young children unwilling to use such facilities even though they did exist? Questions such as these may call for survey work by the students in and around their own homes, for visits to the parents of young children, the police and other civic authorities. In this way, a precise profile of the nature and extent of the need for play facilities may be reached.

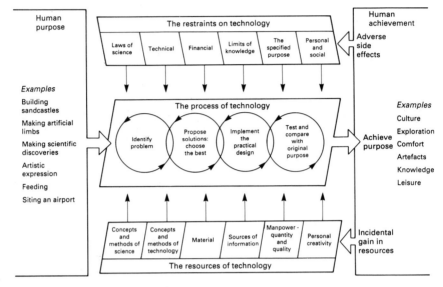

Figure 3.3 The process of technology (Project Technology 1971)

With such a profile compiled, further preliminary work would be called for in which the constraints and resources available could be considered in detail. As with all design processes it is important to explore the experience of the past:

- Were there previous attempts to provide play facilities and, if so, why did they fail?
- Are there problems in their design that, with hindsight, could be remedied or are there inherent difficulties that call for an entirely new approach?
- What of the likely location of the play facilities? Are they to be indoor or outdoor or both? If indoor, who will provide the premises? If outdoor, who will provide the land and ensure that it is suitably enclosed?
- Are the locations available feasible from the point of view of access or do they require parents to bring their children long distances or risk crossing busy main routes?
- Would the location be supervised when in use and, if so, by whom? Would this be undertaken by senior students at the school or would there be regulations that required the presence of at least one trained adult? If the latter, who would be responsible for the recruitment and possible payment of such an adult?
- If supervision was essential could the location be effectively closed off from use when such supervision was not provided?
- Would it be necessary to ensure supporting facilities such as first-aid equipment and toilets?

All these in-depth questions concerning constraints and resources are essential preliminaries to the designing and construction of the play equipment itself. Only if the answers to such questions are satisfactory is there any prospect that the equipment, once provided, can and will be used in the manner envisaged. All of the enquiries are within the scope of co-operating groups of students and teachers. All of them have a relevance far beyond the specific issue at stake – a relevance that is likely to have meaning in the later lives of the students in this or other communities.

Having undertaken this still preliminary work, detailed consideration of the facilities to be provided may be undertaken. Some kinds of facility will already have been readily eliminated such as, for example, soft toys if the location is to be an outdoor one. The next step is to consider precisely what will be provided. Let us assume that the preliminary enquiries have failed to throw up the possibility of an indoor location or adult supervision, but that a sector of a local park is to be made available and surrounded by 'child-proof' fencing by the park authority. It is, however, unlikely to be 'vandal-proof'. In such a situation, the equipment to be constructed will need to be permanent, non-portable, and capable of withstanding weather and possible physical violence as well as normal usage by the young children.

Narrowed down in this way, the design process can take on a sharper focus:

– What sort of equipment satisfying these criteria do young children enjoy? Students may well visit play facilities beyond the community or in schools where they are provided and study children at play, noticing what equipment is popular and the use to which it is put. Detailed measurements may be taken not only of the equipment but also perhaps of the sizes of the children themselves.
– What are the financial resources available? Can the school raise funds to purchase suitable supplies of, say, metal tubing to produce climbing equipment; hardwood, new or second-hand, to provide benches; concrete tubes to make tunnels and obstacles? Possibly the local authority will have funds available for this purpose or a community association may make a donation, or it may even be possible to arrange a sale of work or jumble to raise funds.
– What of the skills available? Does the teacher have competence in the use of concrete? If not, is it possible to attend a course run by the Concrete Development Association, or can assistance be obtained from a local builder or contractor who may even be able to arrange for the loan of a concrete-mixer for a short period?
– Is welding equipment available for the construction of tubular climbing frames? Can the school's circular saw cope with thick sections of hardwood?

- What contribution can the art teachers make concerning the colour combination and the aesthetics generally of the proposed equipment?
- Can the home economics trained teachers advise, from knowledge of the physical development of young children, on the more beneficial kinds of equipment that may be provided?
- And, outside the design and technology department, to what extent can the other departments of the school – social studies, language, mathematics and science – provide resources both of understanding and expertise? Can the project benefit these other departments in turn? Is there perhaps the opportunity for an interesting study by the English students of the way in which language is used during play in the formulation of rules?

Considerations of this kind will have led to a specification of objects of play equipment to be constructed within the design and technology department that take into account as fully as possible the needs and capacities of the users, the resources and competencies of the school and its personnel, the nature and properties of the materials envisaged and, perhaps most importantly, the creative capacity of the participants to devise new solutions that go beyond modifications of existing ones. With such specification, possible solutions may now be explored. Mock-ups of envisaged equipment can be constructed; children of the appropriate age-group can be invited to try them out and their responses recorded; the equipment can be modified and rearranged on site, and the responses compared with those to previous arrangements; the aesthetic consequences of various groupings of equipment can be appraised. This part of the process may occupy an extended period of intense activity as step-by-step modification and improvements to the original solutions are formulated.

Meanwhile, there may be further detailed consideration of the resources of the school for production:

- Do the workshops or studios need modification?
- Is new material or equipment to be ordered and assembled?
- Are production-line arrangements needed, and if so how can they best be planned in order not only to ensure sound production arrangements but also to give students the opportunity of experiencing how such arrangements may be optimised through rational discussion?
- Are there likely to be bottlenecks in certain aspects of the production? If so, how may they be eliminated or at least minimised?
- How may individuals be trained to undertake specific tasks with which they may be unfamiliar? Is a rigid division of labour likely to be the best solution, or will some members of the production group become bored by being involved in more repetitive tasks? If so, does there need to be some system of job rotation?
- How will quality control be maintained? Will there be need for safety testing of the individual components of the swings, climbing frames and

other facilities before they are finally assembled? In all these considerations the underlying need for sound basic craft capability is ever present.

Eventually, when the design is finalised and the production arrangements are
confirmed, the actual manufacture of the equipment can begin. But the
process is by no means over, for not only has the manufacture to be
completed skilfully, but the equipment has also to be installed effectively
and possibly some of the construction work has to take place on the actual
location itself. It is then necessary to ensure that the facilities are satisfactory
in use, to undertake post-delivery checks and maintenance over a period.
Ultimately, the knowledge gained in the post-production period becomes
the raw material for further design and technology processes in the future.
All of this final stage would constitute the evaluation required in attainment
target 4. Taken together the whole process would embrace all four attainment targets at levels of attainment 4–10 and would allow them to be
assessed by the Standard Assessment Tasks and Teacher Assessments.
However, it is important to emphasise that not all aspects of a full design and
technology process have been mentioned in this example. Notably, the
whole question of market research, sales promotion, marketing and account-
ing, items that form essential components of the design process in a normal
industrial company, have not had to be taken account of fully in this non-
commercial example. But in suitable projects these activities too should form
a part of the total process of design and technology education experienced
by students; they too are important components of the industrialised society
in which they will spend their adult lives and in which enterprise awareness
is an essential requirement.

SOME CHARACTERISTICS OF THE DESIGN AND TECHNOLOGY EXPERIENCE

This example of the working out of the design and technology process in a
secondary school shows many of the features of the design process in action.
Readers will be able to draw up their own list of activities that are taking
place. Among others it is important to notice the following:

1 Students have had the opportunity to experience and participate actively
   in an inventive and creative process in which new ideas can be developed
   and old ones modified. In these processes they have also had the experience of responsible decision-making in which not only have their ideas
   been used, but the responsibility for this use and its consequences on the
   lives of others has been unmistakably their own.
2 Students have come to see, in a way often impeded by traditional school
   curricula, the interplay of knowledge and understanding, how the work of
   one 'subject' complements and augments that of another, and how few, if
   any, problems can be solved with a narrow subject orientation. Many

ideas, many resources, and many materials are called for in the solution of almost all human problems.

3 Students have become aware of the social context of human behaviour. This example, like almost all other manifestations of the design and technology process, made it clear that decision-making cannot be undertaken in isolation. The resources and needs of the clients, the parents, the community as a whole, even the wider society, have to be taken into account, and solutions have to satisfy all these participants if they are to be, in any real sense, an adequate response to a problem.

4 The long-standing concerns for skilled performance and the integrity and honesty of workmanship are all honoured in a project of this kind. Skilled work is essential if the equipment constructed is to serve the purpose for which it was intended, and the safety of its users to be ensured. In addition other materials such as concrete, requiring different but still unmistakably skilled handling, may also be introduced. The difference from many previous craft activities is that here skill is being used in a meaningful rather than an artificial context: its acquisition and its employment can be justified to even the most cynical parent or the least sympathetic teacher.

5 Above all, the design and technology process provides a tool of enquiry which, once experienced, will probably have a wide general applicability in the adult life likely to be experienced by the students; it is a process that will link rather than isolate them from the economic and social aspects of adult community in which they live.

In reviewing the consequences of the design and technology process in school we have returned once again to its social justifications, especially those that concern the key decision-making elements and the social integration to which it leads.

CONCLUSION

The experience of design and technology education that has been described in this chapter is nothing less than a preparation for an active participative role in modern society, and it is argued that this constitutes the most sufficient justification for the new subject's identity of design education. Hudson (1966) has noted that 'Our education should create an environment where an individual can discover something of himself, his aptitudes, the relevance of his ideas and of other people's ideas.' The task of subsequent chapters will be to identify more fully the practice of this essential preparation for adult life offered by Design and Technology education.

REFERENCES

Archer, L.B. (1973) 'The need for design education', Paper presented to DES conference N805, Horncastle (mimeo), London, Royal College of Art.

APU (Assessment of Performance Unit) (1983) *Design and Technology Performance (Trent Polytechnic Survey)*, London, DES.

DES (Department of Education and Science) (1989) *Design and Technology for Ages 5–16* (Final Report of the Working Group on Design and Technology), London, HMSO.

DES (Department of Education and Science) (1990) *Technology in the National Curriculum*, London, HMSO.

De Sausmarez, M. (1964) *Basic Design: The Dynamics of Visual Form*, London, Studio Vista.

Design and Craft Education Project (1971) *Design for Today*, London, Edward Arnold.

Hudson, T. (1966) 'Creativity and anti-art', in *Design Education*, Hornsey, Hornsey College of Art.

Jones, J.C. (1970) *Design Methods and Technology: Seeds of Human Futures*, London, John Wiley.

Project Technology (1971) *Final Report*, London, Schools Council.

Chapter 4

Technology in the national curriculum
Getting it right

Alan Smithers and Pamela Robinson

This is the edited version of a much longer paper which severely criticised the way in which the national curriculum order (DES/WO 1990) was implemented in England and Wales. This evaluation was commissioned by The Engineering Council. It makes a plea for a particular emphasis and content for school technology education.

INTRODUCTION

Technology in the national curriculum is a mess. What has emerged seems to be very different from what was intended. Her Majesty's Inspectors are reporting that the standard of work in secondary schools, where national curriculum technology has been running for five terms, is actually declining (in contrast to the other subject areas where improvements have been noted). It is proving extremely difficult to devise the required standard assessment tasks.

How is it that this important attempt to raise the profile of technology in schools and give making and doing their proper place in education seems to be foundering; and what can be done about it? Many of the difficulties seem to be associated with a progressively generalised and abstract notion of 'technology'.

The problem with technology in the national curriculum can therefore be stated very simply: it lacks identity. The first step towards rescuing it would then seem to be to delimit it as a subject saying what technology is and, just as important, what it is not.

THE NATURE OF TECHNOLOGY

Technology in essence is different from the other subjects of the national curriculum, most of which on Hirst's (1974) useful definition are 'forms of knowledge' – that is, approaches to understanding distinguished by their means of establishing the truth. Science, for example, depends on continually re-checking pictures of the world against external reality; mathematics, on logical deduction from axioms; and history, on sifting evidence from the past. Not all subjects are like this, English literature, art and music illuminate through particular creations. English language is the basic communication tool, and geography is defined by its field of interest.

But technology differs from them all. So in inventing it as a subject there is little to go on. Perhaps the clearest analogy for the technologies in higher education is medicine which Hirst categorises as 'a practical organisation of knowledge' – that is, a class of problems that are informed by and are potentially solvable through the application of 'the forms of knowledge' and 'skills'. In medicine, the class of problems is to do with human health and it draws on subjects such as science and maths, and skills such as being able to listen carefully. Technology as a practical organisation of knowledge is implicit in the definition of an engineer adopted by the Engineering Council (1990: 10):

> An engineer is one who acquires and uses scientific, technical and other pertinent knowledge and skills to create, operate or maintain safe, efficient systems, structures, machines, plant, processes or devices of practical and economic value.

Categorising technology as a practical organisation of knowledge is helpful in at least two ways. First, it raises the question of what is the class of problems to be addressed and, second, what is the appropriate balance between practical problem-solving and developing knowledge and skills?

The first exposes a crucial weakness in technology as it has emerged. It is not delimited so we do not know what counts as technology. Defined on problem-solving alone, most activities become technology – writing this report, conducting a scientific experiment, finding one's way to a railway station. What is needed is some statement of technology's domain. Because it has widespread application does not mean that it has to be left as a cross-curricular theme. Like the English language its products may appear everywhere, but it should be possible to organise it as a meaningful and recognisable subject.

CONTENT

The main reason why technology in schools seems so elusive is that it embodies the aspirations of a number of different interest groups which have been kept together only by pitching its objectives and content at such a high level of generality that it can include almost anything. If it is to be given shape and substance as a subject then agreement will have to be reached at the much more difficult level of detail.

But there is one other source of confusion that we have not so far explored and that is the tendency, on occasions, to use the term 'technology' synonymously with 'vocational education'. The National Institute of Economic and

Social Research in a series of papers (Prais and Beadle 1991) has made a powerful case for the closer integration of education and employment opportunities such as occurs in a number of European countries, notably Germany and The Netherlands. This not only brings benefits in terms of productivity, earning power, workmanship and service, but individuals reach much higher levels of attainment in general education, for example, in maths. It is clearly important that Britain should seek to improve its vocational education but this will involve the whole of the upper secondary school curriculum of which technology is only part. The industrial context of technology is important but it only adds to the confusion if 'technology' and 'vocational education' are used interchangeably.

Given the diverse array of interests and the wide variety of ways in which the term 'technology' is being used, what can be done to arrive at an acceptable content? Perhaps a first step would be to seek some agreement on what technology is not. We would suggest that two important areas of educational experience which overlap with technology but differ from it could usefully be treated separately: basic life skills and vocational education.

An important purpose of schooling is to give children practical skills. Among these there are a number which are affected by technology though not necessarily part of it, for example, being able to cook, use a computer and wordprocessor, and fill in forms. These are all important and they should be on the timetable, but to treat them as technology runs the risk of their not being valued in their own right but becoming intellectualised and part of some grand theory. It would be better if they had their own slot. Then much of the difficulty currently being experienced in trying to weave home economics, information technology and business studies into technology would disappear.

If we distinguish 'technology' from 'basic life skills' and 'vocational education', then of what is it to consist? Applying Hirst's categorisation of 'a practical organisation of knowledge' would suggest that we need to settle on the class of problems which it is to address and the associated knowledge and skills. It is probably not possible to define these by drawing a circle and saying everything within it is to be regarded as technology and everything outside is not. But we can attempt to identify 'a centre of gravity', as it were, and say that those things close to it are at the heart of technology and everything is connected but at varying degrees of remoteness.

We would suggest that technology as a school subject should centre on technology as it is commonly understood and is represented in higher education and employment. This would, in essence, be to return to the view of technology first offered to the Working Group in its terms of reference:

> that area of the curriculum in which pupils, design and make useful
> objects or systems, thus developing their ability to solve practical prob-

lems . . . drawing on knowledge and skills from a range of subject areas, but always involving science or mathematics.

(DES 1988: 86–7)

The question is, then, can 'technology' conceived in this way be turned into a subject which adds to the lives of people who want to leave school at age 16 or 18, or who want to continue in education but studying something else, just as much as those wanting to pursue technology further. That is, can technology be created as a subject with a number of different stopping off points which provides a general education as well as specific mastery?

We believe it could, but it would be for those with the necessary expertise to settle the details. Again an analogy with English is helpful since it directs attention to both language and literature. The 'language' of technology is essentially the knowledge areas (including materials, electronics, instrumentation, fluids, structures) and skills (including control, measurement, assembly, construction, project management) applied to a particular class of practical problems, improving or inventing products or systems.

But we should not forget the 'literature', the art of creating. Here, however, as in English, the expectation should *not* be that everyone will invent new and marvellous things, as it were writing like Dickens, Shakespeare or even Alan Ayckbourn. The important point is that everyone should have quality experience in making and designing, the equivalent of composing in prose and verse. An important part of that experience would be to study the creations of others. Among younger pupils, this could involve, for example, the study of toys:

> The pupils brought in from home a range of moving toys some of which were from the 1940s and 1950s and others which were more contemporary. They investigated the movements, linkages, materials of the toys and the energy sources that made them move. The pupils researched some of the history behind the developments of material and toy design and then designed and made a range of moving toys from jumping jacks, push-along animal toys using cams and followers, to other more complex moving toys using syringes for simple pneumatic and hydraulic mechanisms.

(School Inspector, Essex)

In secondary schools, machines such as the Kenwood Food Mixer could be considered. This represents an example of good engineering which held the market lead for a very long time. It is particularly interesting because of the orbital track of the mixing implement, the arrangements of the gear train to take a blender at the top of the machine and further attachments on the front, and the elegance of a design suitable for mass production. The mixer makes use of a number of different materials in the construction, and in consequence the various parts are manufactured by different techniques.

Other examples could be the electric hover mower, personal stereo and fork-lift truck.

Technology on this basis would be a practical organisation of knowledge and skills. It would be a subject capable of bringing a better balance to English education which has been criticised as overly academic and theoretical (Smithers and Robinson 1991). It must be emphasised though – since the criticism is sometimes levelled – that the aim is *not* to go back to woodwork and metalwork for the less brainy but to give all children a firm grounding in skills relevant to today's and tomorrow's world, experience in making and designing, and insight into how things work.

NATIONAL CURRICULUM FRAMEWORK

If this approach were adopted what would it look like in terms of the national curriculum framework of attainment targets, programmes of study and assessment arrangements?

Currently there are four attainment targets in design and technology (other than information technology which we argue belongs elsewhere) – identifying needs and opportunities, generating a design proposal, planning and making, and evaluating. Although essentially part of the same process they have become separated and been given equal weight. We believe this does not give sufficient priority to 'planning and making' which, since technology is a practical subject, should be pre-eminent. Its importance could be signalled by giving differential weights to the existing attainment targets, or reducing them to two, perhaps 'planning and making' and 'the process of making' or just one, as is being considered in Northern Ireland. Here the Ministerial Group is consulting on one attainment target, significantly 'technology and design', which would be concerned with capability developed 'principally through the design and manufacture of products' (Northern Ireland Ministerial Working Group 1991).

The programmes of study would need to be worked out in detail with a clear indication of what progression up through the four key stages would mean in practice. They should also show how the subject would be a stepping stone to A levels and vocational qualifications, and beyond them higher education and employment. As we have argued, the fundamental weakness of technology in the national curriculum is that it has not faced up to these issues of detail. We believe the approach we have outlined based on the 'class of practical problems' and associated knowledge and skills could be the organising principle needed for deciding what should be included.

RECOMMENDATIONS

The logic of the analysis offers a number of pointers as to what might be done to rescue school technology:

- it should be clearly established as a practical/technical subject concerned with the design and manufacture of products and systems;
- its content should be specified as a practical organisation of knowledge and skills;
- it should be distinguished from the overlapping but different areas of basic life skills and vocational education;
- there should be clear progression in content with the subject acting as a stepping stone to higher education and employment;
- curriculum materials should be devised to reflect this sharper focus;
- the tests and examinations should embody the objectives and content as more precisely specified;
- the success of technology as re-defined will depend on a supply of appropriately qualified teachers supported by good in-service education;
- the subject will also require appropriate capitation, resources, workshop facilities and ancillary staff.

Britain is the first country to make technology part of the compulsory curriculum for all pupils aged 5 to 16. It is a pioneering venture and not everything can be expected to go smoothly. But it does seem badly off course at the moment, and corrective action is urgently required. Getting technology right in schools would bring benefits to the education of individuals, the economy, and ultimately the quality of life of us all.

REFERENCES

DES (1988) *National Curriculum and Technology Working Group: Interim Report*, London, DES.

DES/WO (1990) *Technology in the National Curriculum*, London: HMSO.

Engineering Council (1990) *Policy Statement: Standards and Routes to recognition*, 2nd edn, London, The Engineering Council.

Hirst, P. (1974) *Knowledge and the Curriculum: A Collection of Philosophical Papers*, London, Routledge & Kegan Paul.

Northern Ireland Ministerial Working Group (1991) *Proposals for Technology and Design in the Northern Ireland Curriculum*, Belfast, NICC.

Prais, S.J. and Beadle, E. (1991) *Pre-vocational Schooling in Europe Today*, London, National Institute of Economic and Social Research.

Smithers, A. and Robinson, P. (1991) *Beyond Compulsory Schooling*, London: Council for Industry and Higher Education.

Chapter 5

The coming of technology education in England and Wales ·

Robert McCormick

In this chapter, the changing view of technology and technology education implicit in the previous articles is placed within a historical context. The way the subject was re-defined as it was being 'created by committee' is explored in detail.

HISTORICAL BACKGROUND[1]

There was life before the national curriculum and, even in what appears to be a completely new area of the curriculum, there are historical antecedents which are important in understanding the current state of technology education. I will explore these antecedents by giving a brief overview of some of the strands that have contributed to the development of technology education, before going on in the next section to examine the more recent developments that led to the national curriculum for technology. The contributing strands include craft, art and design, science, home economics, and science, technology and society (STS). For each I will identify the traditions and some of the views that each contributes to technology education. It is on to these traditions that the national curriculum was grafted, and from which teachers started as they tried to make sense of the curriculum proposals presented through the Order for Technology (DES/WO 1990). The Order itself had a period of development and only some of the thinking during that period found its way into the final document.

Craft

This tradition is not a single one and differs across time; two strands were important in England and Wales. One strand is (trade) craft stemming from the nineteenth- and early twentieth-century manual training, and emphasising exercises to develop skills with tools. Another form of craft developed from Swedish *sloyd*, that in some forms became aligned with art. *Sloyd*, founded to keep village crafts alive in nineteenth-century Sweden, emphasised creativity and was popularized in England through women elementary school teachers. The trade craft tradition has of course developed from wood to metal, from hand tools to machinery, but has been unable to continue to develop as technology did because the basic model of production was flawed, and because there is a limit to what can be done in schools (Medway 1989: 14–15). The craft model of the single worker in control of the whole production process does not reflect the teamwork of industry. The failure of computer controlled lathes to have a meaningful place in schools is an example of the difficulty of representing modern industrial practice. It is not a parallel of the ordinary lathe because it is a mass-production machine, and exercises which get students to programme its operation, or to use CAD/ CAM links, often ignore the industrial context within which such machines are used. Flexible manufacturing systems, which are often responsive to one-off production (based upon a basic 'model'), are only accessible to pupils through three-dimensional models, computer simulation, video and factory visits. To some the answer to limitations of schools is a process approach, through problem-solving and design, in an effort to free the curriculum from a specific content (a specific technology). Current primary school 'design and technology' practice in the UK reflects this approach.

But the difficulties that the craft tradition may have should not blind us to the important contribution it makes to how to teach skill development, use materials and manage individually-based project work. The emphasis of this tradition on finished products does, however, create problems for the development of modelling skills.

Art and design

There are three main inter-related groups (not all of them homogeneous), those from art and design, design education as part of general education, and craft, design and technology (CDT). In the nineteenth century two groups existed within art and design (Thistlewood 1989). One, the Society of Art Masters (SAM), was a hierarchical, subject-centred association of art school (male) principals dedicated to presenting drawing as an academic discipline, emphasising classical draughtsmanship and design allied to industrial arts. The other, the Art Teachers Guild (ATG), contrasted strongly with SAM. It was mainly made up of female classroom teachers, and was egalitarian, individual-centred (child-centred) in its interests. Its ethos was to support those who considered the creativity, expression, invention and imagination of childhood as important. This, Thistlewood argues, was a by-product of the English Arts and Crafts Movement, with its concern for the spiritual value of craftwork. Industrial art to them suppressed free creativity. The successors to these two organizations combined in 1984 to form the National Society for Education in Art and Design (NSEAD), in a synthesis of their two approaches. NSEAD commented upon the national curriculum for design and technology schools (NSEAD 1990; Steers 1990).

Those seeing design education as part of general education focused initially around the Royal College of Art and Bruce Archer, who was responsible for an enquiry into design in schools (RCA 1989). He viewed design as a third area in education, distinct from, but equal to the sciences and humanities (Archer 1979). It concerns doing and making and includes such things as technology and fine, performing and useful arts; he represented technology as lying somewhere between science and design. As an interest group they are represented by the Design Council and, along with other groups, are represented on the Design Education Forum. This Forum collectively impressed upon the working group which drew up the England and Wales national curriculum on technology in schools, the importance of seeing design, not technology, as the overarching curriculum activity (Steers 1990: 11–12). Such views have contributed to an understanding of design and, in particular, they offer a sophisticated view of design based on what professional practitioners do.

CDT developed under a number of influences, including that of design education (Penfold 1988: Ch. 4), and the view of design which CDT has developed, epitomised by John Eggleston's work (Eggleston 1976), has not surprisingly been criticised by the art and design groups. These criticisms include: a mechanical view of design, expressed through various linear and circular staged models that fail to teach pupils the process, and do not reflect how designers think (Jeffrey 1990); a view of craft that emphasises an outdated woodwork and metalwork view of making, rather than one which develops new ideas and designs (NSEAD 1990: 32); and the problem of modelling I mentioned earlier.

Science

Having started with 'applied' beginnings in the nineteenth century (Layton 1973), science educators in England went through a post-war phase of emphasising 'pure science', and were reluctant to support technology education (McCulloch, Jenkins and Layton 1985: Ch. 6). Now the Association for Science Education (ASE) recognise the importance of technology education, as different from science education, and the role of science teachers in it (ASE 1988; SSCR 1987).

The concern to make science relevant has increased the interest in studying science in meaningful contexts, technology being one of these. Problem-solving therefore becomes important. Science brings to technology education: scientific investigation and experimentation methods including ideas of a 'fair test' (Harrison 1990); a knowledge and conceptual understanding essential to a technologist; the development of new science and technology areas such as biotechnology, that CDT and home economics teachers, for example, are often ill-equipped to handle.

There were efforts to introduce science into technology teaching, through the *Modular Courses in Technology* (Schools Council 1981). Students could study a number of modules on electronics, mechanisms, structures, materials and pneumatics, before completing a more substantial project for GCE O level (i.e. covering what is now key stage 4).

Home economics

This is not a well documented area, but it had developments parallel to that of craft: from needlework and cooking, which emphasised skills by following patterns and recipes, to textiles and food. Textiles work had developed design approaches, while food included investigations along with a good deal of science.

Science technology and society (STS)

This tradition stems directly from the desire to educate for citizenship and to control science and technology. It is one response by those in science education who want to teach science in context, to avoid the irrelevance of 'pure science' and, by implication, to replace 'science for all' in schools by STS (Za'rour 1987: 731). The STS tradition has been responsible for developing value issues in relation to technology and, in particular, has developed teaching material and methods for discussing controversial issues, roleplay activities and games (Solomon 1988: 272–3), methods more familiar to social studies teachers. This tradition also brings in a different kind of problem-solving from that of design and make, one which relates to decision-making about, for example, where to locate a power station.

THE CREATION OF THE NATIONAL CURRICULUM FOR TECHNOLOGY[2]

The first Statutory Order for technology in the national curriculum for England and Wales (DES/WO 1990) defined the attainment targets (against which children would be assessed at ten levels of achievement) and the programmes of study (what they should be taught). As the first legal document to be issued it contained none of the rationale for the curriculum, nor any of the thinking that led up to it. This thinking, encapsulated in earlier reports, is another important antecedent, only some of which reaches the teachers who have to implement it. All teachers get by right is the Order, and few ever saw the earlier documents. In this section, therefore, I will review some of the thinking that appeared through the earlier reports.

The initial moves

The Education Reform Act introduced the title of the foundation subject 'technology' into the school curriculum, although previously HMI had defined a technological area of learning and experience (DES 1985).[3] As with all the subjects, a working group was set up to define the profile components and the programmes of study for the subject. The title of the working group was for 'design and technology' and its terms of reference issued in April 1988 included, along with similar terms given to other subject groups, 'design in all its aspects' (i.e. those not within technology) and 'information technology'. Initially primary level technology had been given to the Science Working Group, which had included it in its interim report, but the Design and Technology Working Group took it on.

The combination of design and technology as a single title was used by the Working Group to indicate a unified activity, indeed they use the term 'design and technological activity'. Medway (1992: 68) puts the change from 'technology' to 'design and technology' down to pressure from the 'design lobby'. The Working Group recognised that there was an overlap: 'most, but not all, design activities will generally include technology and most technology activities will include design' (DES/WO 1988: para 1.5). However, this underplays the complexity of the relationship. There are activities in both design and technology (separately) that do not overlap, and the relationship varies according to what is being designed. Thus in a product cycle (including market research, design, supply of parts, etc., production) design as an activity is not the whole of the cycle, though where it begins and ends is not easily defined. Technology as an activity includes the 'design' phase, and also the supply and production phases. When an individual potter produces a product the phases may not be clear and modelling, prototyping and making run into each other. Here design and technology activity cannot easily be disaggregated. When an architect designs a building he or she will work only on a model (2-D or 3-D) and design is a distinct phase, but technology activity will be part of both the design and the construction of the building. The simplest way to resolve this is actually to use the word 'technology' (and technological activity) and assume that design is part of it. (See McCormick (1993) for a fuller discussion of the relationship.) There may be other aspects of design that are excluded, but they may be covered in other areas of the curriculum. But of course, at the time the Working Group was not necessarily defining *an* area of the curriculum. The final Order for Technology did not resolve the problem and there remains a puzzle as to whether there are *design* activities and *technological* activities, or only *design and technological* activities.

The place of information technology (IT) was also a difficulty. The Working Group in effect proposed a subject of 'design and technology', but that would have been in contravention of the Education Reform Act that used the title technology, and so eventually two profile components were created: *design and technology* and *information technology*. While this may appear a cosmetic change, it is one which caused problems for IT staff who in some schools might on the one hand be part of a technology team, but on the other see their responsibility for IT across the curriculum and hence outside the team. It certainly severed the connection between design and technology on the one hand and computers and information technology as *a technology* on the other. This effectively destroyed the subject technology.

The interim report

The Design and Technology Working Group produced an interim report late in 1988 (DES/WO 1988), which then went out for consultation before a final report was produced in 1989. The interim report contained some interestingly different statements from those which eventually formed the final Proposals and the Order itself. The first chapter was a reflective discussion of the nature of design and technology, and education based on such activities. At this stage there was no implication that design and technology would be a separate subject, indeed the requirement to understand the effects of technological change implied strong cross-curricular links (Barnett 1992: 89). However, perhaps the most significant aspect was the definition of capability:

- pupils are able to *use* existing artefacts and systems effectively;
- pupils are able to make *critical appraisals* of personal, social, economic and environmental implications of artefacts and systems;
- pupils are able to *improve*, and extend the uses of, existing artefacts and systems;
- pupils are able to *design, make* and *appraise* new artefacts and systems;
- pupils are able to *diagnose* and *rectify faults* in artefacts and systems.
                                        (DES/WO 1988: 17–18, my emphasis)

This is a much wider range of aspects of capability than eventually found its way into the attainment targets, which really only focused upon the fourth of the ones above. In other words the interim report saw design as only one of *several* aspects of capability, and a more true reflection of technology in the world outside school, where design, important though it is, is undertaken by only a fraction of those working in technology.[4]

The final report

The Design and Technology Working Group produced their final report in the form of proposals to the Secretary of State for design and technology for ages 5–16 (DES/WO 1989). These proposals took the form of an introduction spelling out some of the rationale for the subject, and complete

attainment targets (and associated statements of attainment) and programmes of study. The rationale was much less specific about the nature of
capability than the interim report, presumably because the attainment
targets (ATs) specified what capability meant. However, it was discussed in
one paragraph, where yet another list of attributes, different from those of
the interim report, were given:

- to intervene . . . to bring about and control change;
- to speculate on possibilities for modified and new artefacts . . .;
- to model what is required;
- to plan . . . ways of proceeding and organize . . . resources;
- to achieve outcomes . . . which have been well appraised;
- to understand the significance of design and technology to the economy and to the quality of life.

(DES/WO 1989: para 1.5)

Four ATs were proposed for the design and technology profile component
and one for the information technology profile component. The design and
technology ATs corresponded to identifying needs and opportunities for
design and technological activities, generating a design proposal, planning
and making the design, and appraisal of it (and the designs of others). For
each of these ATs ten levels of statements of attainment (SoA) were defined.
In addition the programmes of study (PoS) were defined for each of the key
stages under sixteen headings and at ten levels! The headings included:
materials, business and economics, aesthetics, structures, exploring and
investigating, modelling and communicating, making, health and safety,
energy, tools and equipment, systems, mechanisms, imaging and generating,
organising and planning, appraising, social and environmental. Not surprisingly there was a universal reaction against the complexity of the PoS during
the consultation period that followed.

Besides the complexity of the proposals, one of the major problems was
the difficulty in interpreting what some of the statements meant. They had
been deliberately kept at a level of generality to try and avoid prescription
but, even with examples, this meant that the various statements were somewhat abstract or vague (AT1, Level 7: to devise an effective research strategy
for investigating a specific context). There was also a confusion of types of
statements in the PoS compared with those in the ATs. The SoA in the latter
were focused upon the process of designing and making, devoid of any
particular content. The statements in the PoS were a combination of the two,
some on process topics such as 'exploring and investigating' and some on
content such as 'mechanisms'.

Finally, the most significant aspect of the proposals, from the point of
view of implementation, was the idea that design and technology would be
taught by teachers from subject areas of art and design, business studies,
CDT, home economics and information technology. This implied bringing

together teachers who had had no real contact in the past and, as there was no national curriculum subject for most of them (apart from art and design), put them under some pressure to co-operate.

The consultation report

The consultation process revealed a concern about the complexity of the structure (PoS), the difficulty in the language and the CDT bias, and the National Curriculum Council (NCC) was given the task of conducting this process and responding to it. Its position was much less independent of government than the Working Group and so it was mindful of both the responses to consultation and government concerns. The latter is evident in the forward to their consultation report, which as Barnett (1992) notes was very much concerned with wealth creation and enterprise, whereas the Working Group had talked about a range of reasons for teaching technology in schools.

The need to reduce complexity and simplify language (because in many cases, especially primary schools, non-specialists were being addressed), resulted in the PoS having only four headings defined at each of the four key stages:

- developing and using systems;
- working with materials;
- developing and communicating ideas;
- satisfying human needs.

In fact these headings only superficially simplified the PoS, because the original statements under each heading had been retained and redistributed among the new headings. Thus 'developing and using systems' contained items from the original 'organizing and planning', 'structures', 'mechanisms' and 'energy'.

The ATs were much the same as before except that the idea of a specification was added to AT2, but as McCormick (1990b: 42) argues this was poorly interpreted in the SoA and not carried through to evaluation in AT4. One of the problems for the NCC was in trying to learn from the thinking developed by the Working Group over the time of its work. Not surprisingly the NCC misunderstood some of the ideas in technology, and 'specifications' was just such an example.

The NCC did, however, respond to the CDT bias and introduced examples that would appeal to home economics teachers. In so doing they set in train a problem that was to be raised in the first years of implementation of the technology national curriculum, whether design-and-make activities could be extended to those including food. Thus examples included the design of a salad. In itself this is rather a ridiculous example of 'technology', although as part of 'design' there may be some rationale. Inasmuch as designing a salad is a model of, say, catering or industrial activity (e.g. supermarket retailing) then it is a good analogy, but taken on its own it simply says *any* activity can be conceived of as a 'design and technology' activity.

Subject by committee

Most subjects are created by a long process of development, perhaps involving universities. Technology, on the other hand, was created by committee. There were of course a variety of interest groups that had a vested interest in the outcome; I have already mentioned the 'design lobby'. The creation of the Design and Technology Working Group was an opportunity to sweep aside all the special interest groups that might have lobbied for their brand of design and technology and, by all accounts, Lady Parkes, who chaired the group, did just that. However, when it came to operationalising the broad ideas on design and technology, which previously had taken up much of the first chapter of the interim report, the final report, as I have already noted, exhibited a CDT bias. In any case, even discounting the influence of pressure groups, the subject created by the committee is very sensitive to the composition of the committee. The listing in the final report (DES/WO 1989: 102) indicates that of this group only one member represented the world of practising technologists (Denis Filer from the Engineering Council), with another from 'business'. The other ten were, in one way or another, associated with education. It would be unfair to cast any aspersions on the work of the Group, which had an unenviable task, but it is not unfair to ask how such a group could come to grips with an area of activity with so few practising technologists in its number. Such groups should perhaps work more like parliamentary select committees, taking evidence in public and publishing it all, then we could see the sum total of expertise available. Whatever the considered view of the Working Group, the NCC then modified the ATs and PoS of the final report and, though we have access to the way they weighed up the evidence, we do not even know who was involved in drawing up the NCC consultation report. The NCC had to assimilate in a short period of time an understanding of the issues that the Working Group spent a year on. The NCC did an admirable job in taking into account responses to the final report, but how could it be expected to represent adequately the breadth and depth of technology in the short period of time it had?

The first Order for Technology

In March of 1990 the first Order was issued (DES/WO 1990) which did not differ substantially from the consultation report. Thus design and technology, as a component of technology, was launched into schools:

- strong on process (encapsulated in the ATs), but weak in content (not defined in the PoS);
- seeing the process in terms of a holistic design-based activity;
- recognising value issues but scattering statements on this over a variety of levels and ATs;
- asking a diverse set of teachers to work together to provide a coherent area of the curriculum.

Although there was *Non-Statutory Guidance* (NCC 1991a) and in-service material to help teachers to implement the curriculum, they were not adequate to cope with the considerable task of getting teachers to take on the issues required. The difficulties were at the level of the staff team that had to implement the new curriculum, and at the level of individual teachers who had to use a rather vague document to plan their work and, more important, assess their pupils. Thus, for example, the Level 2 statement for AT1 was: 'ask questions which help them to identify the needs and opportunities for design and technology activity'. Assessing a pupil on the basis of this statement would prove different in each of the following starting points for an activity based upon the design of play equipment:

1 using existing play equipment identify needs and opportunities for the design of play equipment;
2 using the given beams and plastic drums identify needs and opportunities for the design of play equipment;
3 identify needs and opportunities for the design of play equipment (i.e. start with a 'blank sheet of paper').

Clearly the last of these starting points is the most open-ended and the demands all three make on pupils depends on any stimulus material that is provided. In fact these statements will take on more life through the way the Standard Assessment Tasks (SATs) are defined but, although they have undergone much development, it seems likely that they will reduce in importance.

The difficulties in implementation were revealed in an HMI report (HMI 1992) and in the NCC's own monitoring of the curriculum (NCC 1992). The political debate was also fuelled by a report prepared for the Engineering Council which opened with the statement 'technology is a mess' (Smithers and Robinson 1992; see Chapter 4 in this volume). The culmination of this was a review process which resulted in another round of reports and draft legislation.

The revised Order

As this article is being written, the first proposals for the revised Order are coming out. These proposals (DFE/WO 1992) will follow a process of consultation and drafting similar to that of the first Order. The changes suggested by the review group of HMI and NCC officers have tried to address the problems of implementation noted above, by reducing the number of SoA and PoS statements and clarifying the content (the skills and knowledge) to be taught. This resulted in two ATs, *designing* and *making*. However, each of these contained strands:

designing
- investigating, clarifying and specifying the design task;
- modelling, developing and communicating design ideas.

making
- planning and organising making;
- using a variety of materials, components, tools, equipment and processes to make products safely;
- testing, modifying and evaluating.

On the face of it, it looks as if four ATs have effectively been replaced by five, except that the review group argued that originally there were twelve. Somewhere along the line I must have missed something – nowhere in the first Order is there any mention of strands. Although the NCC in-service materials (NCC 1991b) talk about strands they are not listed. No doubt the review group are referring to the strands created during the development of SATs, but these had no statutory place. What is a teacher to make of such informal and perhaps not universally shared knowledge? Despite this problem of the number of strands, the number of SoA were reduced by half (to 59!), so at least the Order has been simplified.

The PoS identified the 'skills and knowledge which pupils should acquire' (DFE/WO 1992: 3) through establishing two core sections on *designing* and *making*, and five supporting sections:

- construction materials and components;
- food;
- control systems and energy;
- structures;
- business and industrial practices.

Control systems have a variety of elements, such as electrical/electronic, mechanical and pneumatic. At key stage (KS) 4 the elements, along with 'Construction materials' and 'Structures' or 'Food', are offered in various choice combinations depending upon whether a full course (10 per cent of curriculum time) or a short course (5 per cent) is being offered. Finally, a number of design and make tasks (DMTs) were suggested as the basis of teaching, with the number and content being specified for each key stage.

As in the first Order, we have the problems of 'subject by committee'. 'Food', as a section in the PoS, quite rightly preserves some of the home economics input to technology teaching. But what are we to make of the specific identification of textiles as a construction material? At Level 6 it is listed along with other generic groups of materials (timbers, metals, plastics, composites, etc.), but it is the only construction material that has a DMT specified for it in the proposals (DFE/WO 1992: 27). The purpose is clear; it ensures that those home economic teachers specialising in textiles can have some input. The cost of this is a degree of illogicality and the loss of textiles as a distinct technology, equivalent to that of 'food', which has its own section in the proposal.

It is evident that teachers will have yet another period of learning to understand both the structure, etc. of the Order and the new definition of the subject 'technology'. They will have to analyse the curricula they have recently developed to see how they match the new requirements. Further, they may have to think about their own skills and the school's resources to be able to teach the PoS. Of course the choices of the various forms of control, for example, allow schools to match the teaching to their resources, but in what sense is this a *national* curriculum or 'technology for all'? Those teachers who remember the *Modular Courses in Technology* may feel some sense of familiarity, but wonder what has been learnt over the last twenty years.

NOTES

1 This section of the article is taken from an earlier more extensive account of the evolution of technology education (McCormick 1990a), a shortened version of which is published in McCormick, Murphy and Harrison (1992).
2 This section is based upon a previously published article (McCormick 1990b). Barnett (1992) and Medway (1992) also give background account and analyses of various stages in the creation of the national curriculum for technology.
3 In fact the Assessment of Performance Unit had defined technology as one of the areas of their curriculum model that would be tested (APU 1982).
4 One of the main arguments of Medway (1992) is that the overemphasis on design in the national curriculum was a symptom of the divorce between the curriculum and real technology.

REFERENCES

Archer, B. (1979) 'The three Rs', *Design Studies* 1 (1) 17–20.
APU (Assessment of Performance Unit) (1982) *Understanding Design and Technology*, London, APU.
ASE (Association for Science Education) (1988) *Technology Education and Science in Schools*, Hatfield ASE.
Barnett, M. (1992) 'Technology, within the National Curriculum and elsewhere', pp. 84–104 in J. Beynon and H. Mackay, *Technological Literacy and the Curriculum*, London, Falmer Press.
DES (Department of Education and Science) (1985) *The Curriculum from 5 to 16*, Curriculum Matters 2, an HMI series, London, HMSO.
DES/WO (Department of Education and Science) (1988) *Interim Report of the Working Group for Design and Technology*, London, DES.

DES/WO (Department of Education and Science and the Welsh Office) (1989) *Design and Technology for Ages 5 to 16: Proposals of the Secretary of State for Education and Science and Secretary of State for Wales*, London, HMSO.

DES/WO (Department of Education and Science and the Welsh Office) (1990) *Technology in the National Curriculum*, London, HMSO.

DFE/WO (Department for Education and the Welsh Office) (1992) *Technology for Ages 5 to 16 (1992) Proposals of the Secretary of State*, London, HMSO.

Eggleston, S.J. (1976) *Developments in Design Education*, London, Open Books.

Harrison, M.K. (1990) 'Science in technology: technology in science', in *Proceedings of the 3rd National Conference Design and Technology Education Research and Curriculum Development*, Loughborough, University of Technology, Department of Design and Technology.

HMI (Her Majesty's Inspectorate of Schools) (1992) *Technology at Key Stages 1, 2 and 3*, London, HMSO.

Jeffrey, J.R. (1990) 'Design methods in CDT', in *Journal of Art and Design Education* 9 (1), 57–70.

Layton, D. (1973) *Science for the People*, London, Allen & Unwin.

McCormick, R. (1990a) 'The evolution of current practice in technology education', Paper presented to NATO Advanced Research Workshop 'Integrating Advanced Technology into Technology Education', 8–12 October, Eindhoven, Netherlands.

McCormick, R. (1990b) 'Technology and the national curriculum: the creation of a "subject" by committee?', *The Curriculum Journal* 1 (1), 39–5.

McCormick, R. (1993) *Teaching and Learning Design*, PGCE Pamphlet, Milton Keynes, Open University.

McCormick, R., Murphy, P. and Harrison, M.E. (eds) (1992) *Teaching and Learning Technology*, London, Addison-Wesley.

McCulloch, G., Jenkins, E. and Layton, D. (1985) *Technological Revolution? The Politics of School Science and Technology in England and Wales since 1945*, Lewes, Falmer Press.

Medway, P. (1989) 'Issues in the theory and practice of technology education', *Studies in Science Education* 16, 1–23.

Medway, P. (1992) 'Constructions of technology: reflections on a new subject', pp. 64–83 in J. Beynon and H. Mackay, *Technological literacy and the curriculum*, London, Falmer Press.

NCC (National Curriculum Council) (1991a) *Non-Statutory Guidance for Design and Technology*, York, NCC.

NCC (National Curriculum Council) (1991b) *Implementing Design and Technology at Key Stage 3*, York, NCC.

NCC (National Curriculum Council) (1992) *National Curriculum Technology: The Case for Revising the Order*, York, NCC.

NSEAD (National Society for Education in Art and Design) (1990) 'Current issues in art and design education: the NSEAD response to the Report of the National Curriculum Working Group for Design and Technology', *Journal of Art and Design Education* 9 (1), 23–37.

Penfold, J. (1988) *Craft, Design and Technology: Past, Present and Future*, Hanley, Trentham Books.

RCA (Royal College of Art) (1989) *Design in General Education: The Report of an Enquiry Conducted by the Royal College of Art for the Secretary of State for Education and Science*, London, Royal College of Art.

Schools Council (1981) *Teacher's Master Manual*, Modular Courses in Technology, Nottingham, National Centre for School Technology, Trent Polytechnic/Oliver & Boyd.

Smithers, A. and Robinson, P. (1992) *Technology in the National Curriculum: Getting it Right*, London, The Engineering Council.

Solomon, J. (1988) 'Science technology and social courses: tools for thinking about social issues', *International Journal of Science Education* 10 (4), 379–87.

SSCR (Secondary Science Curriculum Review) (1987) *Better Science: Making it Relevant to Young People. Curriculum Guide 3*, London, Heinemann/Association for Science Education.

Steers, J. (1990) 'Design and technology in the National Curriculum', *Journal of Art and Design Education* 9 (1), 9–22.

Thistlewood, D. (1989) 'The formation of the NSEAD: a dialectical advance for British art and design education', *Journal of Art and Design Education* 8 (2), 135–52.

Za'rour, G.I. (1987) 'Forces hindering the introduction of STS education in schools', in K. Riquarts (ed.) *Technology Education: Science-Technology-Society. Science and Technology Education and the Quality of Life*, Volume 2. Papers submitted to the International IOSTE symposium on world trends in science and technology education, Kiel University, West Germany: Institut für die Pädagogik der Naturwissenschaften.

Part II

Learning technology

Chapter 6

Learning through design and technology

Assessment of Performance Unit

This extract is from the report by the APU of their extensive investigation into the nature of design and technology capability. It reviews the many models of design and technology which have been used to describe the 'progress' of technology and outlines the one developed by the APU to help with their assessment programme.

INTRODUCTION

From the earliest work in this field, there has been general agreement on certain basic tenets of design and technology. It is an *active* study, involving the *purposeful* pursuit of a *task* to some form of *resolution* that results in *improvement* (for someone) in the made world. It is a study that is essentially procedural (i.e. deploying processes/activities in pursuit of a task) and which uses knowledge and skills as a resource for action rather than regarding them as ends in themselves. The underlying drive behind the activity is one of improving some aspects of the made world, which starts when we see an opportunity to intervene and create something new or something better.

MODELS OF DESIGN AND TECHNOLOGY

Early models of the activity described it in simple problem-solving terms that start with a problem and progress through a linear sequence of steps to a solution. Innumerable variants of this basic idea can be found in the literature and gradually – as teachers became more experienced at working with them – the models were themselves refined. The linear track became a 'design loop' on the reasonable grounds that the evaluation of the end

Figure 6.1 A simple linear model

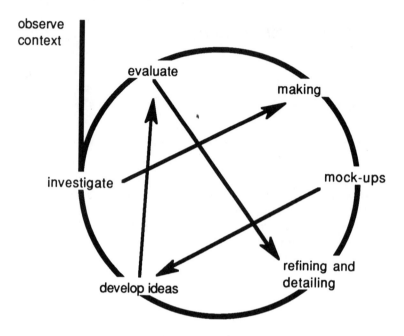

Figure 6.2 An interacting design loop (Kimbell 1986)

production must not only be conducted in relation to the initiating problem, but that, moreover, the results of the evaluation will themselves provide new problems to start the cycle all over again.

Once again, however, familiarity with this process led to dissatisfaction with it as an adequate description of what pupils do when they tackle a task. Do they not have to look things up (research them) when they are making things, or generate ideas (e.g. about testing methods) to evaluate a solution? And do they not have to evaluate ideas as they emerge to see if they are worth pursuing? The models used to describe the process became ever more confused as the subtlety of the process became apparent.

The principal motives behind this drive to analyse the constituent parts of the activity lay in the need to make it possible to *teach* and *assess* it. For these two purposes it became increasingly necessary to try to impose order on what is essentially a confused, interactive process. These models have been helpful guides to the sorts of activity that need to go on in design and technology, but they have equally been dangerous in prescribing 'stages' of the process that need to be 'done' by pupils.

Used unsympathetically, the approach can reveal a greater concern for 'doing' all the stages of the process, than for combining a growing range of capabilities in a way which reflects individual creativity and confident and effective working methods.

(APU 1987: 2.12)

The essence of this problem lies in the transformation of active capabilities into passive products. To take an example, 'investigation' or 'research' is typically one of the stages identified in the process and results in the accumulation of large folders of background material related to the task. In making an assessment of this 'stage' of the process, where should we look for evidence of a pupil's investigative/research capability? Naturally we look at the folder. Inevitably, therefore, the research folder (a product) comes to represent an active capability. There are three related problems here.

First the development of the investigation folder typically assumes that all investigation goes on early in the project, i.e. it is about investigating the task to see what is involved in tackling it. But do we not need constantly to be investigative. Don't we need to investigate user reactions to our early design ideas, or the most appropriate glue for a particular making task? Typically, by allocating 'investigation' to a particular stage of the process, and by committing it to the formality of a separate folder, we prevent pupils from recognising the need *to be investigative* at all times.

Second, because the investigation *folder* becomes the focus of assessment there is an enormous pressure to 'pretty-up' the folder after the event, regardless of its relevance to the developmental process and as if it were to be valued as a product in its own right. Which frequently of course it is.

Third, this line of reasoning results in the efficient packaging and presentation of all the 'stages' of the process. *In fact the process of design and technology becomes a series of products* (The Brief, The Specification, The Investigation, etc., etc.). It has to be said that examination procedures and syllabuses in design and technology have contributed substantially to this unhelpful tendency to convert active capabilities into passive products.

Whilst the analysis of the process into these discrete elements may have helped teachers to get to grips with the parameters of what is involved in tackling a design and technology task, it has frequently emasculated it by ripping it apart in quite unnatural and unnecessary ways. Assessment in design and technology has too often assumed that you can measure the quality of an omelette simply by measuring (and aggregating) the individual quality of the eggs, the milk, the butter and the herbs. As if the cook was irrelevant!

THE INTERACTION OF MIND AND HAND

For APU we attempted to create a different way of looking at design and technology; a way that placed the interactive process at the heart of our work and the products as subservient to that process. To do this, we rejected

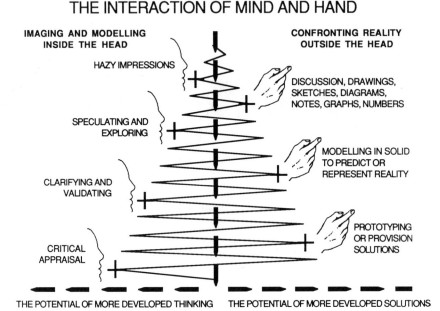

THE INTERACTION OF MIND AND HAND

IMAGING AND MODELLING
INSIDE THE HEAD

HAZY IMPRESSIONS

SPECULATING AND
EXPLORING

CLARIFYING AND
VALIDATING

CRITICAL
APPRAISAL

CONFRONTING REALITY
OUTSIDE THE HEAD

DISCUSSION, DRAWINGS,
SKETCHES, DIAGRAMS,
NOTES, GRAPHS, NUMBERS

MODELLING IN SOLID
TO PREDICT OR
REPRESENT REALITY

PROTOTYPING
OR PROVISION
SOLUTIONS

THE POTENTIAL OF MORE DEVELOPED THINKING   THE POTENTIAL OF MORE DEVELOPED SOLUTIONS

Figure 6.3 The APU model of interaction between mind and hand.

the idea of describing the activity in terms of the products that result from it, and instead concentrated on the thinking and decision-making processes that result in these products. We were more interested in *why* and *how* pupils chose to do things than in *what* it was they chose to do. The pupil's thoughts and intentions were as important to us as were the products that resulted from them.

We gradually came to see the essence of design and technology as being the interaction of mind and hand – inside and outside the head. It involves more than conceptual understanding – but is dependent upon it, and it involves more than practical skill – but again is dependent upon it. In design and technology, ideas conceived in the mind need to be expressed in concrete form before they can be examined to see how useful they are.

Imaging in the mind

It is not uncommon for pupils to believe that, almost from the start of an activity, they have a complete solution sorted out in their mind and this often leads them to try to short-circuit the process of development, 'I know what I want to do – I just need a piece of plywood/felt/clay . . .'. In fact we know that they cannot, in their mind alone, have sorted out all the issues and difficulties in the task – let alone reconciled them into a successful solution. What they have got is a hazy notion in their mind's eye of what a solution is like – and this is a crucial starting point for them. But is is only a starting point, and to enable the idea to develop it is necessary to drag it out of the mind and express it in real form. To demonstrate this phenomenon, simply imagine an 8-year-old girl with spinal injuries lying in a hospital bed. She has to lie flat on her back and not move. She loves doing jig-saw puzzles. Can we develop for her a jig-saw puzzle system that can operate effectively within these constraints? Even with this tiny amount of information we have all begun to image – in our mind's eye – solutions that we believe might work. The solution might involve magnets, or velcro, or possibly a sheet of glass or clear plastic. This internal image is our starting point from which we may – eventually – be able to fashion a satisfactory solution. But it is only a starting point, and our first responsibility is to try to drag this internal image out into the light of day. There are at least two good reasons for this.

First, the process of trying to express a hazy idea forces us to clarify it. We soon see that our vague idea about magnets might mean two very different things. Are we to stick little magnets onto each piece – or should we make a new puzzle out of magnetic material? The former sounds fiddly and time consuming – but the latter would eliminate the use of all existing jig-saws. By trying to express our idea – in words, or pictures, or in concrete reality – we get closer to seeing the difficulties and the possibilities within it.

The second reason for dragging the idea out of our mind and expressing it in some way is that by doing so we make it possible for others to share our idea. As soon as your idea is expressed – in words, or pictures, or in concrete reality – it is something that I can comment on. 'Do you mean . . .', 'Do you really think that . . .', 'But what if . . .'. As teachers, this is one of our major responsibilities, to act as a catalyst by providing helpful, critical but supportive comments on pupils' developing ideas.

For these two reasons, therefore, the act of expression is a crucial part of the development of thinking. Without such expression it is almost impossible for an idea to move very far forward because very few people are able to cope with that degree of mental imaging. It is like playing mental chess. We can all manage the first move or two – but trying to hold in our mind an image of the board after twenty moves (and counter-moves) is impossible for most of us. With the chess board in front of us (as a concrete expression of the current state of our thinking) we can achieve a far more cunning and sophisticated level of thinking. So too with design ideas – the concrete expression of them not only clarifies them for us but, moreover, it enables us to confront the details and consequences of the ideas in ways that are simply not possible with internal images. Cognitive modelling by itself – manipulating ideas purely in the mind's eye – has severe limitations when it comes to complex ideas or patterns. It is through externalised modelling techniques that such complex ideas can be expressed and clarified, thus supporting the next stage of cognitive modelling.

It is our contention that this inter-relationship between modelling ideas in the mind, and modelling ideas in reality is the cornerstone of capability in design and technology. It is best described as 'thought in action'.

Modelling solutions

Expressing ideas is therefore a necessary part of developing ideas. But does it matter what mode of expression is used? Are all means of expression equally applicable to any design circumstances? Clearly not, and part of the art of developing capability in design and technology is to develop a rich variety of modelling strategies that enable ideas to be expressed in the most appropriate ways.

Choosing the most appropriate form of modelling involves thinking not only about what the idea is that needs to be expressed, but equally about how the modelling is supposed to help. If we wish to explore a basic concept for a new product (e.g. a new car radio volume control that adjusts the volume according to the ambient noise level) then, at this level of broad concept, *discussion* (verbal modelling) may be the best way to start. It is very quick and it helps people to get a grip on some of the big issues and difficulties that might need to be tackled. It is interesting to note that in the modelling tests that we developed discussion proved to be a vital element in pupils' responses. For some situations they found it to be the most useful form of modelling.

But discussion alone does not allow us to get into the detail that would be required to evaluate how the noise sensing could best be achieved, let alone confront the details of electronic circuit design. Different types of modelling are needed that may be *diagrammatic*, or *computer-simulated* and that enable fine detail to be explored and resolved. As the electronics is being sorted out it will probably be necessary simultaneously to consider the styling and ergonomics of the developing product, and this needs a different form of modelling again, probably involving a range of *graphic techniques* and *3D models* that fully represent the appearance and feel of the finished article.

With modelling it is a matter of horses for courses. Is speed the priority or accuracy; is the idea qualitative or quantitative; are you trying to sort out the visual details or the mechanical functioning; analyse the stresses in a shelf support or detail the combination of flavours and spices in a new snack product? There are many ways of modelling ideas and each has its advantages and disadvantages. Accordingly, pupils need a rich awareness of the diversity of possibilities for modelling to enable them to grapple with the particular requirements of their task.

But the guiding principle behind the selection of any technique must be

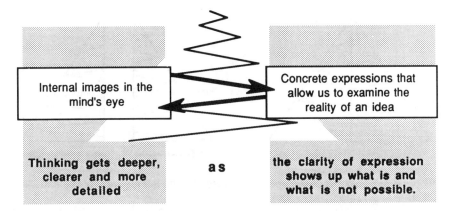

Figure 6.4 Clearer and more detailed expression allows clearer and more detailed thinking

that it enables pupils progressively to confront the reality of their ideas – to get a better and sharper grip on what they will be like (and how they will work) when they are finally completed. We must recognise, however, that the notion of the finally completed product is elusive for there is really no such thing. 'The end' of the process is typically arbitrary and determined not by the task itself so much as by the parameters that bear on it – typically the time-scale of the project. There is nothing particularly special about the 'final' prototype, from the moment it exists it becomes the focus for yet further refinement and is therefore but another extension of modelling activity. In the commercial world, the endless progression of updated versions of existing products bears witness to the possibilities for refining and developing ideas. Whilst the motive underlying these developments will probably be the maintenance of market share in a fickle consumer world, the process of development has modelling at its heart. If scientific innovation (micro-chips, lasers, etc.) often provides the opportunity for product development, it is modelling that provides the dynamic driving force that carries development forward from hazy ideas to refined and detailed working prototypes.

This active, task-centred description of design and technology carries with it a number of implications, the most central of which concerns the dimensions of an assessment framework for design and technology.

THE DIMENSIONS OF CAPABILITY

The model presents us with two completely contrasted ways of looking at the assessment of capability. Traditionally, assessment devices in design and technology have separated the conceptual and the expressive: conceptual

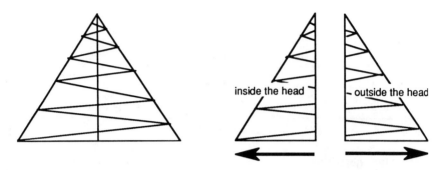

Figure 6.5 Traditional assessment strategies split the interactive process and use different assessment techniques

matters being seen as testable in written examinations, whilst the expressive are equally (though perhaps less validly) testable in graphic/modelling/ making examinations.

We took the view – supported by the brief we had been given – that this approach to assessment is destructive of the essence of capability as we have described it above. We were not interested in conceptual understanding for itself, or in the decontextualised display of any particular communication skill but rather in the extent to which pupils can *use* their understandings and skills when they are tackling a real task. Capability in design and technology involves the active, *purposeful deployment* of understanding and skills – not just their passive demonstration. Isolated tests of knowledge and skills were therefore quite inappropriate and we had to look towards the development of test tasks that could give us a measure of active capability.

This idea, when applied to our model of the activity, meant that we had to consider a completely different way of looking at tests. If the integrity of the imaging and modelling (inside/outside, conceptual/expressive) process were to be maintained, then any splitting up of the process had to be done without destroying this crucial relationship.

Given this starting point, we developed the idea that tests might be constructed that provide a 'window' through which we could observe the process in action – with the size of the window being defined by the time available. It followed that any such test must of necessity contain within it the three dimensions of capability that are represented in the model, i.e.:

– conceptual understanding (inside the head);
– communicative/modelling facility (outside the head);
– their *interaction* through the process in the activity.

By slicing the process in this way we hoped that it would be possible to see (and assess) the central procedures of the activity as well as the extent to which they were resourced by conceptual understanding on one hand and

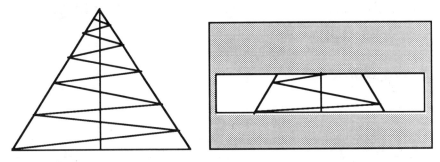

Figure 6.6 Looking at tests as windows, through which to scurtinise parts of the process whilst maintaining the integrity of the model

expressive facility on the other. We thus derived the three principal dimensions of an assessment framework.

More than simply identifying these dimensions, however, the model has further implications. It is as important for pupils to be aware of what they *need to know* as it is for them to actually know it. Accessing new knowledge and skills in response to the demands in the task is a fundamental characteristic of capability in design and technology.

> The designer does not need to know all about everything so much as to know what to find out, what form the knowledge should take, and what depth of knowledge is required for a particular purpose.
>
> (DES/APU 1981: 5)

It therefore became as important for us to probe a pupil's capability in accessing relevant knowledge and skill as it was to register the existing knowledge that they were already using in their task.

REFERENCES

APU (Assessment of Performance Unit) (1987) *Design and Technological Activity: A Framework for Assessment*, London, APU/DES.

DES/APU (Department of Education and Science/Assessment of Performance Unit) (1981) *Understanding Design and Technology*, London, DES/APU.

Kimbell, R. (1986) *Craft design and Technology*, Milton Keynes, Open University.

Chapter 7

The importance of graphic modelling in design activity

Steve Garner

This article describes a research project into the way professional designers use drawing to help them think through, as well as communicate about, their creative ideas.

The NSEAD-funded one-year programme of research set out to examine the functions of drawing for a wide range of professionals engaged in three-dimensional design. It followed the popular method of case study analysis but because of the variety of information this technique generates the opportunities for examining and testing particular hypotheses were limited. Nevertheless, it was a method particularly appropriate to that investigative programme as it provided a very broad foundation upon which later studies could be based. The findings from the research have been presented in a number of papers (Garner 1988, 1990). In these papers drawing is presented as a major influence on the development of designerly thought and comparisons are made between the investigation of drawing and the studies of natural language by researchers such as Bruner (1962) and Barnes (1976).

The case studies consisted of twenty examples of designers and included, amongst others, architects, sculptors, engineers, theatre designers and craftspeople. Some of these held teaching posts in their subject. The analysis involved looking for commonalities of opinion and was based on transcripts of each interview. These transcripts were bound together and submitted to the NSEAD at the conclusion of the work. In one of these transcripts Dick Powell refers to the capacity of drawing to allow a designer to 'converse with themselves'.[1] Such conversation may involve asking the right questions, constructing the right structures and providing conjecture. Assimilation of information may be more important than communication and drawing may provide a means of achieving this. A number of case studies referred to a use for drawings in 'turning over fresh information' or 'consolidating a theme'. This 'homing in' extends the contribution of drawing from a problem-solving to a problem-finding strategy. Client-based meetings were cited as one situation where drawing had an important function in the formulation and definition of requirements.

Exploratory drawing would appear to increase the potential of discovering or seeing new arrangements or directions in old information. Obviously the individuals' creativity will have some bearing on this but there is some evidence to suggest that the development of creativity is in some way encouraged by the implementation of graphic strategies. The technical skills of representation are clearly going to influence the ability to portray what is intended but the development of representational drawing skills demands that the draftsperson looks and 'sees' with greater insight. That is to say, there is a relationship between drawing and visual literacy. Thoroughness of seeing and the development of critical abilities are similarly inter-related. One of the research subjects – a furniture designer – promoted the activity of observational drawing as a means of exploring, understanding, remembering and, particularly, critically judging – and in this way influencing the quality of concept, detailing and proportion. There was some agreement amongst the case studies for this capacity as Claire Webber, a painter, commented: 'I draw to help me understand. It's rarely used to express myself. It's to do with learning about what you are looking at and being surprised.'[2]

There appears to be a deliberate and structured approach in the exploitation of drawing for responding to external and internal stimuli. Drawing appears to be used for the deliberate provocation of responses rather than as a passive medium for externalising, in an intuitive manner, such stimuli. Responses need not be restricted by practicality. A free flow of ideas may be essential and distinct from the evaluative strategies employed in the design process. Roy Axe, Director of Concept Engineering at Austin Rover at the time of the research, sees a long-term future for the notorious marker pen rendering of the automotive industry simply because he can see no other means yet of capturing the essential 'caricature' of the designer's intention.[3] Perhaps the research work into 'computer aided vehicle styling' currently being undertaken by Michael Tovey at Coventry University will change this. The term 'spirit' may be viewed as synonymous with caricature as highlighted by another subject, this time an architect, in referring to one of the great designers of the twentieth century:

> Alvar Aalto did very, very sketchy, embryonic, schematic drawings which were purposely ethereal because he was trying to catch what you could only call the spirit or the essence of the job. He did not wish to compromise solutions by seizing on form too quickly.[4]

Somewhere between the analysis of the problem and the conscious exploration of potential resolutions lies a cloudy perceptual domain within which designers refer to sources of motivation or inspiration that result from quick sketches they have made. Certain sketches would seem to be produced within which resides sufficient ambiguity for the mind to see a variety of subsequent moves. Thus a creative analysis is begun that appears to display some congruity with Tovey's (1986) dual-processing model of activity within the mind. Case-study evidence seems to support this by reference to the importance of drawings which possess 'flexibility', that is, drawings which can be interpreted in a number of ways. Central to this issue is the deliberate reduction of preconceived 'meaning' without the sacrifice of 'feeling'. Closely associated wlth this is 'serendipity' or happy chance. This was so commonly mentioned by subjects that one is led to believe that happy chance can be conjured up at will. Perhaps the immediacy of drawing assists this process. Similarly humour has been proposed as a catalyst in this context whereby drawing may act as a trigger. In the same way that reinterpretation (or misinterpretation) of information may lead to unusual perceptions and subsequently lead to laughter, so interpretation of graphic information may trigger creative insights. The use of the word 'play' occurs frequently – and a little apologetically –within the transcripts, as if there should be no requirement for such apparently unfocused activity. On the contrary, play can be an immensely focused activity (observe young children with a favourite toy). Economists, scientists, ecologists as well as members of the design professions appear to be quite happy with the notion of 'playing' with ideas as an essential stage to creative idea development.

Underlying the exploitation of drawing as an exploratory tool is a considerably more basic foundation. This is the sheer enjoyment in the activity. It appears that the subjects of the research would draw during design activity whether it presented an advantage or not! Even in homes and offices the numerous doodles on telephone pads would appear to indicate that drawing can be organisational, creative and involuntary. It is difficult to isolate the functional requirements to draw from this inner motivation but a great many designers appear to be unable to stop themselves from drawing as they talk, listen or create. Whether drawing ability promotes design practice or vice versa is unclear, but the majority of those interviewed regularly made time to maintain their graphic abilities through recreational sketching or painting. In one discussion Alan Williams of DCA design consultants explored the relationship between recreational sketching and the exploitation of drawing within the pressured, commercial world of product design. His belief is that designers require a constant interest or inquisitiveness in the world around them and that sketching, with its requirements for looking and thinking, is an important way to maintain this.[5] One subject referred to his National Service in this context:

> When I went into the army I continued drawing. I've got sketch books full of drawings simply because it was a way of coming to terms with the world around me; new landscapes, new situations, new people. It seemed to me a way of making contact in a very real way.[6]

The relationship between drawing and designing is further articulated by Norman McNally of Glasgow School of Art:

If you cannot report on what exists, i.e. you do not have an investigative vision of the world around you, then you can hardly be expected to report on what does not exist – things that you are pulling out of your head. Objective drawing constantly informs conceptual drawing.[7]

Drawings produced during design activity may be intended to possess no more than fleeting value and yet they can often display characteristics that make them very precious to the drawer – and the viewer. A blend of serendipity, skill, speed, economy, pleasure, pain, anger and humour can often produce a sketch of more interest to people than the finished product – whether that be a building, a domestic product, a piece of sculpture or a painting. In fact the roughness of a sketch would appear to be an important characteristic of some types of design drawing. A very detailed 'conceptual' sketch might stifle ambiguity and might fix early thoughts which could be improved upon. Subjects were often apologetic for the quality of some sketch work shown but this is likely to result from the general assumption within our society that drawings are meant to convey information. If we suspend the notion that drawings are communicative devices and search for their meaning in developmental strategies of the mind then we may come closer to an appreciation of their role.

The role of drawing as a modelling device within an exploratory strategy is clearly, then, not limited to small patches of application. It lies at the very heart of people's search for understanding. Exploration has been presented as a conglomeration of inter-related activities, some revolving around problem analysis and inquisitiveness, others around creativity or discovery and still others that are concerned with making visible the products of such exploration.

The area within the design process between exploration and idea development is a very grey one. Rarely does one get the opportunity to complete research activity thoroughly before manipulating the information in a response to identified requirements. In fact, a case could be made for the importance of creatively examining the breadth of a problem and the possible responses to it before a systematic research process is completed. Thus, drawing strategies that aim to explore problems, manipulate information and visualise responses have no clear divisions between them. Designing is not a linear process. Its iterative nature is well accepted and this results in differing requirements for drawing at any one stage of the process. To compound this issue skilled practitioners, as represented in the case study subjects, are able to produce drawings which have multiple functions and, more importantly, functions which take place apparently simultaneously. To take an extreme example, a sketch which may have been made to externalise a private and incomplete notion may also quite readily communicate form, detail, scale, etc. It may also facilitate evaluation and at the same time provoke further generation of ideas. In reality, drawing styles and purposes merge gradually into one another and reflect the personal preferences of the designers, engineers, sculptors and architects themselves. Alan Williams again:

> Perhaps in certain circumstances a quality of sketching or scrawling is an indication of a poor or illogical process of thinking but it can reveal a way of using a pencil as a tool to uncover ideas. Few people can actually sit down and draw something they have imagined. It is a natural way of developing ideas. One can usually identify by looking at somebody's scrawlings how hard it is for them to get any ideas. If there is a flow of ideas the sketches, the drawings seem to indicate the lucidity of thinking.[8]

Research into drawing as a modelling tool owes much to Bruce Archer's work three decades ago. He stated then that 'Drawing is a very economical way of modelling, it is the fastest and best way of having a quick idea – a visualisation – of what is in your head and thus leads naturally into solid modelling' (Archer 1976).

The notion of drawing as a modelling device is clearly not new but perhaps the appreciation of its function within the personal and developmental phases of design work is not greatly developed. Modelling through drawing can be a very powerful communicative device but modelling can have private functions too. It can operate in conjunction with other capacities of the mind so as to evaluate, develop and externalise thought processes of an individual. It is plausible that learning to draw may in some way assist the development of conceptual modelling capabilities – revealing and solidifying for the drawer the nature of form and implications of change. If this is so, then surely drawing must be reinstated as one of the major components of design education.

NOTES

1 D. Powell, product designer, London, interviewed 25 Nov. 1987.
2 C. Webber, painter, Loughborough, interviewed 12 Oct. 1987.
3 R. Axe, Director of Concept Engineering, Austin Rover, interviewed 2 Dec. 1987.
4 I. Ballantine, architect and lecturer, Glasgow School of Art, interviewed 20 Nov. 1987.
5 A. Williams, Director of DCA Design Consultants, interviewed 6 Aug. 1987.
6 P. Ashen, then Head of Furniture Design, Birmingham Polytechnic, interviewed 1 March 1988.
7 N. McNally, product designer and lecturer, Glasgow School of Art, interviewed 20 Nov. 1987.
8 A. Williams (see note 5).

REFERENCES

Archer, B. (1976) 'The Three Rs', Lecture delivered at Manchester Regional Centre for Science and Technology, 7 May.

Barnes, D. (1976) *From Communication to Curriculum*, London, Penguin Books.

Bruner, J.S. (1962) *On Knowing*, London, Harvard University Press.

Garner, S.W. (1988) 'The Language of design: drawing on a profound resource', *Studies in Design Education, Craft and Technology* 20 (3), 133–6.

Garner, S.W. (1990) 'Drawing and designing: the case for reappraisal', *Journal of Art and Design Education* 9 (1), 39–55.

Tovey, M. (1986) 'Thinking styles and modelling systems', *Design Studies* 7 (1).

Chapter 8

A comparison between the nature of modelling in science and design and technology

David Barlex

David Barlex considers the use of both mental and physical models to help children's understanding.

INTRODUCTION

Two articles (Burden-Teh 1990, Liddament 1990) concerned with modelling in design and technology and my own interest in the use of scientific understanding in design technology (Barlex 1987, 1991) have prompted me to look at the modelling that may be carried out in science lessons and compare this to the modelling that takes place in design and technology lessons.

To begin with a definition of a model is required. It can be defined as a simplified or idealised version of reality created for a purpose. From this it follows that modelling is the process of creating models which fulfil their intended purpose successfully.

To put modelling into an appropriate context it will be necessary to explore three areas:

1 the nature of scientific activity in the 'real' world and in school science;
2 the nature of design and technological activity in the 'real' world and in school design and technology;
3 the nature of modelling in school design and technology and school science.

THE NATURE OF SCIENTIFIC ACTIVITY IN THE 'REAL' WORLD AND IN SCHOOL SCIENCE

Scientific activity in the real world

Let us begin by looking at the image of the scientist. The prevailing stereotype of the scientist, particularly among school pupils, is as follows: male, wearing a white coat and spectacles, obsessively interested in science, unworldly, and unaware of persons and events outside science (see Head 1985).

However representative of real scientists this image may or may not be is open to question, but it does contribute to a common cultural view of the scientist and what he (as opposed to she) does. Scientists do experiments to find things out; sometimes they go wrong with disastrous results as in science fiction films (*The Fly* and *The Blob*) or as in real life (Chernobyl and Bhopal) although these may perhaps be better described as technological blunders rather than scientific ones. Nobody was trying to discover a new or elusive scientific truth when these disasters occurred, but the media certainly talked about and blamed the scientists working at the establishments concerned.

An informed and perhaps sympathetic layperson's view of scientists and their work might be as follows: a scientist carries out lots of observations through activities called experiments. She/he sets up models that can be used to explain observed phenomena and predict future observations. The phenomena that are observed are those that are 'reliable' in that they can be observed by others who may or may not believe the explanatory model that the scientist wishes to invoke in explaining those phenomena. Eventually the models carry sufficient weight that they become embodied in scientific theories such as the atomic theory. The work of Thomas Kuhn (1962) has described the development and acceptance of a major scientific theory as establishing a paradigm in which the majority of the scientific community trust and work. When the scientific community builds a body of reliable data that cannot be explained in terms of models derived from the prevailing theory a scientific revolution occurs in which the old theory is discarded in favour of a newer theory which can accommodate this new data as well as that accommodated by the previous theory. This is the paradigm shift and, like all revolutions, is uncomfortable and involves power battles between conservatives who hold to the previous theory and radicals who advocate the need for a new theory. The revolutions in moving from Newtonian physics to Einsteinian physics and from classical physics to quantum physics are examples. Note that these are rare occurrences and that most of the time most scientists are simply gathering data that informs and conforms to the current paradigm.

Scientific activity in school science

We can suppose that the purpose of school science is to engage pupils in the methods of science so that they can know and understand a significant body of scientific knowledge, understand how science contributes to our understanding of the world and take an informed interest on those issues facing society that have a scientific dimension.

The work of Rosalind Driver (Children's Learning in Science Project based at Leeds University) has given great strength to the constructivist view of learning and insights into the nature of school science from the pupil's perspective. This view of learning requires the learner to construct his own meaning by reconciling new information with existing beliefs. This reconciliation is much more than simple remembering. It is quite possible for a learner to learn off by heart great chunks of information without understanding any of it or for that information to make any difference to the set of beliefs by which the learner explains the world around him. Driver and her co-workers have described a phenomenon known as pupils' alternative frameworks. These are sets of beliefs held by pupils that are at variance with the accepted scientific view. Alternative frameworks for a variety of scientific explanations – electricity, energy, gravity, force dependent phenomena – are well documented across pupil populations in Western Europe, USA, Australia and New Zealand (Driver et al. 1985). From a teaching point of view, the most challenging feature of pupils' alternative frameworks is that they are very resistant to change. It is only the pupil who can change her/his set of personal beliefs in response to new information. This requires both a willingness to do so and an awareness that an inconsistency exists. This is further complicated by the fact that many pupils have been shown to apply what is called 'local reasoning'. They are inconsistent in the way they apply their set of beliefs, often to avoid any fundamental shift in position. So the question arises, how can the scientific modelling required by science education be reconciled with pupils' alternative frameworks?

If a teacher sets up any of the significant and accepted scientific models for explaining the physical world there is the immediate problem that it is at such variance with the pupil's alternative view that it will be rejected out of hand with minimal consideration. Some would argue (see for example Arnold and Millar 1988) that children should be allowed to postulate their own models and explore them for inconsistencies. With appropriate guidance they will move to an accepted scientific view and, although this looks as if it will take longer than a more didactic or expository form of teaching, if fundamental concepts are developed in this way during primary and early secondary school, then later progress will be much faster and we will not be in the current position of 70 per cent of 15-year-olds experiencing difficulty in interpreting the circuit diagram for a simple torch (see APU 1984). Others, myself included, take a less extreme view and would introduce the models but give pupils sufficient time and a wide range of activities related to the models, including those perhaps not normally associated with science education – dance, music, drama, creative writing, making flic books, small group discussion – for the pupils to establish such an ownership of a model that they can use the model to confront the inadequacies of their current (alternative) set of beliefs.

Let us look at one of the most fundamental models used by scientists – the particle model of matter. This model starts by postulating that all matter –

solid, liquid and gas – is made of particles. Such particles are so infinitesimally small that a single particle cannot be seen using the most powerful light microscope. (At a rough estimate there would be about one million, million, million, million such particles in a tablespoon of water, i.e. 1,000,000,000,000,000,000,000,000.) A further condition of the model is that the particles of a single substance are all alike – same mass, same size, but different from the particles of all other single substances. Now, at first sight this does not seem a very useful way of looking at the world. It certainly requires a large dose of imagination and mental effort to begin to take it seriously; after all it does sound preposterous. The strength of this model lies in its powers to explain everyday phenomena, make predictions and to be developed to explain more complex phenomena. The model is so powerful that it is, as far as most scientists are concerned, not a model but a statement about what the world is really like, i.e. it is a theory.

The development of this theory has its roots in ancient Greece; it has had periods of acceptance and rejection. As recently as 1906, Boltzmann, a scientist of great repute and historical significance who believed strongly in the particle model of matter, committed suicide because the model was under such strong attack. Many texts trace the development of this model but this is not strictly relevant to what follows (see Mellor 1971).

Let us try to use this model to explain the properties of solids, liquids and gases. First we must establish the observed nature of these: solids have a fixed shape and volume; liquids have a fixed volume but no fixed shape – they take up the shape of their container, are incompressible and form into droplets quite unaided. Gases have no fixed shape or volume, they spontaneously spread out to fill the available space and are compressible.

Now can we imagine a solid, liquid and gas as being made up of these minute particles so that the arrangement we envisage explains the properties that we observe to be true? If we can, then surely this is imaging and modelling worthy of any design and technology lesson?

Comparing 'real' world and school science

Given the resistance to change of alternative frameworks it is tempting to argue that as children progress in their scientific understanding they go through a series of personal paradigm shifts that eventually leads them to a publicly acceptable set of scientific beliefs (that required by the National Curriculum perhaps). Given also that responding to a paradigm shift is an uncomfortable and agonising experience for the professional scientist (most of whom do not, most of the time, actively seek out data to challenge the prevailing paradigm anyway) we should not be too surprised that many children go to great lengths to avoid such shifts in allegiance. It is becoming increasingly apparent that helping children to reconcile inconsistencies in their beliefs and the way they are used to explain the observed world would be an important role for the science teacher as she/he guides pupils to the publicly accepted view. I will return to a modelling perspective on this later.

THE NATURE OF DESIGN AND TECHNOLOGICAL ACTIVITY IN THE 'REAL' WORLD AND IN SCHOOL DESIGN AND TECHNOLOGY

Design and technology in the 'real' world

It is the outcomes of design and technological activity that are significant in 'real' world design and technological activity. The procedural competences that are developed and utilised by those producing the outcomes are insignificant compared to the outcomes themselves. The motivation for the endeavour is the production of an outcome that is seen as responding to an opportunity or meeting a need.

An opportunity is linked to the notions that design and technology may be innovation driven or market led. It may involve the production of a new product as in the case of the 'Walkman'. This did not exist before 1975 and no part of the human race was excessively deprived because of this. Technical developments in earphones rendered a Walkman possible and intelligent marketing rendered the Walkman an object of desire. Now it (and a variety of clones) are produced and sold in millions world wide. Or an opportunity may involve developing a product that exists already. The safety razor has existed since the early twentieth century. It clearly meets a need but the development of a variety of 'innovative' forms over the past thirty years is in response to market pressures from competing manufacturers.

A need is linked to the notion that design and technology is benign in that it responds to needs by developing products that meet those needs. Some designers such as Papanek (1985) have argued that design and technology has failed by being innovation driven and market led and that the only honourable function for design technologists is to identify 'real' needs, on a global scale, and to use their talents to meet these. Papanek polarises the distinction by asking questions like 'If two-thirds of the world is hungry how can any sane person spend his time developing convenience food for the over-fed?'

Design and technology in school

Although pupils produce outcomes (artefacts, systems and environments) as the most obvious 'end product' of design and technology in schools in trying to meet needs and grasp opportunities it is the intentions (meeting the need or grasping the opportunity) and the procedural competences developed and utilised in response to those intentions that are significant. Current models of good practice require that the pupil has significant responsibility for the nature and quality of the response she/he makes and that she/he is required to reflect on and evaluate both the nature and quality of her/his response. Without product there can be no design and technology process but it is the process that is educationally significant although it is the nature of the product at varying stages within the process that reveals much about the process.

THE NATURE OF MODELLING IN SCHOOL DESIGN AND TECHNOLOGY AND SCHOOL SCIENCE

Modelling as a pupil design/technologist

It is all too easy to see the end result of the modelling activity, 'the models', as the most significant part of the activity. They are only significant to the extent that they help the designer, be they pupil or professional, develop a clearer picture of that which she/he is designing and that, in the case of education, they reveal to the teacher the mental processes of the pupil in coming to grips with the design task. While it is convenient to classify the models in terms of their form it is important for the teacher to see them for what they are in educational terms – insights into pupil thinking. Modelling as used by pupils in schools may lead to the following outcomes:

1 *2D representations on paper*
    These include progression from 'rough' exploratory sketching of overall concept, through part details and assembly considerations to full rendering of finished form and working drawing allowing making by someone else.

2 *3D representations*
    These include simple paper, card, straw, lollystick, paper fastener explorations of mechanisms and structures as well as the use of kits such as Lego and Fischer Technic. Similarly explorations of overall form can be developed using simple materials without any attempt to achieve final finish as opposed to detailed block modelling which is the 3D equivalent of a rendered drawing.

3 *Symbolic representations*
    These come in the form of mathematical formulae, calculations, concept diagrams and graphs. They can be used to calculate details of mechanical arrangements, geometric drawing may be used to plot loci of moving parts. Displacement vs time and velocity vs time graphs may be considered in developing the correct profiles for cams. Vector diagrams may be constructed to reveal the nature and size of forces in frameworks.

4 *Computer simulations*
    These can be used:

to explore a variety of finishes or decorative schemes – paint programmes,
to explore a variety of forms – 3D modellers,
to animate a mechanism, e.g. crank and con rod, and explore variations
on key variables – animation programmes,
to generate working drawings – such as CAD packages.

Whatever form the model takes, it is important that it moves the pupil
towards a clearer detailing of the design proposal.

Modelling as a pupil scientist

Using the mind's eye to conjure the particle picture is an activity that can be
described by the APU model for design and technological activity (APU
1987); where the iterative process of developing a detailed design proposal
can be seen as paralleling the iterative process of acquiring ownership of a
scientific model – one that means something to the learner and is moving
towards that which is deemed acceptable in terms of prevailing scientific
views. Note that the model only becomes examinable when it comes out of
the head and appears in concrete form. Engaging pupils with expressing
themselves about the particulate nature of matter can lead to a variety of
interesting outcomes – flic books, models and creative writing (Barlex and
Carre 1985). None of these are prescribed outcomes, each pupil in a class set
such tasks will produce their own unique responses. As in the case of the
pupil as designer, what is important about the model is that it moves the
pupil towards clearer detail, in this case a clearer appreciation of the atomic
model.

In conclusion I believe that I have shown that teachers of science and
design and technology share both an opportunity and a responsibility to
involve pupils in modelling – an activity that is central to both disciplines. A
consideration of a joint approach to this as opposed to who is covering what
content might provide an interesting strategy for co-operation between
science and design and technology in the school curriculum.

REFERENCES

APU (Assessment of Performance Unit) (1984) *Electricity at 15: Science Report for
   Teachers 7*, London, DES.
APU (Assessment of Performance Unit) (1987) *Design and Technological Activity: A
   Framework for Assessment*, London, HMSO.
Arnold, M. and Millar, R. (1988) 'Teaching about electric circuits: a constructivist
   approach', *School Science Review* 70 (251), December.
Barlex, D. (1987) Project work: case studies module 4 units 5–6', *Teaching and
   Learning Technology in Schools*, Milton Keynes, Open University Press.
Barlex, D. (1991) 'Using the energy concept in DAT', *Design and Technology
   Teaching* 23 (1).

Barlex, D. and Carre, C. (1985) *Visual Communication in Science*, Cambridge, Cambridge University Press.

Burden-Teh, P. (1990) 'What form of modelling?' *International Journal of Technology and Design Education* 1 (2).

Driver, R., Guesne, E. and Tiberghein, A. (1985) *Children's Ideas In Science*, Buckingham, Open University Press.

Head, J. (1985) *The Personal Response to Science*, Cambridge, Cambridge University Press.

Kuhn, T. (1962) *The Structure of Scientific Revolutions*, Chicago, University of Chicago Press.

Liddament, T. (1990) 'The role of modelling in design and technology', *Design and Technology Teaching* 22 (3).

Mellor, D.P. (1971) *The Evolution of the Atomic Theory*, Amsterdam, Elsevier.

Papanek, V. (1985) *Design for the Real World*, London, Thames & Hudson.

Chapter 9

The relationship between 'modelling' and designing and making with food as a material in design and technology

Jane Murray

Jane Murray continues the discussion about the use of models in design and technology education and makes a particular case for including food as a possible material for this activity.

INTRODUCTION

This chapter explores five topics related to modelling and to food as a material in design and technology. The topics are: the different interpretations of the term 'modelling'; the function of modelling in design and technology education; modelling and forms of representation; the part that modelling plays in cognitive processes and the significant teaching and learning implications of these topics. Each topic will be considered using 'food' as a material.

DEFINITIONS OF THE TERM 'MODELLING'

To develop an understanding of the relationship between modelling and designing and making with any material it is necessary to explore the meaning of the term 'modelling'. A dictionary offers definitions of the term 'model' giving a variety of usages which cover a replica or representation of:

- a concrete object to show what it looks like or how it works;
- an abstract idea to make it more intelligible;
- a blueprint, design or plan for others to follow or imitate;
- different brands or versions of the same product.

This definition is referring to the word model as a noun; in design and technology the active form of 'modelling' is more commonly used. Modelling is a term used to embrace:

- modelling inside the head – cognitive modelling or imaging; and
- modelling outside the head – concrete modelling.

Modelling inside the head includes the activities of imaging thoughts and ideas and shaping and forming those ideas using images and representational forms. These representational forms might be mental pictures: in stills, in series or moving; in the spoken or written word; or using other forms of language such as number or symbols.

Concrete modelling is the taking of the ideas inside the head and developing them outside the head by sketching, drawing, explaining, planning, exploring, experimenting and manipulating materials and communicating the ideas in a tangible form. Both forms of modelling can be used to develop ideas, explore what things look like or how they might work and test them. The tangible evidence of modelling outside the head are referred to as models, mock-ups or prototypes depending on their stage of development.

'Food' has been identified as one of the materials in design and technology for designing and making outcomes. Much comment and prejudice has been expressed over this and people have questioned whether food is a material that can be used for modelling. There is no conflict between the definitions given here and food. The dictionary definitions can be exemplified using food, for example, a replica or representation of:

– a concrete object to show what it looks like or how it works – any food product;
– an abstract idea to make it more intelligible – nutrition;
– a blueprint, design or plan for others to follow or imitate – a recipe;
– different brands or versions of the same product – a cheesecake.

In relation to modelling, foods can be imaged in the mind and the images can be transformed, and food materials can be shaped, formed and represented through and with other materials and media.

THE FUNCTIONS OF MODELLING

The Assessment of Performance Unit design and technology project explored the concept of imaging and modelling, and the relationship with design and technology activities: 'As soon as we begin to perceive the outline of a task, pictures or images of solutions start to appear in our minds' (APU 1987). This relates closely to modelling inside the head, 'in the mind's eye', imaging, capturing and holding the images or 'temporary spatial displays' (Kosslyn 1978) and then manipulating and modelling them outside the head to produce tangible results. Modelling activity is a tight iterative relationship between imaging and modelling as designing and making proceeds, it is at the crux of all 'practical' activity combining the human ability for thought and action. The concrete modelling fuels the ideas for further cognitive modelling which then need to be tried out in a concrete form.

How do people engage in imaging of ideas with foods? Can these ideas be manipulated by cognitive modelling? The following quote shows the possibility of the former:

Each wine we tasted was accompanied by an imaginary menu, described with much lip-smacking and raising of the eyes to gastronomic heaven. We mentally consumed ecrevisses, salmon cooked with sorrel, rosemary-flavoured chicken from Bresse, roasted baby lamb with creamy garlic sauce, an estouffade of beef and olives, a double loin of pork with spiked slivers of truffle.

(Mayle 1990)

Use the 'mind's eye' to do the following. Image the food on the table at a children's party; the children are 6 years old. What type of potato snack products are on the table? Are they savoury and crisp in texture? Think of a new product that is an interesting shape for the 6-year-olds. What texture, what smell, what taste? Could they be a different colour? Does that work, or is it unappetising? Will the children eat them?What might need changing? This type of guided imagery could be used as teaching strategy to help students appreciate the way in which they can engage in modelling designs for 'new' food products.

MODELLING AS REPRESENTATION

The national curriculum Order for Technology uses the term 'modelling' in the programme of study and the statements of attainment. The references demonstrate a limited definition of the term and imply that modelling is not fundamental to all design and technology activity, but is somehow restricted to representing ideas in drawings and a narrow range of materials. A broad interpretation that acknowledges the source and development of ideas, and the range of representational forms is required.

The range of forms of modelling as representation includes language, both oral and written, and other symbolic forms: number, signs, notation, drawing and three-dimensional forms using available, substitute and specific materials.

Modelling of thoughts, ideas or images is essential for demonstrating, developing, clarifying, expressing and communicating ideas with oneself and with other people. Taking the images that have been modelled inside the head to a point outside the head makes them more accessible for oneself and others to predict, to test, to confront, to transform and to appraise. What is expressed by modelling is a result of images in the mind, these are influenced by what can be expressed by modelling outside the mind.

How can images of design ideas in food be drawn out of the mind and shared with others? Sketches of early ideas could be in the form of language as in the spoken or written word. For example, could you describe the foods that you would imagine to be on sale in a truck drivers' cafe? What happens when someone enters the cafe who requires a vegetarian meal that is low in fat? Ideas for suitable foods could be described in the written or spoken word or through other forms of representation using number, symbols, drawings. As more detail emerges these might need the clarification of, for example, measurement, detail of appearance or make-up, a recipe. Teaching strategies to help foster this type of thinking can be devised. Less easy is still the question of where the images in the mind are coming from. Are they stored snapshots of previous observations? If so, how does someone who has never observed a 6-year-old's party or a truck drivers' cafe, fare?

MODELLING AND COGNITIVE PROCESSES

Does this concept of modelling tie in with theories of cognitive development? Vygotsky wrote that words follow from objects in speech development. Language, signs and symbols are used for action, and have the potential for reverse action. Vygotsky also writes of the importance of tools in child development. By handling tools and mimicking tasks carried out by others the child learns through observation, action and thinking about what is being done.

> Consequently, the child's system of activity is determined at each specific stage both by the child's degree of organic development and by his or her degree of mastery in the use of tools.
>
> (Vygotsky 1978: 21)

This correlates very closely with the tight iterative process described by the APU and the way in which imaging and modelling is used by humans in order to imagine the world, image how it might be different and externalise these imagings through modelling using tools (including, language, signs and symbols) and materials.

Eisner writes about the importance of symbol systems in the 'process of concept formation'.

> We can construct models of the world from which we can derive verbal or numerical propositions or from which we can create visual or auditory images. The point is that, while the sensory system provides us with information about the world in sensory form, our imaginative capacities – when coupled with an inclination toward play – allow us to examine and explore the possibilities of this information.
>
> (Eisner 1985: 204)

These writings on cognitive development serve to demonstrate the importance of modelling in relation to all concept formation, and in considering, rehearsing and engaging in practical activity – which is at the very heart of design and technology.

The visual sense is significant but the other senses are also used to observe, interpret and represent thought. Eisner (1985: 166) points out that:

Basic to the understanding of mind is the importance of understanding the functions that the sensory systems perform in the realisation of consciousness. . . . Our sensory system performs an active role in this process by putting us in contact with the world.

Food, as a material interacts with the visual senses and those of touch, taste and smell. This is important for cognitive modelling in food and responses to these senses can be represented in language and two-dimensional forms. In order to pursue the modelling 'outside the head' to develop design ideas and the function of modelling, food materials must be used to bring the ideas into a form where they can be tested and modelled to a point of satisfaction in terms of the outcome being developed. Some have argued that using similar materials or the same materials in different ways undermines 'representation', but to engage the senses fully in concrete modelling with food usually requires the use of edible materials. The interaction between thought and action is enhanced by the use of food as it enables the breadth of senses to be used and the possible outcome being represented to be appraised appropriately.

MODELLING AND TEACHING AND LEARNING

What are the issues and implications for teaching and learning concerning students and teachers? If modelling is fundamental to the development of capability in design and technology how should teachers address the issue of supporting students' development of modelling strategies?

An important aspect of modelling in design and technology is that both students and teachers need tangible evidence of cognitive modelling. Students use modelling to bring their ideas into the 'real world' and test them; teachers observe the modelling procedures for evidence of the conceptual modelling that the student has engaged in. However, there is a danger that the outcome of the modelling activity becomes the most significant part of the experience at the expense of the process. Modelling then becomes a series of prerequisite steps that students are expected to take to provide evidence for teachers.

The most important teaching and learning points must be that teachers encourage students to engage in imaging and modelling and support future situations by providing opportunities for observation, drawing upon as many experiences as possible. Modelling images in a rich range of representational methods and materials, not a sterile, hoop jumping, linear route that merely requires conforming to a prescribed convention, is necessary.

Gunstone writes of science:

Traditional practical work has features which can inhibit the possibility of students restructuring personal theories. . . . For these students, successful assembly of the apparatus became the only significant task. Once this was achieved the rest of the practical was completed in ritualised fashion, with little or no serious thought.

(Gunstone 1990: 74)

This could equally apply to traditional school-based work with food. Working to recipes and methods prescribed for particular situations is not necessarily going to foster the imagination in designing with food as a material. Students need to be considering the properties of food materials and how they can use, develop, extend or change those properties in the designing and making of 'new' products.

The references to modelling in design and technology seem to be largely based on the conventions of a part of the process used historically in craft, design and technology. These raise similar issues to those highlighted above in reference to science and traditional home economics. The wider concept of imaging and modelling is something that all teachers of design and technology need to embrace. The range of representational materials must be broad and appropriate for the actual materials being represented. Modelling in food serves the purposes of minimising waste and expense in terms of materials as ideas are developed, trialed and tested; or finding out if the ideas that are being taken out of the head and into 'concrete' form will actually 'work'. However, food materials are distinct with some very specific qualities and properties that require handling different from other materials. Foods are nearly always designed and made to be eaten. This raises the issue of the appropriateness of models. Will a beautifully modelled food item made of a non-edible material be of much value for testing?

A particular symbolic system is useful for some types of information, but not for others and vice versa. Thus when we choose to become 'literate' in the use of particular symbol systems, we also begin to define for ourselves what we are capable of conceiving and how we can convey what we have conceived to others.

(Eisner 1985: 125)

CONCLUSION

In conclusion, modelling is at the heart of design and technology. This is not just in its facility to enable students to image the world in which they live, consider changes and use thought and action in designing and making responses to these changes; but also in the development of understanding in relation to all the activities being engaged in.

The iterative processes of thought and action, imaging and modelling inside and outside of the head are fundamental to design and technology when working with any of the materials identified in the statutory order (construction, graphic media, food, textiles). Food designers, technologists and home economists engage in modelling with food when they image possibilities for new products and develop and test those images both inside and outside the head. Some interpretations of 'modelling' seem to have excluded using food as a material for modelling. The difficulty is not with the material but with the narrow interpretation.

There are implications for teachers and for students. Students must develop the capacity to handle a range of images and use modelling strategies to do this, either by concentrating on snapshot images in the mind, or by encouraging the ideas to flow and synthesising them, then communicating them. Teachers should take responsibility for setting up situations and activities that require students to think and be analytical, to give them opportunities for creating images and for modelling those images in a range of ways that are appropriate to the student, the intended audience, and the materials and outcomes being considered. This involves methods of teaching that contextualise activities, encourage creativity, support designing, reflecting and evaluating and the use of appropriate modelling strategies and representations.

Teachers of design and technology could benefit from appraising their understanding of the term 'modelling' as used in national curriculum design and technology. The range of materials is broad and there are significant differences between all of them, which means that narrow definitions and interpretations of the terms used in designing and making are unhelpful and restrictive. It is essential that 'modelling' is interpreted in such a way to clarify its breadth, and that the interpretation encompasses the range of materials in design and technology, the range of methods of representation and the functions required from the activity of engaging in modelling.

REFERENCES

APU (Assessment of Performance Unit) (1987) *Design and Technological Activity: A Framework for Assessment*, London, DES.

Eisner, E. (1985) *The Art of Educational Evaluation: A Personal View*, London, Falmer Press.

Gunstone, R.F. (1990) *Reconstructing Theory from Practical Experience*, Oxford, Oxford University Press.

Kosslyn, S.M. (1978) 'Imagery and cognitive development: a teleological approach', in Siegler, R. (ed.) *Children's Thinking: What Develops*, Lawrence Erlbaum Associates.

Mayle, P. (1990) *A Year in Provence*, London, Pan.

Vygotsky (1978) *Mind in Society*, New York, Wiley.

Chapter 10

A critique of the design process

John Chidgey

In this short chapter a practising teacher relates his personal experiences of teaching the 'design process' which coincides well with the research perspective of both the APU and Hennessy and McCormick.

My experience as a practising CDT teacher spans fifteen years – a period of rapid development during which the notion of 'the design process' has remained central to the teaching of CDT. The idea is that there exists a systematic 'design process' and that such a process can be learnt by pupils and subsequently applied to solve particular problems of design. The purpose of this chapter is to examine this notion.

First, let us consider two cases where pupils may be said to have engaged in 'successful' design. Pupil A was a 16-year-old girl whose experience with the original choice of topic for her final project in the 'CDT: Design and Communication' course had come to nothing. However, I discovered that she was interested in looking after hamsters in the science department, and that in her spare time she had been attempting to improve their environment by redesigning their 'home' which included making models of objects for them to play with. I suggested she might consider continuing with these experiments as part of her coursework for the CDT examination. Her reaction was positive and resulted in the successful design of a new 'home' and the construction of play objects for hamsters.

By comparing pupil A's process of designing with the generally recognised stages of 'the design process': Problem – Research – Development of Ideas – Making – Evaluating, it is possible to identify a number of discrepancies. This pupil's experience of designing came as a result of an interest, or an opportunity to pursue an interest. She developed her first ideas in cardboard models, tested them out with the hamsters, modified them and remade them from plastic (they thought the cardboard models were food!) and then retested them. During this process she gradually formulated her own specific design brief and generated her own ideas. The communication of her ideas graphically and the gradual formulation of a brief evolved 'naturally' as it were. The concepts of 'problem' and 'solution' did not seem to be helpful tools in organising her 'design' experience. It is true that the identification of a problem in this case could have been the hamsters' 'home'. However, this problem had been considered some time before by a member of the science department who had solved that problem by constructing the current hamster 'home'. In other words, this 'solution' was also a 'problem'.

What has changed is the perspective from which the situation is viewed. Context is dynamic and non-linear – problem and solution may coincide; linear models may therefore be inappropriate. A cyclical model may be more realistic since it suggests greater flexibility. Pupil A's design experience, rather than being a step-by-step systematic approach, revealed a more complex interaction between some of the 'design process' stages.

Pupil B was a 16-year-old boy who took and passed the O level technology course between the years 1983 and 1985. He had become interested in learning about computer control and decided to pursue this interest by constructing a model of a crane which he could operate using his own computer program.

When he had overcome some initial design problems and completed his initial construction of the crane, he began his testing procedure. This highlighted further design problems, the main one being the rotation of the turntable. Initially he thought that a single geared DC motor would operate the turntable successfully, but in the end he made several modifications before finally deciding upon stepper motors which gave him the precise control he wanted. During this process of investigation/evaluation and modification of ideas he was also teaching himself more advanced programming skills which would enable his crane to simulate more complicated manoeuvres.

The time spent in learning the necessary programming skills and modifying the crane meant that the meccano model had to be his final 'solution'. As the weeks passed he had been spending most of his time building his model, only doing the minimum of communication of his ideas on paper. I had been concerned because I knew that the assessment procedure was formulated around the stages of 'the design process', marks being allotted accordingly. Being aware of how well motivated and engrossed this pupil was in his work, and of how much and how quickly he was learning, I felt that to have tried to enforce a rigid procedure for satisfying assessment criteria might have been counter-productive. However, I insisted during the last few weeks of the course that he prepare notes and sketches in a manner acceptable for examination assessment.

Both case studies are typical examples of CDT design projects I have been involved with over the years. While it has to be agreed that some pupils follow a process model inflexibly, many others do not, often changing their minds and making modifications and improvements in a seemingly ad hoc manner. Although many of the stages of the design process used by pupils A and B corresponded with those common to many of the models portrayed in

CDT literature, their appearance in the projects seemed to be more complex. Indeed, some of the authors of the CDT literature that I examined (none of whose models are precisely alike) do acknowledge that their models are simplications of the process of designing.

A small survey I conducted into how heads of CDT departments use the design process models, strongly indicated that many of their staff and they themselves follow the stages of the models and expect their pupils to learn them (Chidgey 1988). However, from my own experience of working with CDT colleagues, I am aware that in practice some teachers do interpret these models as being simplifications of design processes, and use them more flexibly as a structure for teaching CDT.

Writers of CDT 'official' guidelines and criteria aimed at teacher education have, over the years, expressed in progressively strong terms the notion of general areas of design skills. In 1979 the DES referred to these as 'seldom achieved in isolation'; in 1983 their expression was 'It is the quality of the pupils' unified experience of designing, making, testing and evaluating that is of fundamental importance rather than any ability he or she may acquire in a specific competency' (DES 1983). More recently the AACDT said 'CDT is an holistic activity-based subject that integrates cognitive and manipulative skills through designing, making and evaluating' (AACDT 1987). It seems, therefore, that the thinking is moving towards broader concepts.

When I examined the question, 'How effective is the use of the design process model in learning the skills, knowledge and desirable attitudes associated with CDT?' (as portrayed in the statements above), my attempts to match CDT learning experiences with discrete stages common to various design process models were unsuccessful (Chidgey 1988). While it was possible to identify some of the skills and attitudes relating strongly to specific stages (for example, it is highly likely that a pupil will experience manipulation during the making stage), it was impossible to pair up many other skills and attitudes with specific stages. Materials can, for example, be manipulated during investigation, solution and modification stages. The skill 'discussion' as a means of communication is likely to percolate throughout the design experience, particularly in a group exercise. The same applies, for example, to discriminating, evaluating, observing, commitment and determination. (This is consistent with the 1979 DES statement that 'CDT is more concerned with the development of desirable attitudes than with an end result or with the acquisition or the retention of a body of knowledge' (DES 1979).) In particular, it seems evaluation cannot be reduced to a single stage which comes at the end of the design activity; it is systemic and all-pervasive – how could we progress otherwise?

Designing is a creative activity. Attempts to equate design with science have been unsuccessful due to the ineffable ingredient of craft knowledge gained through non-scientific experience. Ryle's concept of 'knowing how', like Polangi's 'tacit knowing', cannot be made explicit. It is only 'knowing that' which can be made explicit and formulated into rules. They argue that since 'knowing how' and 'knowing that' are mutually exclusive and interfere with one another, knowledge of the explicit rules of design can actually inhibit practice (Cross *et al.* 1981). Since designing involves making decisions and judgments to bring about change from the existing to the new and uncertain situation, following rules is inappropriate. It is contradictory, then, to suggest that one can be creative by following or learning rules.

But while the concept of design is developing, as already shown, CDT teaching is still hampered by current GCSE assessment procedures. Although pupils at this level are encouraged to identify and tackle problems themselves, there is a tendency for what should be a creative experience to be diluted by attempts to satisfy the assessment criteria (hence the 'artificial' means by which I ensured that pupil B gained appropriate reward for his coursework). The case studies indicate that some pupils, given teacher guidance and encouragement, can develop their individual process of designing, and it ought to be subsequently possible to develop a more valid means of assessment which gives due credit to the development of their design skills and achievements.

Would we, as CDT teachers, not be better employed focusing our attention for assessment purposes on the characteristics of the learning experience, rather than attempting to satisfy stages of 'a design process'? One possible way of doing this would be to replace the notion of 'stages' (which implies a particular order) with 'aspects' of designing. This would still provide us with the necessary structure to aid learning while shifting the emphasis towards the development of individual pupil profiles.

In the foundation years, where the context of a design experience is often provided by the teacher, I would suggest that design briefs need to be rigorously articulated to identify the possible/probable design skills learnt from each experience. This would facilitate pupil-oriented assessment, contribute to the preparation of further teaching packages, and provide some opportunity for continuity, progression, reinforcement and differentiation through the age and ability range. The 'aspects' of designing would provide the essential framework for lower school work.

It is unlikely that 'a' or 'the' design process exists, and that even if it did, the learning of a systematic approach to designing would assist pupils in developing the necessary skills for solving particular problems of design. Instead, a more flexible framework based on 'aspects' of designing, adopted to assist in developing the skills, attitudes and knowledge associated with CDT, may encourage teachers and pupils to concentrate their thoughts and efforts towards the design activity itself while providing the essential structure to aid and monitor progress. At the same time, exam boards and assessors should adopt a more pedagogical approach to monitoring and recording pupils' progress in designing in CDT.

REFERENCES

AACDT (Association of Advisors in Craft, Design and Technology) (1987) *Craft, Design and Technology. Policy Paper*, Sleaford.

Chidgey, J. (1988) *An Examination and Critique of the Notion of 'The Design Process' as Used in Teaching of Craft, Design and Technology*, Bulmershe College of Higher Education.

Cross, N., Naughton, J. and Walker, D. (1981) 'Design method and scientific method', *Design Studies* 2 (4), 195–200.

DES (Department of Education and Science) (1979) *Aspects of Secondary Education: Craft, Design and Technology*, London, HMSO.

DES (Department of Education and Science) (1983) *CDT – A Curriculum Statement for the 11–16 Age Group*, London, HMSO.

Chapter 11

The general problem-solving process in technology education

Myth or reality?

Sara Hennessy and Robert McCormick

In this chapter the products of educational research into how pupils learn technology are shown to inform everyday practice.

INTRODUCTION

'Problem-solving' is a much abused term in many areas of the curriculum, including the relatively new area of technology. A basic confusion exists between *problem-based learning* and teaching *problem-solving methods*. Most areas of the curriculum give pupils problems to solve as one approach to learning, where the main purpose is to help pupils understand certain concepts or ideas in the subject. The actual *process* of solving the problem may be unimportant. In technology education, problem-based learning could be used to teach about mechanisms by, for example, setting a problem of transforming one kind of movement into another (perhaps dressed up in some 'realistic' context of someone needing to produce a toy with an electric motor to make the hair rise up and down on a puppet). For those who take a learner-centred approach to education, this pedagogic strategy is very important because the learner is active and the problem makes the learning meaningful.

When teaching problem-solving methods, on the other hand, the processes involved in solving the problem are the focus, and understanding of concepts (*conceptual* knowledge) is usually of secondary importance. Those who are concerned to teach problem-solving consider it to be of more lasting relevance to pupils than content. Often they characterise problem-solving as some kind of idealised process involving the sub-processes of recognising a problem, generating and implementing a solution, and evaluating the results. Knowledge of these sub-processes (*procedural* knowledge) is seen as applying across a variety of areas of the curriculum. In technology education, such a set of sub-processes is used to unite five previously separate curriculum areas (art and design, business studies, CDT, home economics and IT).

This approach depends upon some idea of a general problem-solving process that can be used in a variety of contexts and, if such a process exists, it is an important part of education. National curriculum technology intends to develop general practical capability, preparing students to handle complex problems in their future personal and working lives (NCC 1989: 1.47). This idea of a general problem-solving capability is an attractive one, but is it just a myth? What is the evidence for a general problem-solving capability that can be taught, and that can be used in a variety of curriculum areas, and indeed in adult life? In this chapter we examine the evidence that derives from studying what both experts and ordinary people do in their everyday activity (what is called 'situated cognition'), and from the research in science education on children's 'alternative frameworks'. We also look at the specific difficulties of a process-based area such as design and technology, where the main concern is to learn to use the 'design and make' process.

EXPERT PROBLEM-SOLVING

One obvious source for considering what we teach pupils about problem-solving is to look to see how experts solve problems. The sub-processes identified earlier for technology are based upon some idealised view of what experts do, but experts themselves disagree about this view (NEDO 1976). In fact, those who have studied how experts solve problems find that they do not follow a generalised decontextualised process (Glaser 1992). How experts work evidently varies according to the context in which they are working. In particular, they use considerable knowledge (much of it informal) about the problem area, and vary what they do according to the changing needs of particular problems. Significantly also, in actual work situations, experts work collaboratively, and have goals which they want to achieve and which they may even set. This makes the whole activity more meaningful to them.

Pupils in school (novice problem-solvers as they are called in the research literature) work in quite different situations from experts. They are not so goal-directed in solving a problem, nor do they work under the same constraints, and the task is less meaningful. More importantly, novices are continually working in unfamiliar contexts, where the nature of the problems and the knowledge required to solve them may not have been encountered before. Taken as a whole, the research on problem-solving challenges the idea of a general problem-solving process which is independent of the particular nature of the problem.

SITUATED COGNITION

Recent evidence from researchers taking a 'situated' perspective (predominantly in the area of mathematics learning) provides a similar challenge. This work spans several cultures and characterises successful problem-solving strategies used in everyday life outside school. It has investigated mathematical capability in the workplace and in domestic life, documenting the craft apprenticeship of tailors in Liberia (Reed and Lave 1981), the everyday practice of arithmetic and manipulation of quantity relationships in grocery shopping, cooking, dieting and money management (Lave 1988), street vending in Brazil (Carraher, Carraher and Schliemann 1985; 1987), dairy workers' calculation strategies (Scribner 1984), and construction work (Carraher 1986). Researchers in this tradition have consistently found that concepts and relationships which appear complex to learners in a classroom context are dealt with inventively and effectively in everyday situations, and that problem-solving is structured into, and by, ongoing activity (Lave, Smith and Butler 1988). In other words, rather than applying some specialist procedure specifying how to solve a problem (e.g. identify the problem, generate solutions, etc.), people use a *variety* of methods that change appropriately according to the circumstances. Some key examples are as follows.

Most adults and children spontaneously invent their own, reliable mathematical procedures, and they rarely use the standard written methods outside school (Fitzgerald 1985; Shuard 1986). Two large-scale survey reports on adult numeracy have concluded that formal teaching lacks relevance to mathematics as commonly practised in daily life; many adults have forgotten those methods or they lack the confidence to use them (ALBSU 1983; Sewell 1982). By way of illustration, Lave (1988) has shown that personal methods are commonly invented and used successfully by adults in a practical situation (calculating the 'best buy' in a supermarket) with a very high degree of accuracy (98 per cent), whereas the same people solved only 59 per cent of similar calculations correctly in a written test. This finding and that of Reed and Lave (1981) indicated that two distinct systems of arithmetic procedures and practices (symbol- or rule-based versus meaning-based) are functioning independently within the same culture, with different procedures and rates of success. This conclusion is corroborated by studies contrasting the calculation strategies employed by the same children selling produce in Brazilian street markets, in solving word problems and in computation exercises (Carraher *et al.* 1985; 1987). Similarly, construction workers have been found to demonstrate greater skill in applying proportional reasoning when interpreting blueprints than students who learned the principles in formal mathematics; the presence of physical objects in the builders' environment rendered the task more relevant to them (Carraher 1986).

Collectively this work shows that out-of-school problem-solving in mathematics can be sophisticated, but that it is intimately connected with the specific context, and it is the familiarity with this context that gives meaning to the activity. This contrasts with the school situation where mathematical operations are divorced from reality, have less meaning and hence appear more difficult. Skilled practical thinking varies to adapt to the changing circumstances of problems, and to the changing conditions while the problems are being solved (Scribner 1984). Formal procedures for solving problems are therefore largely unhelpful.

CONSTRUCTIVIST RESEARCH IN SCIENCE EDUCATION

Students' mental models are similarly flexible and context-specific. Evidence for this comes from the wealth of research over the last two decades into 'alternative frameworks' in children's understanding of science (e.g. Driver 1989; McDermott 1984). There is conclusive evidence that children construct intuitive beliefs about natural phenomena (such as heat or forces) that conflict with the scientific viewpoint and that these beliefs are highly resistant to instruction and evidence to the contrary. These frameworks, and similarly lay adults' mental models of science and technology (Wynne, Payne and Wakeford 1990), often appear to be partial, incoherent or internally inconsistent (Champagne, Gunstone and Klopfer 1985). This is because, as with everyday mathematics, pieces of knowledge or cognitive models (e.g. of electricity in a circuit) are being drawn upon flexibly and according to their appropriateness and usefulness in a *specific practical context*. These models provide a sensible framework for understanding and describing phenomena which fit with a person's existing beliefs and ideas about how the world works. For example, our common experience of moving objects is that they remain still unless we push them, yet we have to convince pupils that this model of motion is limited to a world with gravity and friction. Rather than such an Aristotelian view, we want pupils to use a Newtonian one that opposes their experience (i.e. to realise that a body continues moving at a certain velocity unless acted upon by a force). In this sense pupils act in the same way as experts do, except that their models are derived from a different everyday experience. Research on problem-solving indicates the importance of such models in understanding and hence solving problems (Glaser 1984).

The idea that we teach pupils correct conceptual models ('correct' because they have universal application and are shared by the scientific community) that they can then use in situations they meet in ordinary or working life ignores their experience of alternative models that work in particular situations. Formal knowledge, such as that taught in science and mathematics, is not in a form that can simply be 'applied'. As Layton (1991) reminds us, formal scientific knowledge needs to be reconstructed, integrated and contextualised for practical action in everyday life. The expectation that pupils solving problems (such as they would encounter in technology education) can draw upon knowledge from other subject areas (e.g. science and mathematics) is therefore likely to be unrealistic. The pilot work we have recently carried out at the Open University indicates that Year 8 pupils working on design and technology activities are unable to use, for example, elementary mathematics (e.g. simple arithmetic and geometric drawing) in their tasks, and confirms the informal work of Job (1991) on similar difficulties in using scientific knowledge.

In addition to the unrealistic demand for transfer of conceptual knowledge across curriculum areas, design and technology activities place a clear expectation upon pupils to assimilate an all-purpose 'design process' and apply it in up to five different subject areas which previously had little connection. However, the research on expert problem-solving and situated cognition points to the conclusion that the idea of a general problem-solving capability that can be used in a variety of contexts and subject areas again has little empirical justification. The earlier discussion of the literature from cognitive psychology and situated cognition indicates that problem-solving in the areas of mathematics, science and technology will be different. Indeed, even within each of the three areas, particular problems and situations will require different approaches – that is the implication of the doubt that research casts on a general problem-solving ability. However, this notion that there is such a general ability has a long tradition and there are instructional programmes specifically based upon it. What is the evidence for a general transferable problem-solving capability that can be taught, often independently of the prior acquisition of subject knowledge, and used flexibly in a variety of contexts? The next section examines this question.

EVIDENCE FOR TRANSFER

The development of programmes of instruction in higher order skills is based upon the assumed existence of universal cognitive skills of problem-solving and thinking. A well-known example is de Bono's CoRT (Cognitive Research Trust) Thinking Program. The CoRT programme uses generally familiar knowledge and is intended to foster problem-solving, interpersonal and lateral thinking skills, including metacognitive skills (i.e. reflecting upon one's own learning, planning a task, and apportioning time and resources) and a wide variety of idea- and solution-generation techniques and evaluation techniques. Although the programme has been widely used in USA and elsewhere for over fifteen years, very little systematic evaluation of it has taken place and there is minimal support for its lofty claims that students will transfer their new thinking skills to 'a variety of real-life situations' (de Bono 1985). While anecdotal evidence is often positive and short-term gains have been reported by Edwards (1991), the first substantial evaluation of de Bono's classroom materials by the Schools Council (Hunter-Grundin 1985) failed to demonstrate any significant transfer. Although there is some other evidence to support the notion of general cognitive skill development (Adey and Shayer, in press), the limitations of transfer theory and the importance of context in the application of knowledge and skills have increasingly been recognised and demonstrated empirically (Glaser 1984; Lave 1988).

In sum, research shows that what problem-solvers of all ages in everyday and workplace situations actually do and know depends on the context in which they are asked to work, and bears little relation to what goes on in the average classroom. Why, then, has the traditional classroom environment become an alien culture which lacks relevance to the everyday problem-solving practices and thinking which take place outside it?

PROBLEM-SOLVING INSIDE AND OUTSIDE THE CLASSROOM

The findings reported above are not altogether surprising when we explore the differences between problem-solving processes in classrooms and everyday situations. These differences include individual as opposed to group activity, the nature of incentives and the way problems and their solutions are formulated:

1 In school, a premium is placed upon what individuals can do by themselves and without external support (Resnick 1987). Yet teamwork is the norm in practical settings outside school (especially in technological activity), where learning is characterised by the sharing of informal knowledge and the construction and negotiation of meaning (Wenger 1991).
2 The incentives outside school lead to learning that is self-motivated or commercially driven and the problems encountered are hence authentic and relevant to the learner rather than artificially constructed, as are computation or even some 'design and make' exercises.
3 In school, many problems are pre-formulated and accompanied by the requisite data, whereas outside school, problems are seldom clearly defined initially and the information necessary for solving them must be actively sought from a variety of sources (Maier 1980).
4 Although the same subject topics arise in both contexts, the methods used are quite different; school mathematics relies heavily on paper and pencil, for instance, and the greatest premium is placed on pure thought activities – what individuals can do without the external support of books, notes, calculators or other complex instruments. In contrast, most mental activities and actions in everyday life are intimately engaged with the physical world – with objects, events and with some form of tools. The resultant cognitive activity is shaped by and dependent upon the kinds of tools available (Resnick 1987).

The result of the differences between problem-solving inside and outside the classroom, and the devaluing of pupils' own informal knowledge, is that pupils are likely to ignore the formal methods taught in school. They secretly adhere to their own reliable and far more flexible intuitive methods whilst presenting a 'veneer of accomplishment' (Lave, Smith and Butler

1988). This phenomenon is explored further below in the context of technology education.

DESIGN AND TECHNOLOGY AS A PROCESS-ORIENTED CURRICULUM

In England and Wales, the design and technology component of technology in the national curriculum defines capability in terms of the ability to employ the sub-processes of: identifying and clarifying tasks or problems; investigating; generating and developing solutions; evaluating (DES/WO 1990). These correspond to the kinds of general processes in the literature discussed earlier. Design educators maintain that these broad processes are universal, and proponents of this approach make great claims about the variety of potential outcomes. Examples include discovery, critical assessment, decision-making, problem-solving, planning, evaluating, reflecting and collaboration (deLuca 1992). Eggleston (see p. 34) makes the claim that such skills will have a 'wide general applicability in the adult life likely to be experienced by the students'. Sellwood (1990) asserts that the value of the process approach lies in its structuring and organising of thinking skills, and that it will ideally become second nature to pupils (and teachers) to organise a means of successfully achieving objectives which can then operate at all levels and in all situations. How realistic are these claims, especially in the light of the evidence examined earlier in this chapter?

The answer is far from clear. The only substantive published research was not based upon what pupils did, but upon the records of their design-and-make activity (sketches, notes, drawings, 3-D models, prototypes and finished products), along with interviews with the pupils and their teachers (APU 1991). Our research at the Open University is investigating the question of whether or not pupils are assimilating and developing a coherent view of the design process. One of our central hypotheses is that pupils may merely try to accommodate teachers' aims through superficially and mechanically following the prescribed procedures, whilst simultaneously adhering to their own product-oriented agendas, thus creating a 'veneer of accomplishment'. We believe that a 'veneer' could be encouraged by an over-emphasised design process and the focus of the assessment system within design and technology upon: (a) systematic procedures clearly demonstrated through notes, sketches, artefacts, etc.; (b) the style and quality of project folders/reports. This belief is supported by prior work showing that assessment procedures can lead pupils to omit unsuccessful designs from their project folders (Anning 1992) and to describe a logical, systematic procedure rather than the actual development of design ideas (Jeffery 1990). The Hayes Report (1983) indicates that the 'veneer' extends to professional designers who can be observed to doctor their portfolios too, as a consequence of working under the same frustrating constraint of having to offer several alternative solutions to a design problem.

Our preliminary observations during the initial stage of secondary teaching highlight the possibility of the opposite problem arising, namely that pupils may in general remain unaware of the processes they are supposed to be learning and doing. Although the ways in which tasks are presented and adapted to pupils' needs and the degree of explicitness about the values of the task, are known to be crucial factors in performance (Black 1990; Roazzi and Bryant 1992), we found that teachers frequently did not initially make clear their aims and assessment criteria. Consequently pupils were not even aware that they were undertaking 'processes' such as modelling and evaluating, nor were they taught any specific techniques to enable them to carry out the processes. For example, when faced with evaluating a model or a final product they had designed, they had no criteria to judge it against, because they had not been made aware of the need for a specification at an earlier stage. We suspect that, as in other subject areas such as mathematics, there is a degree of mismatch between teachers' and children's agendas, perceptions and beliefs concerning technological activities (Simpson 1988; Wittrock 1977). The children we have observed engaging in technological activity seem to emulate the novice problem-solvers characterised by Schoenfeld (1987); they spend far more time doing rather than thinking or planning, neither analysing the task adequately nor monitoring their own performance. This characterisation is not derived merely from pupils' lack of competence, but from the ways in which we believe activity is structured in schools.

A critical insight derived from the situated cognition literature discussed earlier is that in rich problem-solving contexts, 'problems' emerge out of dilemmas presenting a personal challenge. Learning arises when means are sought to resolve those dilemmas (Lave *et al.* 1988). Design and technology has greater potential than any other curriculum area for problems to be formulated in the context of authentic activity, so that pupils might engage in both reflective and active participation (two aspects identified as important by Kimbell and his colleagues, APU 1991). New or 'emergent' problems often arise during the course of design and technology activities, which present unique opportunities for learning through open-ended project work. (Thus, producing a stable structure for a kite might become for the pupil the 'problem' that emerges during construction, superseding the more global 'problem' presented by the teacher of creating a kite for a special occasion.) The popular idea that 'problem-solving' in technology must be confined to a holistic 'design-and-make' process is hence under challenge. Our position is that 'design and make' is instead a complex and iterative process of refining problems; various kinds of tasks, and stages within them, present different problems which require different approaches. According to Lave (1988), authentic problem-solving activity is commonly represented as a systematic sequence of recognising a problem, representing it, implementing a resolution and evaluating the results. Unfortunately this ignores the multitude of ways of tackling a problem and the fact that some activities take place simultaneously or structure each other differently on different occasions.

Unfulfilled ambitions

To summarise, there appears to be a conflict between the problem-solving literature and the ambitious assumptions made in technology education, particularly that of a generally applicable design and problem-solving process. The research evidence casts doubt on any one general model of problem-solving, and design and technology activities may therefore not be fulfilling the ambitious aims of applicability of their proponents. The technology curriculum covers an impossibly wide range of activities and cannot prepare students for all kinds of future problem-solving, but is applicable only to those problems with related content (Medway 1992). Pupils have difficulty in operating with decontextualised knowledge, in using knowledge acquired in other subject areas and in bridging with problem-solving outside school. The present demand for pupils to conceive and develop an explicit design proposal bears no relation to expert practice and the demand for the artificial generation of several design ideas may be counter-productive. These demands could lead to children mechanically following a sequence of systematic procedures. To avoid this, more explicit attention needs to be given to developing students' problem-solving skills (Johnson 1987). 'Problem-solving' in technology is in fact much more than a straightforward sequence of 'design and make'; it requires a complex range of different approaches according to the changing nature and requirements of the activity undertaken, the information available, the stage reached and individual learning style. Rigidly fostering a single all-purpose process is inherently unproductive, and children need to realise that there are inevitably multiple ways to solve any problem.

A WAY FORWARD?

Despite the evidence that most forms of everyday problem-solving require context-specific forms of competence, there is nevertheless evidence that global problem-solving strategies may also have a role to play. After all, situation-specific learning by itself can be very limiting, precluding transfer when familiar aspects of a task are changed. Decontextualised knowledge is potentially a powerful aid which helps us master complex situations and results in far greater flexibility.

A major implication of the research literature is that instruction needs to achieve a balance between subject matter knowledge, general problem-solving strategies and strategies for effective learning (Glaser 1984).

Encouraging steps have indeed been taken in this direction in the form of the recently publicised work on 'cognitive acceleration' across the curriculum through science learning (Adey and Shayer, in press), and a series of highly successful 'cognitive apprenticeship' programmes for mathematics and language learning (Palincsar and Brown 1984; Scardamalia and Bereiter, in press; Schoenfeld 1985). These promote situated learning by giving students the opportunity to observe, engage in and invent or discover expert strategies in context. They also aim to extend situated learning to different settings, decontextualising knowledge by explicitly conveying cognitive and metacognitive strategies for monitoring its use. The time is right to explore the potential of similar instructional approaches in other subjects such as technology. Johnson and Thomas (1992) have pointed out that apprenticeship programs could easily be adapted for technological problem-solving, with teachers serving as role models for students, solving unfamiliar problems without fear of making errors or of encountering difficulties in finding solutions. Technology teachers could thereby show students how to collect and use information to solve technological problems and help them realise that not all problems have straightforward solutions.

IMPLICATIONS FOR THE TEACHER

The above discussion yields several implications for educational practice in the context of the requirements of the national curriculum. First, if teachers believe that the general design and problem-solving process is useful and can be transferred across many different contexts (as the national curriculum technology asks them to do), then they must endeavour to make it explicit. Children will *not respond* to a process approach otherwise. This has at least three consequences.

1 Teachers must have a clear idea or model of the component processes involved and how they are inter-related

Such an idea has to be developed in the knowledge that there is disagreement about the various models put forward. (See McCormick 1993 for a discussion of some of these models.) In particular, the degree of iteration in the process is controversial among engineers (NEDO 1976) and educators, who disagree about which models to follow and whose choices reflect their different motivations (e.g. working in industrial settings or developing creative potential in children). Unfortunately it is common practice to interpret the problem-solving sub-processes as ordered steps in a linear process (HMI 1992: 18), despite warnings in the *Non-Statutory Guidance* (NCC 1991) and in the first report of the APU Design and Technology Project (1987: 2.12):

Used unsympathetically, the approach can reveal a greater concern for 'doing' all the stages in the process, than for combining a growing range of capabilities in a way which reflects individual creativity and confident and effective working methods.

A sympathetic approach may allow the use of a sequence of some sub-processes, but would encourage interaction and flexibility in their use.

2 Teachers must attempt to structure and resource activities so that all pupils can exercise the sub-processes

'Design and make' activities that always include a holistic process, with little or no focus on particular sub-processes (such as generating design ideas) are likely to make it difficult for pupils to build up their understanding and skills at using the processes. We have already pointed out the importance of emergent problems, which may cloud pupils' view of the overall process. This, combined with the fact that activities stretch over a number of weeks, will tend to reduce the importance of the holistic process and fail to help pupils in exercising specific sub-processes that could be used at a variety of stages in their activity. Thus some activities should have a specific focus on particular sub-processes. For example, an activity could focus on evaluation, requiring pupils to draw up a specification and use it to evaluate their product. Such sub-processes can be introduced at different stages to show that they need to be used flexibly; an activity might begin by evaluating an existing product as a way of identifying a need in the market or to help generate ideas for a new design (in addition to using evaluation to assess alternative designs or finished products made by pupils).

3 There must be some method by which pupils are supposed to recognise, reflect on and use these sub-processes

This is essentially an issue of teachers talking about their teaching with pupils, who should be informed what the emphasis of the activity is and what the teacher is aiming to do. Self-assessment and group discussions about the process they have used could play a crucial role in getting them to reflect upon the sub-processes. If pupils are to learn about processes, they must be conscious of them and actively engage in developing their own capability in employing them.

The second teaching implication concerns the way knowledge is used in design and technology tasks. If pupils are required to be able to use scientific knowledge, for example, then some deliberate effort will be needed to facilitate and support this. Teachers must help pupils apply such knowledge in the context of a specific problem. At its simplest level, this means a teacher being aware in general terms of what science and mathematics pupils have encountered, and realising that the inability to use this knowledge can prevent pupils from using the problem-solving processes. More problematic is the need to spend time with individual pupils when they appear to be stuck, helping them to access and use their knowledge. For most teachers there is only time to give a quick fix by telling a pupil what to do or 'providing' the knowledge, without being able to get pupils to make the transformation discussed earlier in this chapter.

Next, there is a need for pupils to develop 'metacognitive strategies', to 'think about their thinking'. In teaching mathematical problem-solving, Schoenfeld (1985) encouraged pupils to ask themselves questions about what they were doing, what they were trying to achieve and what they would do next. Continual asking of such questions eventually led pupils to internalise them and this improved their problem-solving performance. Requiring children to assess and monitor their own progress and perform-ance in this way should help make pupils aware of what they are doing and why.

The fourth pedagogic implication follows up the idea of 'cognitive apprenticeship' introduced earlier. This requires pupils to be able to work with and observe an expert solving design and technology problems, or at least aspects of them. The expert could be the teacher undertaking design and technology activities or an outside expert (designer or engineer) could be brought in to work with pupils so they can see how he or she works. In most design and technology classrooms, the teacher rarely takes part in activity, and usually only demonstrates particular skills rather than modelling problem-solving strategies. This is often to ensure that the pupil becomes involved in the task rather than just getting the teacher to do the work, but the result is that the pupils never see the teacher solving the kinds of problems they will encounter.

Apprenticeship can also take place in the context of peer interaction and collaboration. A situation where pupils are working together is both ben-eficial to learning and reflects most technological activity outside of school. To overcome the problems of individual assessment as part of a group, specific roles and division of labour may be necessary. Certain parts of the design and technology process become more significant in group work. For example, a pupil group acting as the market research department can draw up a specification that is used with a concept design team, a detailed design team, and a manufacturing group. Thus the specification acts as the common terms of reference for several teams, just as it does in industry. Similarly the communication function of modelling (2-D or 3-D) can be exploited when, for example, the design team produce their ideas for the detailed design team, and the detailed design team produce manufacturing drawings. Discussions and negotiations in these kinds of situations will make more explicit many of the processes that design and technology teachers are anxious to encourage. The group work will provide a more meaningful engagement with these processes as a means to solving the problems as they occur within the 'design and make' task.

Finally, the most successful technology education programmes strive to promote pupils' 'ownership' of problems. These problems should be ones pupils want to solve, which are real and relevant *to them*, and for which they can take responsibility. This means providing opportunities for discovery and invention of problems, as well as solutions. We believe that 'problem solving' must come to denote the resolution of meaningful problems and dilemmas in the context of guided social interaction and negotiation with teachers and peers.

To conclude, we would ask teachers to examine their own views on problem-solving in the light of the evidence we have presented. The fact that the research base on how pupils solve technological problems is as yet relatively weak, means that teachers must carry out such an examination in a spirit of exploration.

REFERENCES

Adey, P. and Shayer, M. (in press) 'An exploration of long-term far-transfer effects following an extended intervention programme in the high school science curriculum', *Cognition and Instruction*.

ALBSU (Adult Literacy and Basic Skills Units) (1983) *Literacy and Numeracy: Evidence from the National Child Development Study*, London, ALBSU.

Anning, A. (1992) 'Learning design and technology in primary schools,' in R. McCormick, P. Murphy and M.E. Harrison (eds) *Teaching and Learning Technology*, London, Addison-Wesley.

APU (Assessment of Performance Unit) (1987) *Design and Technological Activity: A Framework for Assessment*, London, HMSO.

APU (Assessment of Performance Unit) (1991) *The Assessment of Performance in Design and Technology*, London, School Examinations and Assessment Council, HMSO.

Black, P. (1990) *Implementing technology in the National Curriculum: Key issues in implementation*, London, The Standing Conference on Schools' Science and Technology and DATA.

Carraher, T.N. (1986) 'From drawings to buildings', *International Journal of Behavioural Development* 9, 527–44.

Carraher, T.N., Carraher, D.W. and Schliemann, A.D. (1985) 'Mathematics in the streets and in schools', *British Journal of Developmental Psychology* 3, 21–9.

Carraher, T.N., Carraher, D.W. and Schliemann, A.D. (1987) 'Written and oral mathematics', *Journal for Research in Mathematics Education* 18 (2), 83–97.

Champagne, A.B., Gunstone, R.F. and Klopfer, L.E. (1985) 'Instructional consequences of students' knowledge about physical phenomena', in L.H.T. West and A.L. Pines (eds) *Cognitive Structure and Conceptual Change*, London, Academic Press.

de Bono, E. (1985) 'The CoRT Thinking Program', in J.W. Segal, S.F. Chipman and R. Glaser (eds) *Thinking and Learning Skills*, Vol. 1, Hillsdale, NJ, Erlbaum.

deLuca, V.W. (1992) 'Survey of technology education problem-solving activities', *The Technology Teacher*, February, 26–30.

DES/WO (1990) *Technology in the National Curriculum*, London, HMSO.

Driver, R. (1989) 'Students' conceptions and the learning of science', *International Journal of Science Education* 11 (5), 481–90.

Edwards, J. (1991) 'The direct teaching of thinking skills', in G. Evans (ed.) *Learning and Teaching Cognitive Skills*, Hawthorn, Victoria, Australian Council for Educational Research.

Fitzgerald, A. (1985) *New technology and Mathematics in Employment.* Birmingham, Department of Curriculum Studies.

Glaser, R. (1984) 'Education and thinking: the role of knowledge', *American Psychologist* 39 (2), 93–104.

Glaser, R. (1992) 'Expert knowledge and processes of thinking', in D.F. Halpern (ed.) *Enhancing Thinking Skills in Sciences and Mathematics*, Hillsdale, NJ, Erlbaum.

Hayes Report (1983) *The Industrial Requirements of Industry*, A report commissioned by the DES and undertaken by Chris Hayes Associates and Keller Dorsey Associates, London, Design Council.

HMI (Her Majesty's Inspectorate of Schools) (1992) *Technology at Key Stages 1, 2 and 3*, London, HMSO.

Hunter-Grundin, E. (1985) *Teaching Thinking: An Evaluation of Edward De Bono's Classroom Materials*, London, Schools Council Publications.

Jeffery, J.R. (1990) 'Design methods in CDT', *Journal of Art and Design Education* 9 (1), 57–70.

Job, G.C. (1991) 'The relationship between science and technology in the school entitlement curriculum', in M. Hacker, A Gordon and M. de Vries (eds) *Integrating Advanced Technology into Technology Education*, Berlin, Springer-Verlag.

Johnson, S.D. (1987) 'Teaching problem solving', *School Shop*, February, 15–17.

Johnson, S.D. and Thomas, R. (1992) 'Technology education and the cognitive revolution', *The Technology Teacher* 51 (4), 7–12.

Lave, J. (1988) *Cognition in Practice: Mind, Mathematics and Culture in Everyday Life*, NY, Cambridge University Press.

Lave, J., Smith, S. and Butler, M. (1988) 'Problem solving as an everyday practice', in J. Lave, J.G. Greeno, A. Schoenfeld, S. Smith and M. Butler (eds), *Learning Mathematical Problem Solving*, Institute for Research on Learning Report no. IRL88-0006, Palo Alto, CA.

Layton, D. (1991) 'Science education and praxis: The relationship of school science to practical action', *Studies in Science Education* 19, 43–79.

Maier, E. (1980) 'Folk mathematics', *Mathematics Teaching* 93, 21–3.

McCormick, R. (1993) *Teaching and Learning Design*, PGCE Pamphlet, Milton Keynes, Open University.

McDermott, L.C. (1984) 'Research on conceptual understanding in mechanics', *Physics Today*, July, 24–32.

Medway, P. (1992) 'Constructions of technology: Reflections on a new subject', in J. Beynon and H. Mackay (eds) *Technological Literacy and the Curriculum*, London, Falmer.

NCC (National Curriculum Council) (1989) *Design and Technology for Ages 5–16: Proposals of the Secretary of State for Education and Science and the Secretary of State for Wales*, York, NCC.

NCC (National Curriculum Council) (1991) *Non-Statutory Guidance for Design and Technology*, York, NCC.

NEDO (National Economic Development Office) (1976) *The professions in the Construction Industries*, London, NEDO.

Palincsar, A.S. and Brown, A.L. (1984) 'Reciprocal teaching of comprehension-fostering and comprehension-monitoring activities', *Cognition and Instruction* 7 (2), 117–75.

Reed, H.J. and Lave, J. (1981) 'Arithmetic as a tool for investigating relations between culture and cognition', in R.W. Casson (ed.) *Language, Culture and Cognition: Anthropological Perspectives*, New York, Macmillan.

Resnick, L.B. (1987) 'Learning in school and out', *Educational Researcher* 16 (9), 13–20.

Roazzi, A. and Bryant, P. (1992) 'Social class, context and cognitive development', in P. Light and G. Butterworth (eds) *Context and Cognition: Ways of Learning and Knowing*, Hemel Hempstead, Harvester Wheatsheaf.

Scardamalia, M. and Bereiter, C. (in press) 'An architecture for collaborative knowledge building', in E. De Corte, M. Linn, H. Mandl and L. Verschaffel (eds) *Computer-Based Learning Environments and Problem Solving* (NATO-ASI Series F: Computer and Systems Sciences), Berlin, Springer-Verlag.

Schoenfeld, A.H. (1985), *Mathematical Problem Solving*, Orlando, FL, Academic Press.

Schoenfeld, A.H. (1987) 'What's all the fuss about metacognition?' in A.H. Schoenfeld (ed.) *Cognitive Science and Mathematics Education*, Hillsdale, NJ, Erlbaum.

Scribner, S. (1984) 'Studying working intelligence', in B. Rogoff and J. Lave (eds) *Everyday Cognition*, Cambridge, MA, Harvard University Press.

Sellwood, P. (1990) 'The national project: practical; problem solving 5–13', *Proceedings of the 3rd National Conference on Design and Technology Education Research and Curriculum Development*, Loughborough University of Technology.

Sewell, B. (1982) *Use of Mathematics by Adults in Daily Life*, Leicester, Advisory Council for Adult and Continuing Education.

Shuard, H. (1986) 'Primary mathematics towards 2000', *Mathematical Gazette* 70, 175–85.

Simpson, M. (1988) 'Improving learning in schools – what do we know? A cognitive science perspective', *Scottish Educational Review* 20 (1), 22–31.

Wenger, E. (1991) 'Communities of practice: where learning happens', *Benchmark*, Fall, 6–8.

Wittrock, M.C. (1977) 'Learning as a generative process', in M.C. Wittrock (ed.) *Learning and Instruction*, Berkeley, McCrutchan.

Wynne, B.E., Payne, S.J. and Wakeford, J.R. (1990) *Frameworks for Understanding Public Interpretations of Science and Technology*, End of Award Report for ESRC grant A09250008.

Part III

Teaching technology

Chapter 12

Planning for capability and progression for design and technology in the national curriculum

Pat Doherty, John Huxtable, Jane Murray and Ed Gillett

The design and technology advisory team from Somerset provide a link between concerns about how children learn and ideas about how teaching should be planned.

NATIONAL CURRICULUM DESIGN AND TECHNOLOGY – IS THERE A MISSING LINK?

National curriculum design and technology calls for the tackling of open-ended activities in designing and making to meet particular needs. Issues encountered whilst designing and making are likely to demand the interaction of new and developing concepts that take students beyond their previous personal and educationally provided experience. They will be required to make increasingly more complex decisions and judgments and to develop concepts related to design and technology. Students will build their own platform of experience by drawing upon knowledge understood, skills developed and values formulated. Design and technology capability will enable students to cope with, participate in and make informed decisions about the values and purpose of technological change.

Education in design and technology should recognise this complex interaction and develop learning opportunities accordingly. If this educational experience is to be developmental then it must not be based on repetitive design process tasks or specific practical skills alone. Fundamental to engaging in design and technology activity is the relationship between the concepts drawn from specific knowledge, skills and values. Design and technology capability is the management of the complex inter-relationship between these concepts, in a way that facilitates the positive procedures of designing and making to achieve outcomes in response to human need.

The profile component for design and technology in the Statutory Order is design and technology capability. The 1990 national curriculum requirements state that students should be assessed using the statements of attainment as general objectives. The heart of the procedures for design and technology is exemplified by the four attainment targets, but a holistic design and technology experience should offer more. Such an approach calls for interaction between all of what we describe as the 'ground rules'. This can also be the key to both assessment and progression.

The ground rules for design and technology in the statutory orders cover:

- contexts,
- programmes of study,
- range of materials,
- attainment targets,
- outcomes.

WHAT DO THE STATUTORY ORDERS OMIT?

The Statutory Orders make no reference to:

- An understanding of children's conceptual development in design and technology;
- the relationship between the 'ground rules';
- How holistic design and technology will be taught.

This leaves teachers to address the following issues:

- How do children manage their design and technology experiences?
- What are the concepts handled in design and technology and how they inter-relate?
- How can a student's grasp of the concepts of design and technology be ascertained; how can progression be planned for effectively?
- What does capability in design and technology really 'look' like and how does it develop?
- How can a student's *capability* be assessed?

HOW DO CHILDREN DEVELOP IN DESIGN AND TECHNOLOGY?

The role of the teacher is to improve the learning of the child. Design and technology activity must enable students to engage in activities that continuously develop essential concepts whilst working within contexts towards tangible outcomes.

To be effective in the development of this learning, an understanding of the way in which children achieve the progress in design and technology capability is essential.

In the past the focus for activity and learning in the 'practical' areas of the curriculum has been very much on the practical activity and the product; recently the emphasis has swung almost entirely towards the requirements for students to record in detail much of their thinking, research, ideas and planning. It is vital that in design and technology both the reflective (thinking) and active (doing) aspects are given full consideration as they are inextricably linked parts of a dynamic, interactive iterative process. This is exemplified by the holistic nature of the attainment targets.

Each activity/experience builds upon a platform of personal experience. The level of capability we bring to each new activity is characterised by that platform of experience. How much the personal platform is extended will depend upon the degree to which capability is developed within each activity.

A MODEL FOR UNDERSTANDING THE DEVELOPMENT OF DESIGN AND TECHNOLOGY CAPABILITY

The following model of the conceptual development in design and technology capability can help when formulating programmes of activities for children by enhancing the opportunities provided through their learning experiences to develop capability in a planned and progressive way.

This model of conceptual development demonstrates a manner in which pupils will not only 'develop their attainments' but also develop holistic design and technology capability. It is critical that experiences in design and technology are not wholly 'driven' by the attainment targets and programmes of study. This would give a narrow experience and miss many opportunities for a 'full and rounded' design and technology experience.

DESIGN AND TECHNOLOGY CAPABILITIES

Design and Technology is an essentially practical activity, concerned with developing pupils' confidence to tackle a variety of issues, drawing on a broad base of knowledge and skills. It is developed in response to perceived needs and opportunities, takes place within a context of specific constraints, depends upon value judgements at almost every stage and enables the individual to intervene to modify and improve his or her environment.

(Somerset 1990)

KNOWLEDGE SKILLS AND VALUES IN DESIGN AND TECHNOLOGY

The knowledge required for national curriculum design and technology is laid out in the programmes of study and complemented by aspects of the attainment targets. The skills are laid down in the attainment targets and complemented by aspects of the programmes of study. The values will determine the attitudes being taken by students when confronted with issues and constraints in design and technology activities.

Education in design and technology concerns the relationship between

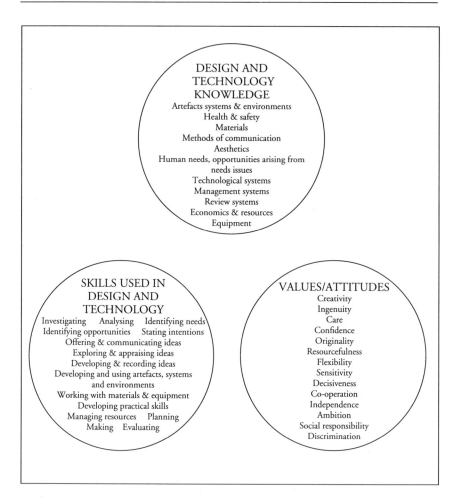

Figure 12.1 Concepts in design and technology

knowledge, skills, values/attitudes when producing outcomes in response to perceived human need. It would seem therefore that there must be some fundamental concepts that facilitate activity in design and technology.

DESIGN AND TECHNOLOGY CONCEPTS

Concepts can be defined as organised but ever-changing groupings of thoughts or notions used to understand, classify and manage knowledge, skills and values.

Conceptual development in Design and Technology requires the assimilation of knowledge, practise of skills and the formation of values and attitudes. Obviously the three are very much interlinked, but it is the identification of the concepts at the heart of design and technology that enables the relevant inter-relationships to be made.

Some concepts are simple, some more complex and they appear to have a hierarchy. When exploring some of the 'words' identified as describing design and technology 'concepts' it is apparent that they fall into 'categories'. It seemed that the categories could be further grouped as follows:

1 What resources go into a design and technology activity?
   (The human, physical, financial and technical resources that influence the procedures)
2 How is a design and technology activity handled?
   (Processes, techniques and methods employed in the generation and manufacture of outcomes)
3 Why issues/actions need consideration?
   (Human interaction and the way in which people are inextricably linked to the processes and resources)

Design and technology concept groupings

When considering a design and technology activity it seemed that these three broad concepts of *what* resources a design and technology activity, *how* a design and technology activity is handled and *why* issues and actions need reflection were those that needed to be handled and inter-related. These three broad concept groups take on relevance *when* set in contexts that determine *whatever* outcomes are realised to meet perceived human need.

It is only when an inter-relationship is established between the above elements of design and technology that capability is achieved.

THE DIFFERENCE BETWEEN ABILITY AND CAPABILITY

The following figures demonstrate a model of conceptual development in design and technology. The graphic description shows that if the concepts of *how*, *what*, and *why* are developed separately they foster *ability*. This ability can be to a very high level, but if the concepts are developed in such a way that inter-relation is enabled then *capability* is achieved.

The growth of an individual concept is shown in Figure 12.3. It uses the analogy of a 'window' into a concept determining the degree to which that concept is accommodated in the mind. As knowledge feeds that concept so the window opens, increasing the degree to which that concept is accommodated in the mind.

Managing and inter-relating the three individual concepts of *how*, *what* and *why* is shown in Figure 12.4. The 'window' analogy is used again to show the varying degree of assimilation, and the 'swivelling of the lamps' models the cognitive adjustments that need to be made to facilitate

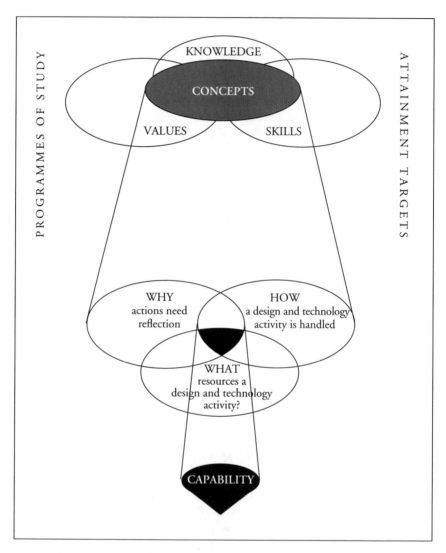

Figure 12.2 Inter-relating the concept groupings results in design and technology capability

conceptual links. The three stages show an increasing accommodation of each concept with its associated increase in ability. However, though some inter-relationships are being made, as yet it is not with all three concepts.

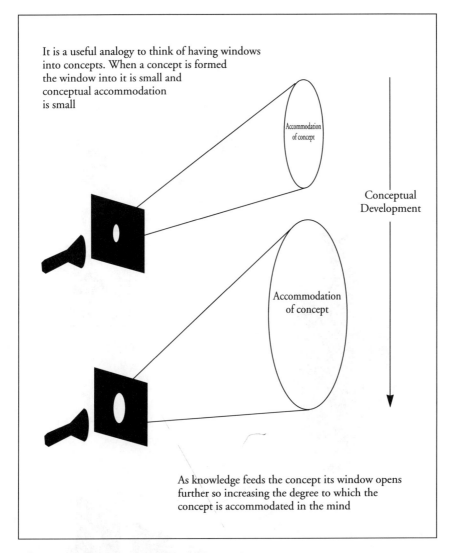

It is a useful analogy to think of having windows into concepts. When a concept is formed the window into it is small and conceptual accommodation is small

Accommodation of concept

Conceptual Development

Accommodation of concept

As knowledge feeds the concept its window opens further so increasing the degree to which the concept is accommodated in the mind

Figure 12.3 The growth of an individual concept

THE GROWTH OF AN INDIVIDUAL CONCEPT

It is only when the concepts are managed to enable inter-relationships to be made between all three as shown in Figure 12.5 that one can feel that design and technology *capability* is being developed.

Progression in design and technology capability encompasses:

– The development of the ability of pupils to handle individual concepts of increasing breadth and depth;
– The ability to handle a larger number of increasingly complex concepts.

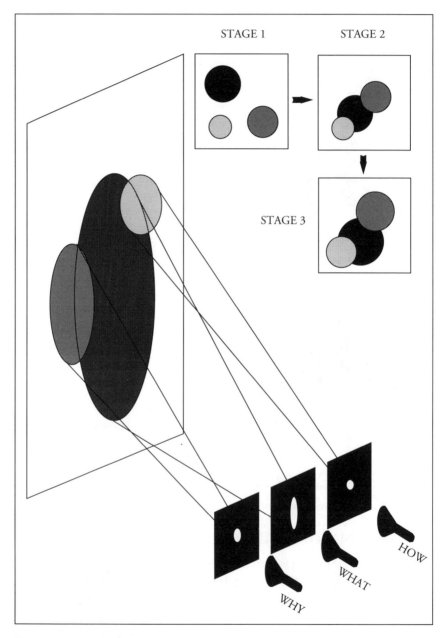

Figure 12.4 Managing and inter-relating individual concepts

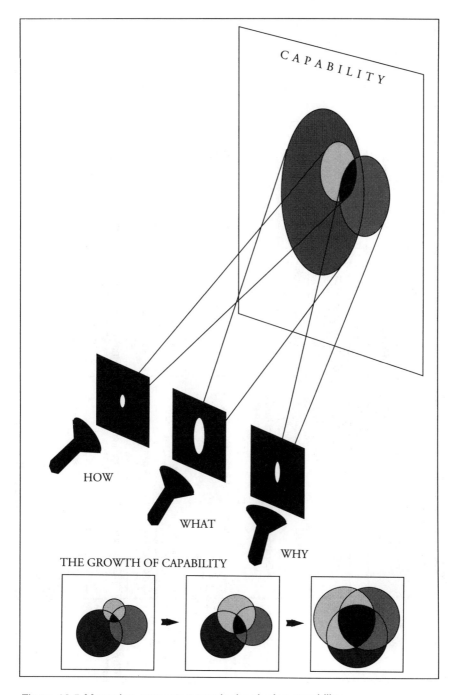

Figure 12.5 Managing concepts towards developing capability

Table 12.1 This matrix is an attempt to provide an holistic 'template' for design and technology activities

		from self and close peer group	working with others from extended peer group	working with others from outside school	working with increasing autonomy
What resources a design and technology activity	Human				
	Personal	working from personal experience	working to extend personal experience	continuing to establish and extend personal limits realistically	willingness and confidence to commit oneself
	Energy	use, sources	control, transfer	release, conservation	generation
	Materials	a selected range of materials, equipment and components	a wider range of materials, equipment and components	a greater breadth of sources	diverse operational characteristics
	Finances	simple costings of materials	costing time, people, skills, budgets	cash forecasting, pricing, incomes	business systems, financial management
How a design and technology activity is handled	Exploring	generation of ideas, creativity, information handling	developing ideas, innovation, investigative	design, prediction	transfer, hypothesis
	Communication	imaging, expression of ideas, proposals, modelling	responding, plans, graphicacy, technological vocabulary, audience	specifying plans and methods, use of data	use of information technology, detail
	Making	practicality, organisation	techniques, prototypes, adjustments	management, production, procedures	specialist conventions
	Evaluating	testing, choices	selection, analyse, appraise, justify	review, set objectives, question, interpret	intuition, review, distinguish, determine
Why actions need reflection	Constraints	competence, time, economics, properties	fitness for the purpose, environment, conservation, efficiency	ethics, market forces, external requirements, opportunity	capabilities, technologies, legality, conflicts
	Human needs	of self, of others	opportunities, safety, health, protection, satisfaction	historical, cultural, social	human dimensions, ergonomics
	Considerations	preference, improvement, aesthetics	value, conservation	finish, function	optimisation, quality, efficacy

When set in the context of:				
Home	me and my responsibility for the needs of my home/family	my own home/family, my roles in these needs	homes and families of other times and cultures, needs, form and function	social and developmental needs of different family units and their homes
School	me and my needs in my own school	the needs of others in my school and schools like mind	the functional needs of schools and those who use them	a range of learning environments and the needs they generate
Recreation	me and the things I need in my games and hobbies	the needs of others in their games, hobbies and sports	the physical, social and recreational needs of people of all cultures	the purpose and provision of facilities, intellectual, emotional
Community	the needs of people that I meet in my local environment	the needs of others that I meet in my local environment	the social needs of people in communities of all times and cultures	the external influences on the needs of all in the community
Business and industry	local shops	small businesses, local industries and factories	national industry and commerce	technologies, economics and management
Whatever outcomes meet perceived human need				
Artefacts	objects from food textiles graphic media construction materials	objects for the needs of others, with increasing quality	objects meeting a wide range of needs from a variety of materials	quality objects matching knowledge to task
Systems	putting together sets of objects or activities	combination of component parts for a single output	combining and managing a variety of systems to achieve outputs	rigorous application of a range of systems
Environments	creation of surroundings for known people and creatures known them	development of surroundings for a range of people and situations	developing and selecting appropriate surroundings in response to real need	sophisticated provision for the real world

The matrix in Table 12.1 is an attempt to provide a holistic 'template' for design and technology activities.

All aspects of the programmes of study and attainment targets can be found in this matrix/'template'. Teachers have found it useful when read vertically to give a 'holistic feel' for design and technology activities, which can tend to be lost if experiences are just AT or POS driven. The matrix, when read horizontally can begin to give indicators or pointers for structuring progression of capability. It is not implied that the progression spans 5–16; it is likely to be very different for individual children, groups and activities.

IMPLICATIONS FOR PLANNING AND ASSESSMENT

It is only possible to flag up pitfalls and 'educated' guesses at this point in these areas.

However as far as planning is concerned experience in Somerset has shown that it is critical to plan a structured range of progressive activities in advance for any key stage giving careful consideration at the planning stage to the following points:

- The *how*, *what* and *why* of design and technology for each activity (as discussed in this chapter).
- Focusing on particular aspects of attainment targets and programmes of study in an activity.
- The opportunity across a range of activities for specialist enrichment.

For any activity to be truly design and technology, all attainment targets must be present. It is, however, unrealistic to target to the same degree each AT in every activity. To make the task *manageable* teachers should be encouraged to focus on particular aspects of each attainment targets to a high profile whilst covering the remainder to a lower profile. It makes teaching and ultimately assessment possible. Across a range of activities in a key stage it is possible to *structure* experiences that develop design and technology capability through integrating the diversity of specialist methods, techniques and materials and their related knowledge, skills and associated values.

Assessment of design and technology needs to be approached in two ways: that of 'holistic' assessment where an 'overview' method is adopted, looking globally at the way children engage in design and technology activities. Second, 'focused assessment' where aspects of activities are used for the basis of assessment over a key stage. A combination of the two methods will provide the desirable balance if built up progressively. It is important not to lose sight of the current position on the 'development scale' of design and technology. The DES advice (DES 1990) recommends teachers to build on existing assessment and recording procedures [and] build up a bank of relevant information about a pupil's progress, including possibly samples of work on which to draw in the context of any discussions about the level that pupil is judged to have reached at the end of the key stage.

SUMMARY

We must guard against giving children experiences that are narrow and prescriptive – a trap that we fall into if experiences are purely attainment target and programme of study driven. It is vital to ensure that children receive full and rounded experiences, and we believe the key to this is to take a holistic view of the provision. The way into this is to identify and understand the concepts that underpin the way in which children manage and develop that management of the design and technology procedures. The development of programmes of work that target a focus for activities which contribute individually to a collectively structured experience is the way to progressively develop capability.

REFERENCES

DES (1990) *ERA 1988 Section 4 Order Technology; Design and Technology and Information Technology*, London, HMSO.
Somerset (1990) *Somerset County Curriculum Statement*, Taunton, Somerset LEA.

Chapter 13

Organising project work

David Barlex

This chapter is an edited version of a much longer booklet on project work written for the Open University Course 'Technology in Schools'. The advice offered is clear and 'down to earth' but not linked to any specific national curriculum document or examination syllabus.

WHY PROJECT WORK IS IMPORTANT

Project work has been seen to be important in a number of curricular areas, but particularly so in technology. This is because it provides the opportunity for pupils to experience genuine technological activity. The activity can be in response to a human need or problem; it can use technological processes (e.g. design or systems analysis); it can be multidisciplinary. The extract below highlights some of the reasons for the inclusion of project work in technology courses:

Project work in technology develops:
(a) skills in the application and use of knowledge and expertise in solving particular problems;
(b) the ability to work with others;
(c) divergent and convergent thinking by giving due consideration to intuitive inspiration, guesses and accidental developments as well as those achieved by means of a logical step-by-step progression;
(d) self-discipline and responsibility, as the success or failure of the project is pupil-centred;
(e) creative abilities and encourages enterprise and dedication;
(f) speculative thought and exercises ingenuity.
(Cross and McCormick 1986: 254)

It is worth noting that, underpinning the fact that project work is centred around the individual pupil, and that pupils take responsibility for their own work, is the idea that pupils will be self-directed in tackling much, if not most, of the learning. Although other teaching methods might individually develop the features quoted above, project work is seen as particularly valuable because, under self-direction, pupils integrate these into a capability demonstrated by successful completion of the project.

CLARIFYING THE LEARNING IN PROJECT WORK

Project work involves the following categories of learning – knowing, understanding, skills, attitudes and values. Black and Harrison propose the idea that task–action–capability depend on three related features:

(a) *Resources* of knowledge, skill and experience which can be drawn upon, consciously or subconsciously, when involved in active tasks.
(b) *Capability* to perform, to originate, to get things done, to make and stand by decisions.
(c) *Awareness*, perception and understanding needed for making balanced and effective value judgements.

(Black and Harrison 1985)

It is important for you to be clear on what you wish to achieve by project work and one way to do this is to try to relate these three features – resources, capability and awareness – to the categories of learning. Figure 13.1 attempts to do this. As you can see, most of the categories contribute to more than one feature.

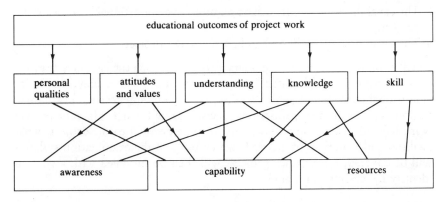

Figure 13.1 Categories of learning related to resources, capability and awareness

At the beginning of a project pupils will start with their own individual collection of resources, awareness and capabilities. It is then important to ask whether there is any progression, during the time a project is tackled and completed, in the extent to which a pupil possesses these three features.

Engaging in the project will enable pupils to utilise their existing resources and, in so doing, reinforce and extend their skills in using them. If, in addition, successful completion of the project requires a pupil to acquire new resources then progression will have taken place.

In applying values to a project, pupils will also become aware of their own existing values, if these are reassessed in the light cast by the project, then progression will have again occurred.

The demonstration of an existing and, perhaps, unsuspected capability and the acquisition of a new capability as the project moves forward will show progression in capability. It is in this area that personal qualities are so important and it is through project work more than any other form of learning that such qualities are revealed.

PLANNING PROJECTS

Introduction

In this section I shall examine how the design of a project is governed by the educational outcomes you, as the teacher, require from the project. When planning project work it is important that you are clear on the following:

1 The capabilities, resources and awareness that pupils are likely to bring with them to the project;
2 The resources the pupils will reinforce and develop by means of the project;
3 The capabilities the pupils will be required to demonstrate by means of the project;
4 The awareness that will be highlighted by the project.

I shall examine one typical 'beginners' project in which the last three features were deliberately orchestrated by the teacher in order to achieve particular educational outcomes. I shall also discuss the consequences of this orchestration in terms of the organisational decisions that teachers planning project work have to make – how much time is to be devoted to the project, what facilities and materials are needed, which parts of the examination syllabus will be covered, etc.? Other projects will then be surveyed with a view to identifying expected outcomes.

Educational outcomes for a key stage 3 project

The control project you are to consider is typical of many carried out in upper primary or lower secondary schools. The brief given to pupils might read:

Design and make a ring-can buggy which:

1 Uses an electric motor, battery and belt drive to move;

2 can be controlled – start/stop at least; forwards/backwards, fast/slow, left/right are also possible;
3 is visually pleasing and/or has an element of 'fun' in the way it works.

The results of such a brief are shown in Figure 13.2. Think about the learning that you might wish to take place.

Skills

The practical skills are: simple but accurate measuring; comparing and marking out; the cutting to length of a wooden strip, metal rod and plastic tube; drilling for tight and sliding fits; cutting, scoring and bending paper and card. Many lower secondary pupils have these skills when they reach secondary school. The use of pupils who do have the skills to demonstrate to those who do not is one way to cope with a class of mixed ability.

Intellectual skills

Most of the intellectual skills listed below will be utilised.

1 *Knowing* Pupils will need to know about simple circuitry and the use of an on and off switch. The desire to control the buggy will drive some pupils to investigate reversing switches, steering mechanisms and speed control. They will learn to appreciate the use of a belt drive with reduction in speed of rotation, which will, perhaps, lay the foundation for later work on belt drives and gears.
2 *Understanding* Design and problem-solving figure largely in this project. The design can be tackled in two phases (chassis/control and the visual/'fun' elements), although they are clearly related. It is likely that pupils will develop visual ideas quickly and then hold them in abeyance while they design and produce a chassis to which the visual elements may be added.

Two extreme approaches are possible with chassis design. First, pupils may be given a standard chassis design which they all make. This will specify the materials to be used and the positions of the axles/ring-cans, motor and battery. Once the chassis has been made, pupils can add their own control features and visual elements.

This approach will leave little room for problem-solving in chassis design – where do I want the cans? How does this effect the position of the axles and the motor? Have I got room for the battery? It precludes any investigative 'tinkering'. It has the advantages that pupils will take less time to construct the chassis and there will be little risk of failure. Designing the control features may then become the major focus of the design activity.

The other extreme is to give pupils almost complete freedom over chassis design; simply specify the materials available and then leave it to

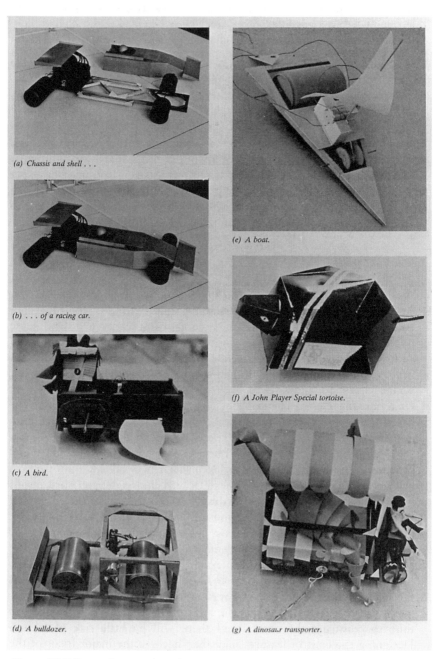

(a) Chassis and shell . . .

(b) . . . of a racing car.

(c) A bird.

(d) A bulldozer.

(e) A boat.

(f) A John Player Special tortoise.

(g) A dinosaur transporter.

Figure 13.2 Some ring-can buggies

them. Pupils will spend a lot of time attempting to solve problems, but the chances of failure will be high.

A middle approach might be to establish with the class important critical dimensions (ring-can size, clearance, motor size, battery size, belt drives available) and develop a chassis design that takes these into account and can be altered to suit individuals' particular needs. This leaves considerable room for problem-solving and investigative tinkering, but reduces the risk of failure.

3 *Attitudes and values* In deciding on the overall appearance of their buggies, pupils will bring a wide range of visual values to bear. The 'fun' element may be due to overall appearance, or may be achieved by building in mechanical devices, such as cams to make wings flap, off-centre axles to simulate wave motion.

If the teacher wishes pupils to explore a wide range of visual possibilities then stimulating materials must be provided and the time for their use must be built into the project's schedule. Similarly, the inclusion of a mechanically driven 'fun' element will need to be supported by the pupils' existing resources. They will need to have already been taught about levers and linkages or cams and followers, say. Otherwise, provision will need to be made for them to acquire the necessary knowledge and understanding within the project's schedule.

4 *Personal qualities* Clearly, the successful completion of this project requires the integration of the areas already discussed. To achieve this, pupils have to operate in a self-directed way, moving through the different phases of the project as is appropriate for their own designs. This means that they will be deciding for themselves what to do now, what to do next and how to do it.

To help them make sensible decisions the teacher can develop a timing scheme for the project in which deadlines for the completion of various stages are identified. This can, and should, be shared with the pupils at the outset of the project. Pupils will then be in a position to organise their own progress through the project.

The success with which they do this when they are new to project work will depend on their existing personal qualities – industriousness, perseverance, realistic appraisal of their own abilities, meticulousness and confidence. It is only by giving pupils the chance to demonstrate such qualities that they can be revealed or seen to be lacking and, more importantly, developed.

As pupils become more experienced in project work they can begin to negotiate their own deadlines for completion of the stages in the project and eventually plan the entire timing for a project.

It is almost impossible for a single lower secondary school project to feature equally prominently all the characteristics of technological activity. Clearly, the ring-can buggy project fails to meet the following considerations: economic criteria; manufacturing as opposed to making; issues concerning the interface between technology and society; working as part of a team and the necessary communicating and co-operating.

As such the buggy project needs complementing with other projects where the above and other elements are considered and enhanced, while those adequately covered in the buggy project can be featured less prominently.

DEVELOPING PROGRESSION IN SUCCESSIVE PROJECTS

In the project just analysed, the path taken by the pupils was clearly laid out by the teacher, although pupils were for much of the time operating in a self-directed manner within these constraints. The whole range of skills needed for self-directed project work was, however, *not* used. This was deliberate, as a 'beginners' exercise should build confidence by gradual initiation into the skills required for project work.

To achieve gradual progression through a series of projects, each project needs to be analysed in terms of the types of task to be performed.

Below is a list of the activities that need to be tackled in order to complete a constructional technology project:

1 *Researching* Finding out from second-hand sources such as books, journals or magazines.
2 *Investigating* Finding out by experiment and observation.
3 *Specifying* Stating clearly the criteria that the chosen solution has to meet.
4 *Developing ideas* that might make a contribution to the chosen solution.
5 *Optimising ideas* to formulate the details of a chosen solution.
6 *Planning* the making or manufacture of the chosen solution.
7 *Making/manufacturing*.
8 *Evaluating*.

In planning for progression it is useful to look at each activity and to see the extent to which it is promoted in a particular project and over a sequence of projects.

For example, at first sight there seems to be little scope for researching in the buggy project. However, consulting scrap books and printed resource sheets are the first steps in developing research skills. Eventually, this can lead to a pupil being able to visit a public library and use catalogues and the Dewey decimal classification to find and make notes from books written at a level appropriate to a project's requirements. In fact, if you compare the buggy project and the activities listed above you will see that all the activities are present in the project to some extent.

For any technology project you could present, by means of a bar chart, a profile of the project in terms of the depth of engagement associated with

Figure 13.3 Project profile for the ring-can buggy project

each of the activities. The length of each bar will be an indication of the depth of engagement. For the buggy project the profile might look like Figure 13.3. It is whether an activity is present or not and the relative, rather than absolute, depths of engagement that are important. A clue to the depth of engagement will be how long pupils spend on a particular activity.

Of course, it is possible to deliberately enhance a particular activity within a project in order to give pupils a deeper experience and appreciation of it. This will be an important strategy for developing the competence of pupils to undertake project work. I think it is preferable to attempting to advance on a broad front across all aspects of project work by, say, making successive projects more demanding all round. This latter approach makes it difficult for the teacher to concentrate on a particular activity and requires pupils to get better at everything all the time.

PROJECT BRIEFS FOR GCSE

Paul Burton has outlined two approaches to project work: the TCP approach and the SDP approach. The TCP approach covered 'Teacher-direct problems', 'Closed-end problems' and 'Pupil-oriented problems'. SDP stands for 'Stimulus, Discussion, Problem' (Cross and McCormick 1986: Ch. 25).

SDP is seen as providing a suitable stimulus for pupils to discuss and so derive a problem that all pupils can tackle on an individual basis. The advantages of this approach are that a single problem emerges and it is pupil-centred because it has been identified by pupils. The disadvantages are twofold:

- The arrival of the stimulus can be unpredictable – a grandmother having an accident, or a newsworthy event – so the teacher needs to be in a position to respond rapidly and flexibly to such occasions.
- Teachers need to have a very clear and detailed overall view of the course within which the project work is taking place so that they can decide very rapidly (almost overnight) whether the problem likely to be derived from a particular event will provide project work that meets syllabus, examination and coursework requirements within the time available. This is a high-risk, demanding venture for the teacher, especially when compared with a safe teacher-decided project that already has the necessary resources available, has been successfully taught for several years and is known to meet syllabus requirements within time constraints.

Teacher-decided projects

Many pupils of lower ability often experience particular difficulty at the initial stage of choosing a major project. Two extreme responses are often encountered: 'I can't think of anything', or the over-ambitious, completely unrealistic proposal, 'I know, Miss, I'll do a rocket-powered, remote-controlled skate board!' A list of briefs suggested by you, the teacher, may prove very useful in starting a discussion with such pupils.

It will be important to develop ways of probing a pupil's commitment to a brief drawn from such a list. There is considerable danger that a pupil coerced into tackling a project chosen by the teacher will not be sufficiently committed to it to maintain interest and motivation in the face of problems and difficulties.

Briefs derived from knowledge bases

One way to engage pupils in the formulation of their own project briefs is to consider briefs from the view point of the knowledge base they are likely to use. With this approach, it is possible to deliberately exploit areas of knowledge acquired in curricular areas other than that in which the project is taking place. One danger is that it is all too easy with this approach to fall into the trap of carrying out a project that is technically interesting, but has no wider appeal.

Briefs arising from events

Using the unexpected or accidental event as a starting point for a project has a great potential for motivation, but the attendant problems of the need for a rapid response and of ensuring appropriateness can be overwhelming. There is, however, no reason why a planned event may not stimulate a discussion from which a problem may be identified. Visits by a whole class or a group are clearly such planned events.

It is possible for all the pupils in a class to concentrate on one of the briefs and to develop their own unique response. Equally, pupils may be allowed to choose from the range of briefs generated. In this case, it looks as if there will be organisational problems similar to those encountered when a project is stimulated by an accidental or unexpected event. This is not so, because the teacher will have chosen the visit with the revelation of particular problems in mind; problems that will generate project work that meets syllabus requirements. After the visit there will be several follow-up lessons in which discussion will lead to briefs being formulated. This slow build-up to identifying a brief gives you the chance to assess the likely needs of the briefs as they emerge and to plan the provision of materials and equipment accordingly.

Briefs derived from pupils' interests

You have seen that considerable motivation can be achieved if a project is concerned with a pupil's personal interest or hobby. There is sometimes the danger that the project can become too technically focused, but there are ways to avoid this.

A situation in which a large number of very different hobby-based projects were being tackled within a single class could present organisation problems, but it is possible to envisage a situation in which one or two pupils were pursuing such highly individualistic projects while the rest of the class were following a brief derived collectively from, say, a visit. The motivation resulting from the hobby will enable the pupils to operate independently from the rest of the class.

In summary four ways to help pupils decide on briefs for major project work have been explored:

1 *Teacher-decided projects*   Important for less able pupils, but with the risk of motivational problems due to coercion.
2 *Briefs derived from knowledge base*   There is the risk of being too technically focused.
3 *Situation-derived briefs*   With the possibility of control by the teacher over the diversity of briefs to be tackled within one class.
4 *Briefs derived from personal interest*   These have high motivational possibilities.

Whatever method is used, and it is likely that more than one will be needed for a whole class, it is clear that the pupils' involvement in any decision, and commitment to it, are essential.

Support in the face of difficulties

It is a consequence of pupils being self-directed and taking on responsibility for their work that they experience disappointment and frustration when pursuing promising ideas that prove unsuccessful. One of the problems facing teachers supervising major project work is the disillusionment and consequent loss of motivation that can then occur.

As a teacher, you may see struggling through a sticky patch as an important part of the learning process: for the pupil this process can cause great dismay. Therefore it is here that the relationship with the teacher is vital. Encouragement and support that helps pupils solve the difficulties for themselves are required rather than the teacher's instant solution. On some occasions, however, it might be important to provide a solution in order to prevent a pupil floundering.

It is worth noting that pupils can help each other with their problems and an atmosphere that encourages pupils to share their experiences will provide support.

A clear commitment to the project from the outset is also important. Some schools insist that the decision as to which project to tackle is taken by both pupil and parents together, particularly when it appears likely that expensive materials or components may be involved. There can be little doubt that parents' awareness of project work and the support and encouragement they can give, will, at times of crisis, help teachers maintain a pupil's commitment and motivation.

Possibilities are:
- as consultants to technology projects;
- as sources of cheap or free consumable materials;
- as fund raisers for equipment;
- as visitors who talk to pupils pursuing project work.

Pitfalls to avoid are:
- consultants who mislead pupils;
- free consumables that are stolen goods;
- clients who will be very disappointed when a project succeeds educationally, but fails to produce the desired artefact.

GROUP WORK

It is universally accepted in all industries that success in any technological venture, by the very multidisciplinary nature of the activity, requires the participants to work in groups. It is surprising, then, that most examination schemes aimed at assessing technological ability concentrate almost exclusively on determining performance on an individual basis, paying scant attention to how an individual uses acquired knowledge and skill resources in a team or a group. Here, therefore, we look at the qualities that can be displayed and developed by pupils engaged in group work and how to design group-work activity for technology projects.

Group-work qualities

To work successfully in groups, pupils will need a range of overlapping and related interpersonal skills. The list below provides five broad categories for you to consider:

- co-operation;
- communication;
- leadership;
- empathy/sympathy;
- reliability.

This is not meant to be a complete description of all the quantities required for group work.

The extent to which individual pupils have to show these qualities when working in a group will depend on the role they take within the group. Here is my attempt at describing, in terms of such criteria, the behaviour that indicates whether a pupil has, or does not have, these interpersonal skills.

1 *Co-operation*   Helps with holding together component parts while one individual makes final adjustments. Refuses to help on the grounds that 'I don't like him, so he can do it on his own.'
2 *Communication*   Explains clearly to others in the team what they have all agreed to do by next lesson. Refuses to discuss the problem in hand.
3 *Leadership*   Makes sure others in the group can get on with their allotted tasks before tackling his or her own. Although a group is spending too much time on a task will not draw attention to this.
4 *Empathy/sympathy*   Shows understanding when a team member is below par. Responds aggressively when a team member meets failure.
5 *Reliability*   Always comes to lessons well-prepared, having carried out what was agreed. Often arrives late and usually without the necessary equipment.

I am struck by the sometimes overlapping and interdependent nature of the categories. It is difficult to be an effective leader without being both a good communicator and reliable, but it is possible to be a good communicator and reliable and still fail to be an effective leader. It is certainly not a simple task to analyse each of the broad categories into their unique individual component interpersonal skills. It is possible, however, to tell from pupils' behaviour whether or not they are displaying or developing the qualities necessary for group work. Providing you have a set of broad categories as a reference against which to consider the behaviour of pupils, you are in a position to assess how well pupils are performing in group work and to design activities that develop the skills required for group work.

Designing group-work activity

Paul Burton's SDP approach (Cross and McCormick 1986: Ch. 25) used group work in CDT projects. Each group had a project director, secretary and project co-ordinator. Burton does not indicate how, or if, pupils were instructed in their roles, but it would certainly be unwise to set up such group-work without giving clear guidelines on what is expected. Such an approach has the following key features:

- A clear job description for each member of the team.
- Support given by means of a planning sheet, although no specific instructions are given.
- The possibility of changing the plan of action in response to early findings is acknowledged and even encouraged.
- Pupils are required to present their results in a format that facilitates both the drawing of conclusions and the presentation of these conclusions to others.

Clearly, the production of printed resources will help you to structure group work. The provision of such resources, however, is only the beginning. Each working group must be supported through the different stages of the activity. You will need to prevent certain individuals from dominating and others from opting out. In the case of dispute, you may be required to act as arbitrator.

In planning pupils' group work over a long period of time, several terms say, you will also be concerned with variety and progression. Variety can be achieved by ensuring that pupils take on different roles in successive projects. This will entail keeping a record of who did what in each group for each piece of group work and assigning roles accordingly. Progression can be achieved by gradually lessening the structure the teacher imposes on the group; moving to a position where pupils decide what jobs are necessary and who takes on those jobs.

PROJECT ASSESSMENT FOR GCSE

This concerns the assessment of the performance of pupils *throughout* a project. It is clearly more complex than evaluating a product, but it is of particular importance if pupils are to develop an overall view of their experience of technology project work. It is also important that you should actively engage pupils in this type of assessment and not just assess their projects on your own.

In assessing a pupil's performance on the various stages of a project you have to consider *when* such assessment should take place in addition to *how* it should take place. Ideally, the assessment should take place as the project develops. In this way the rose-coloured hindsight of both pupils and teachers can be avoided. The reality of the situation is often that all concerned are so busy with the tasks in hand that a conscious, on-the-spot assessment does not take place. However, given that clear markers concerning likely progress through a project have been established with pupils, it is possible for both teacher and pupils to use a simple check list to assess a pupil's performance continually. This could be used as a reminder when assessing a pupil's overall performance at the end of a project.

When assessing performance at the end of a project, using data collected during the project if possible, it is important for pupil and teacher to share their perceptions of the pupil's performance. The most significant learning will occur when there is a mismatch in perceptions *and* there is the opportunity to resolve it. I think it is important to share such a marking scheme with pupils taking the examination course, but it is highly unlikely that they will make any sense of it unless they have been regularly involved in both evaluating what they have made and assessing their own performance over a long period of time.

Clearly, it makes sense to try to introduce this performance assessment in the lower school and one school's attempt to provide a form for making an assessment at the end of project is shown in Figure 13.4. You should note the following features:

- It is much simpler than that used for examination purposes.
- Both teacher and pupil use the same criteria.
- Pupils are required to assess their performance before the teacher.
- Any mismatch in perceptions of a pupil's performance is highlighted and can form the basis for discussion.

The use of a folio or workbook written by the pupil to 'tell the story of the project' is common to much project work and is an essential element in assessing pupils. The London and East Anglia Examining Group's regulations for CDT technology state:

> Candidates will be required to produce a folio on their project. The folio should give a full account of the whole design process, including an analysis of the problem, research carried out, possible solutions, design details, problems encountered and modifications made during the realization of the solution and an evaluation of the whole project. Information from a wide range of sources should be available and evidence of reference to it should be recorded. Candidates should be encouraged to evaluate continually their project work as it progresses and to use a variety of presentation techniques, including colour.

It is clear from this that the intention of the workbook is to reveal the pupil's

		PUPIL	TEACHER
FINDING OUT Did you find out	a lot?		
	a little?		
	not much?		
USEFULNESS Was what you found out	very useful?		
	useful?		
	not much use?		
IDEAS Did you have	lots of ideas?		
	a few ideas?		
	only one?		
CHOSING How many reasons did you give for deciding which was your best idea	lots?		
	a few?		
	only one?		
MAKING PLANS Are your plans	very clear?		
	clear?		
	a bit muddled?		
THE PRODUCT Is it	well made?		
	well finished?		
EVALUATION Does your evaluation include	how well it works?		
	how good it looks?		
	things to improve?		

Name _____

Tutor Group _____

Figure 13.4 Assessment format for lower secondary school project work

thinking and decision-making as it has developed through the project. It is not intended that it should be produced retrospectively once the practical work has been finished, although such practice is, unfortunately, not uncommon. If the workbook is to meet these requirements it is important to establish clear guidelines for pupils to encourage written and graphic work that is appropriate.

For pupils, assessing their own performance will be even more intimidating than evaluating a product they have designed and made. The relationship with the teacher will probably be the most important factor in building the confidence to tackle this. In developing technology project work it is therefore important for you to build into the project sufficient time for both its evaluation and assessment.

While product evaluation can be carried out by group activities it is essential that a pupil's performance is assessed individually with the teacher. This poses interesting logistical problems. If, at the end of a project, you allocate each pupil 5 minutes for a personal tutorial and have twenty pupils in your class, this assessment will take the best part of two double lessons. At any one time there will be nineteen pupils working on their own while the teacher deals with the tutorial.

Preparation for the next project is a useful way to deal with this potentially difficult situation. Three possible activities are:

- Comprehension exercises – newspaper or magazine articles to be read with questions relevant to the next project to answer.
- Making up questions to ask during 'user trips' appropriate to the next project.
- Making entries into a design and technology scrap book.

There are many problems about project assessment yet to be resolved. Even what is known about these problems tends to be locked up in teachers' and examiners' heads and so it is only possible to point to some of the issues.

How do you take into account, if at all, the help given to a pupil by the teacher? It would be a tragedy if the prospect of being penalised in assessment prevents a pupil from asking for help at critical stages in a project. Apart from the effect this has on the relationship between the pupil and the teacher and, hence, on the learning, it does not reflect the way people are expected to work in industry, etc., which projects are at least in part supposed to simulate.

The second problem concerns the pupil being penalised for the fact that the problem chosen does not allow him or her to exhibit the criteria being used in the marking scheme. The scheme assumes that every project has each of the stages identified. What, though, of the pupil who starts with a specification and puts considerable work into solving detailed problems and aspects of realisation, but has not carried out the problem recognition and analysis stages? A pupil who has chosen to make a cheap version of a piece of weight-lifting equipment (with various levers, pulleys, etc.) will have to solve a large number of problems and take many decisions, though the project, as a whole, would not be seen as one where the problem was more open.

The third problem is that many schemes still leave a lot unassessed. For example, they do not actually assess capability in terms of the personal qualities and organisational and planning abilities required. These may, of course, colour a teacher's view of the work of a pupil, but may not be taken into account formally; rather, they operate as 'hidden criteria'. If projects are centrally about capability, as is usually argued, then it is a curious omission. Aligned with this is the neglect of attitudes and values. You might also wonder about the lack of assessment of knowing and understanding.

There is also a lack of concern for: the non-ethical values brought to bear in judging pupils' products; the ethical questions that could be asked about whether the choice of a project was one worth spending the time and effort on; and the value judgments involved in any technological solution arrived at by a pupil. Could pupils be asked to comment on any value issues relevant to their project? For example, in developing an electronic security system for a house, could a pupil comment upon this as a solution to burglary? Issues of energy, resources and environmental conservation, as well as safety, are obvious aspects which might be relevant to many projects.

Finally, group work is usually discounted in assessed project work, because of the difficulties in identifying individual contributions.

Most of these problems can be put down to general inexperience in assessing technology project work and, perhaps in time, solutions will be found to them.

PROBLEMS WITH PROJECT WORK

It is here that I must acknowledge that technology project work is an inherently tricky business. In the primary school and the early years of secondary education the measure of risk can be kept to a minimum by skilful organisation and direction by the teacher, but in trying to solve real problems chosen by pupils there is no guarantee of success, only degrees of risk. This is particularly true for pupils embarking on major technology projects that may take two or three terms to complete. Here I shall look at areas that are known to cause problems and offer some possible solutions.

Matching pupils' ability to project difficulty

If the projects tackled are to be technological there will be large areas of uncertainty and pupils will almost certainly have to develop an understanding of areas of knowledge and practical skill that they have not previously encountered. It is one of the teacher's roles to guide pupils so that they tackle projects of acceptable risk: that is, projects suited to their abilities and inclinations.

In giving this guidance there is no substitute for knowing the pupil well. This includes not only knowing details of the pupil's previous technology experience, and performance in a wide variety of related subject areas across the curriculum, but also an awareness of the home background and the level of support a pupil is likely to receive.

In my experience, the most useful information is locked in colleagues' heads and the most effective way of releasing it is to hold a meeting where proposed projects for pupils are discussed. Any inappropriate or over-ambitious projects will quickly be revealed. Then appropriate support strategies for weak pupils can be developed or they can be redirected. In addition, such a meeting gives the teachers supervising technology project work an overall view of the projects being undertaken and allows them to start planning with this in mind.

Finance

Often the bulk of consumables used in a major project has to be paid for by pupils or their families. It is disappointing and frustrating for pupils to find a successful project halted because, 'I'm sorry, but we can't afford it.' This can lead to bitter and angry exchanges within the family, so a realistic assessment of the likely cost of materials should be shared with pupils and their families.

Even if financial support cannot be given, parental interest is still of crucial importance in maintaining a pupil's motivation. For pupils without significant home financial support there are other support mechanisms available:

– Tackling problems in conjunction with local industry. This is particularly appropriate for technology projects for pupils in the sixth form and both funding and expertise can be forthcoming in such ventures.
– Tackling problems within the school where negotiating with head teachers and school governors can lead to appropriate funding.

Expertise

One problem that is often encountered is that pupils need access to knowledge that is unfamiliar to both the teacher and the pupil. This should neither surprise nor daunt you: the very nature of the exercise should lead you to expect it. It is your response to this situation that is important. There are three well-tried avenues.

The first concerns utilising the available teaching expertise. Clearly, each teacher will have particular strengths as well as all-round skills. It is important to make pupils aware of these, so that they can discuss their project with an appropriate teacher.

The second avenue is to use local industry. The availability of an education–industry liaison officer is a tremendous boon, but many useful contacts can be built up by using Yellow Pages and the local Chamber of Commerce.

The third avenue is to use local further and higher education establishments. My experience is that when approached properly they seldom fail to respond positively and often make equipment available for use, thereby enhancing the pupils' experience of project work considerably. Indeed, the very act of contacting outside experts and negotiating a convenient time for explaining the project and its problem is a venture with no guarantee of success, but the possibility of considerable gain. Such opportunities are the very stuff of technology projects.

Class size

The complex role played by teachers in supervising project work requires energy, enthusiasm and quiet determination. A technology project class supervised by one teacher should not consist of more than twenty pupils, preferably fifteen. In an over-large class, the teacher's energy and enthusiasm become diffused and quiet determination becomes grim crisis management. There is little to be done in the face of too large classes other than reduce risk to a minimum (and hence learning opportunities) by advising pupils to investigate standard problems in a way that leads to conventional, well-worked-out solutions with little flair or innovation. In examination classes, results for such projects will be on the low side and the very reasons for tackling technology projects will have been denied.

Perhaps the most serious effect of a large class other than seriously damaging the teacher's health and sanity is the way it mitigates against consistent effort from the pupils. Strategies for supporting pupils through project work have been discussed; none is more important than regular, frequent, consultation with the teacher. The larger the class, the less frequent the consultation, an over-large class and the situation becomes ragged and the regularity of the consultation disappears as well.

Ancillary support

One major factor influencing the success of technology project work is the presence of technicians who understand the nature of the enterprise. Without the support of technicians the organisation of consumables and specialist facilities for individual projects becomes a major headache which detracts from the teacher's prime task of guiding pupils through project work.

The duties of a technician supporting major project work are significantly different from those of a technician servicing standard course work. The technician will be dealing with individual pupils and their requirements from session to session. It is therefore important to organise a system for effective communication between pupils and the technicians – notes at the end of a lesson listing the requirements for the next lesson, for example – and to avoid long queues 'waiting for the technician'. The clear corollary to this is that the technician must have time between lessons to meet the listed requirements. Lack of adequate technical support will have similar effects to large classes on the quality of pupils' experiences of technology project work and their motivation.

Concluding remarks

You have seen that some of the problems associated with technology project work in schools can be solved by good organisation and co-operation between those involved in the endeavour. The difficulties caused by other problems can be lessened, but not eradicated, by adopting less adventurous project work. Above all, it is important that technology project work should be a positive experience for those involved, both teachers and pupils. If this is not so, many of the educational advantages to be gained from such work will be lost and the considerable effort needed from both teachers and pupils to maintain the activity will not be forthcoming. It is difficult to capture the breath of spring that successful technology project work brings to a wintry curriculum. Perhaps it's the risk of failure and uncertainty with no right answers, only possible solutions.

The rage and disappointment when things don't go as planned can be hard to handle. The tug at the elbow and resulting conversations in the corridor have to be experienced to appreciate the immediacy of the learning. The cries of joy when something works must be heard. The 'standing tall' by pupils of all abilities when they have done something they thought beyond them has to be seen. Analysis, design and planning have their place, but the key is the teacher; the teacher who is prepared to let pupils tackle the unknown and prepares them to do so.

REFERENCES

Black, P. and Harrison, G. (1985) *In Place of Confusion: Technology and Science in the School Curriculum*, London, Nuffield Chelsea Curriculum Trust.
Cross, A. and McCormick, R. (1986) (eds) *Technology in Schools*, Milton Keynes, Open University Press.

Chapter 14

The role of group/team work in design and technology
Some possibilities and problems

Howard Denton

This chapter builds upon the general advice on project work given by David Barlex to address the specific issue of working and learning as a team.

INTRODUCTION

By using group work appropriately it is possible to help people both learn and achieve far more than through working individually. The evidence for this statement comes from both research and the practical experience of many industrialists, for example Peacock, Research Director of Phillips (Peacock 1989). This evidence has influenced the national curriculum with a number of references to forms of group work in the design and technology, science and English documents (DES/WO 1990).

Some teachers are daunted by the multitude of terms group work proponents use; 'group work', 'teamwork', 'collaborative group work', 'co-operative group work', 'autonomous groups'. Similarly, there are many descriptions from industry, e.g. 'problem-solving teams', 'special purpose teams', 'self-managing teams' (Hoerr 1989). Some researchers have used these phrases without defining them, some documents appear to interchange terms without clarification.

In this article 'group' is a generic term which relates to any situation where two or more people work together. This could be passively, by sharing a resource but working independently, or actively where there is collaboration. The distinction between collaboration and co-operation has not been adequately defined by those who use these terms. They appear to have been used in an interchangeable way to imply a situation where learners have actively experienced a learning resource together. For example, a Bible study group or two pupils solving a pnuematics problem together.

'Team' can be used when there is distinct delegation for part of the time; each member would complete a different aspect, but together they tackle a greater task than would be possible if working individually. In contrast a group may work together, each member completing the same task in his or her own way. Group work may involve co-operation but there is replication, teamwork involves co-operation with little replication. In group work communication will be largely explanation and discussion. In teamwork communication will also involve reporting back. A further possible indicator of teamwork is the introduction of competition at an inter-team level. Groups, whilst they may have internal competition (perhaps informally and not due to teacher planning), do not compete externally without becoming a team. When using teamwork the teacher cannot ensure identical learning of bodies of knowledge, however there are other benefits explained below. There will be cases where members of a team act as a group or vice versa. This will vary as the task unfolds.

HMI (DES 1987) suggest that the following 'qualities' are important in developing group/team work

- value co-operation,
- responsibility towards other members,
- readiness to listen to others' points of view
- willingness to support the view which seems to carry best hope of a solution,
- willingness to lead or follow as appropriate,
- perseverance.

Barlex (see page 135 in this volume) puts this simply as co-operation, communication, leadership, empathy/sympathy and reliability. Members need more than simply intellect. Bradshaw (1989) observed teams with high mental ability scores completing a task in comparison with random teams. Often the high ability teams finished last because members spent too much time persuading others to adopt their own view. Similarly, they tended to identify flaws in others arguments whilst failing to build a solution. Whilst we must beware generalising from a specific case this point is of interest.

Many writers suggest that roles be adopted within a team, e.g. manager, secretary, and that the qualities required will differ accordingly. This writer's experience is that the use of specific roles is often counter-productive and that the team may develop some of the limitations of 'scientific management' (Buchanan 1989) for example, lack of flexibility in responding to a developing task. Fieldwork (Denton 1988) indicates that children often prefer a co-operative model of working, though leadership may emerge from various members at different times as the individual's experience becomes central to the task as it evolves.

POSSIBILITIES

Social benefits

The social benefits of group work have generally been accepted which is why it is so often used by special needs teachers. Yeoman (1983) looking at 'collaborative groupwork' feels that self-concept and self-esteem can be enhanced, reporting an improved identification between learner and school and mutual concern between group members. Similar findings are reported in other studies (Cowie and Rudduck 1989; Miller and Davidson-Podgorny 1987).

Group work can have benefits in racial/minority integration. Miller and Davidson-Podgorny looked at integration in American schools where racially mixed group work helped develop empathy. Cowie and Rudduck (1989) also note these effects in gender and social class.

Vocational benefits

Cowie and Rudduck (1989) indicate that there is confusion amongst industrialists as to what they want in their recruits. There is, however, an emerging consensus that the ability to work effectively in a team is important.

Group work has been well established vocationally in this country, particularly through TVEI and enterprise type exercises (Denton 1988) which often use teams rather than groups. An aspect of such work is the introduction of competition. Competition makes many teachers fear for the self-esteem of lower achieving children. There are others who actively challenge the competitive nature of society and feel that many ills develop from it. This concern is clearly both morally and professionally defensible. However, if we could protect children from the effects of competition, how would the young adult manage on leaving school and joining the society of today? By introducing the element of competition within a controlled environment we may help children come to terms with the problems and possibilities it raises.

Learning benefits

Perhaps the least understood advantage of group work lies in achievement. Many are familiar with the concept of synergy, the way in which a group can generate more and better ideas than the same individuals working alone. There are simulations such as 'Lost on the moon' or 'Life raft' which invariably show a better score for groups than the sum of individual scores (Ginifer 1978). Driskell et al. (1987) refer to this as an 'assembly bonus effect' in that pooling thinking minimises errors. This may be true but is not adequate to explain synergy, as people who have used effective brainstorming techniques will know. The ideas of others can be used to 'leapfrog' to further ideas much as De Bono (1982) proposes.

We need to recognise that working in groups can aid academic attainment. Yeoman (1983), concluded that when children learn in groups the effects can be significantly better than learning individually and at the very least no worse. She pointed out that for low level cognitive tasks there is a positive effect on learning and that for high level work there again appears to be a positive gain though this effect needs clarification.

Bennett and Cass (1988) found that when children of different ability worked in groups the lower ability worked better and achieved more if with higher ability children, providing they were supported by having another lower ability peer in the group. A low ability child alone with higher ability children tended to withdraw. High ability children appeared to achieve just as well when with high or low achievers, they were not 'held back'.

The design and technology Orders (DES/WO 1990) do not mention groupwork within AT2 (generating a design). Is this a lack of vision or another example of assessment convenience over-ruling educational practice? Note how the original Science AT 18 'working in groups' (DES 1988: 56) was removed in those final orders.

PROBLEMS

Parlett and Hamilton (1983) showed how the 'scientific paradigm' of evaluation tends to make us value the easily measurable. Less easily measurable qualities tend to be ignored by external examination boards because they are difficult to measure with any reliability. Many examination boards do accept group work but they do so on the basis that work is clearly identifiable to individuals. They do not address group/team skills or the synergetic effect.

When some teachers use group work it may be by children 'working in groups rather than as groups'. This is an important distinction; we often use groups for administrative and logistic convenience, not recognising the educational benefits.

Group work experience needs to be planned for progression. Teachers tend to be successful products of our education system which at secondary and higher levels tends to avoid group work for the reasons outlined above. So we tend to perpetuate this situation. Saba (1989), Chairman of Toshiba, considers much of the relative economic performance of this country and Japan to be due to the fact that Japan is a group oriented culture in comparison to the UK.

Buchanan (1989) notes how 'scientific management' in industry breaks tasks down into small sub-units. This has been shown to have serious drawbacks such as worker dissatisfaction and poor production. Industrial experiments with production teams such as at Volvo showed promise but many failed, Buchanan feels, due largely to management fears of teamwork.

Human beings need more than basic extrinsic rewards. People have social and intellectual needs which must be met in their work.

UNDERSTANDING THE FACTORS

Some users of group work report very positive results (Cowie and Rudduck 1989) but current fieldwork at Loughborough indicates that there are teachers who have failed to get the results they hoped for. Often noise levels have been 'too high' and children have not focused enough on their work. This often leads to the teacher abandoning group work. Group work is a complex area which needs understanding before it can be made to work effectively.

Not all members of a group may contribute fully. Ingham *et al.* (1974) described the 'Ringelman effect' based on the simple task of rope-pulling. Ringelman found that individuals tended to pull with less effort when they were part of a team and that as team size grew the effect was more significant. This work does not mention what rewards there were for the task but it is clear that there was little social or intellectual reward and therefore the validity for an educational context looks poor. Harkins (1987) describes the concept of 'social loafing', where individuals may lower their effort if they feel that their individual performance will not be identified within the group performance. Harkins also showed that when evaluation potential was held constant, pairs out-performed singles in many tasks. He called this 'social facilitation'. This appears to be close to synergy.

Salomon and Globerson (1989) highlighted other negative effects possible within groups. For example, the 'freerider effect' when a member simply goes through the motions, leaving the real effort to others. They reported that this was observed with lower ability members when completion of the task was dependent on higher ability members. All members of a group must have a positive role to play and be needed.

A talented member of a group may slow down if he/she feels that they are being left to do all the work. This is the 'sucker effect'. Similarly pupils may see certain tasks in a sexist light and not perform fully if they feel they do not fit the role.

There is evidence (Salomon and Globerson 1989) that if a group does not like or value a task they put less effort in.

PRACTICAL LESSONS FOR TEACHERS

The task

This must be seen as challenging. It should not be dependent on the abilities of one member but needs the contribution of all members. There should be no roles which children see in a sexist manner and teachers must be sensitive to this in the way they introduce the task.

A group base

The group should have a base where direct communications are possible for the whole group. Individual members may well move off to complete specific, delegated tasks, but the base must always be available.

Roles

Many enterprise-type simulations use traditional structures such as a managing director, sales director, etc. The writer's own experience suggests that staff should sometimes allow groups to decide how to allocate roles. They usually do this on a co-operative basis, though a natural leader may emerge. Certainly experience shows that a co-operatively managed group can react more readily to developments. A strong leader can help, but the rigid demarcation into several roles can be negative in that individuals may disengage at times.

Group size and composition

Starting with young children in small groups we should progress and give experience of larger groups. We may start with self-selected groups and slowly introduce elements of teacher selection as they gain experience. The teacher should then consider putting children who would not normally work together in one team. Gender and race are other factors to consider. Remember that a single boy or girl with two or more of the opposite sex may feel uncomfortable, and lower ability children should similarly be given the support of a peer if in a group with higher ability children.

Assessment

Children need to see that they are being assessed as a group but also as individuals. Records of achievement or profiles can be used. It should be possible to identify the work of individuals within the task. Such identification can never fully account for the contribution of the individual in a synergetic sense but it will maintain motivation and help prevent 'social loafing'.

Group composition

In forming a group staff need to be sensitive to the fact that it takes time to become effective. Tuckman (1965) describes four stages: orientation, when members identify the task and their new colleagues; emotionality, where members struggle to establish the team and their role within it; relevant opinion exchange, where the group has established itself; and emergence of solution, where the group moves into a directly operational phase. These phases cannot be rushed and staff need to be particularly sensitive and supportive in the first two.

CONCLUSION

Group work, when effective, can have dramatic effects in terms of learning. Those that have witnessed such work recognise it instantly and appreciate the benefits.

Establishing such situations is not, however, straightforward. Teachers need to appreciate the limitations as well as potential benefits. Above all group work must be planned in a progressive sense. As Ghaye (1986: 55), put it 'The social and intellectual skills that children need in order to work together in a cooperative, egalitarian and supportive manner, need to be taught in a sustained and systematic way.'

REFERENCES

Bennett, N. and Cass, A. (1988) 'The effects of group composition on group interactive processes and pupil understanding', *British Educational Research Journal* 15 (1), 19–32.

Bradshaw, D. (1989) 'Higher Education, personal qualities and employment: teamwork', *Oxford Review of Education* 15 (1), 55–71.

Buchanan, D. (1989) 'High performance: new boundaries of acceptability in worker control', Chapter 12 in Sauter, Hurrell and Cooper (eds) *Job Control and Worker Health*, London, J. Wiley & Sons.

Cowie, H. and Rudduck, J. (1989) *Cooperative Groupwork – An Overview*, London.

De Bono, E. (1982) *De Bono's Thinking Course*, London, BBC Publications.

Denton, H.G. (1988) 'Group task management: a key element in technology across the curriculum?' *Studies in Design Education, Craft and Technology* 20 (3), 130–2.

DES (1987) *Curriculum Matters 9. Craft Design and Technology from 5–16*, London, HMSO.

DES (1988) *Science for Ages 5–16. Proposals for the Secretary of State for Education and Science*, London, HMSO.

DES/WO (1990) *Technology in the National Curriculum*, London, HMSO.

Driskell, J., Hogan, R. and Salas, E. (1987) 'Personality and group performance', *Group Processes and Intergroup Relations 9. Review of Personality and Social Philosophy*, USA.

Ghaye, A. (1986) 'Outer appearances with inner experiences: towards a more holistic view of groupwork', *Educational Review* 38 (1), 55.

Ginifer, J.H. (1978) 'Decision-making in task orientated groups', *Perspectives on Academic Gaming and Simulation* 1, 2.

Harkins, S. (1987) 'Social loafing and social facilitation', *Journal of Experimental Social Psychology* 23, 1–18.

Hoerr, J. (1989) 'The payoff from teamwork', *Business Week*, 10 July, 56–62.

Ingham, A. *et al.* (1974) 'The Ringelman Effect: studies of group size and group performance', *Journal of Experimental Social Psychology* 10, 371–84.

Miller, N. and Davidson-Podgorny, G. (1987) 'Theoretical models of intergroup relations and the use of cooperative teams as an intervention for desegregated settings', in *Review of Personality and Social Psychology 9. Group Processes and Intergroup Relations*, USA.

Parlett, M. and Hamilton, D. (1983) Evaluation as Illumination: A New Approach to the Study of Innovatory Programmes. Occasional Paper 9, Centre for Research in the Educational Sciences, University of Edinburgh.

Peacock, R. (1989) 'An industrialist's view', Second National Conference, DATER, Loughborough.

Saba, S. (1989) 'The Japanese style of doing business', *RSA Journal* 137 (5399), 715–22.

Salomon, G. and Globerson, T. (1989) 'When teams do not function the way they ought to', *International Journal of Educational Research* 13 (1), 89–98.

Tuckman, B.W. (1965) 'Developmental sequence in small groups', *Psychological Bulletin* 63 (6), 384–99.

Yeoman, A. (1983) 'Collaborative groupwork in primary and secondary schools: Britain and the USA', *Durham and Newcastle Research Review* 10 (51), 99–102.

Chapter 15

Teaching STS
Games, simulation and role-play

Joan Solomon

The national curriculum encourages pupils to consider moral, economic, social and environmental issues when designing. Teaching about science, technology and society (STS) using techniques developed in science education enables technology teachers to raise the 'technological awareness' of pupils.

INDUSTRIAL AWARENESS AND VALUE ISSUES

Economic and industrial awareness and the students' discussion of values are two aspects of the teaching of science, technology and society (STS) which are miles apart, with one set in the hard-nosed world of industry and commerce which is largely unknown territory to the students, and the other having its existence so deeply within their own feelings about what is right and wrong, that articulation may be hard for quite different reasons, related to shyness in talking about feelings, or lack of appropriate vocabulary. What binds values and industrial awareness together is only that in STS issues such as pollution or power generation, both are involved. In addition there is a view, which will be challenged in parts of this chapter, that learning about both – industrial management and personal values clarification – can be handled in the classroom by the same strategies of role-play and simulation.

There are those who deny the need for any special technological or industrial understanding in dealing with science-based social issues. Mary McConnell (1982: 13), for example put her view in uncompromising terms:

The problems associated with technological development may not primarily be problems of technology. Rather, they may be problems among us and between us, problems in a large measure the result of a pluralistic society in which common purpose, common values, and common images are no longer present. They are issues involving conflicts between values and goals within persons and among persons, rather than conflicts between dams and people, or industry and the environment. Resolution of conflict requires communication and creative problem solving to facilitate mutual understanding and effective interaction between people and groups that have different values, different images of the future, and different images of trade-offs and benefits and costs.

We may all agree that in our pluralistic society there are great potentialities for inter-group conflicts of interest and values, but might not be so sure that the basis for resolution of these is simply to be found through communication about values. There is a suggestion here that students do not need to learn about technology, or industry, or economics. All they require is a nose for sniffing out trade-offs, benefits and costs which do not conform to their values, and a facility for effective communication. Sadly there is now a real conflict between industry and the environment in a sense which transcends the caricature of the evil polluter who does not care about people, and the spotless environmental purist. As people, the groups cannot fail to share many objectives; it could be lack of a shared understanding which separates them.

STS education is dedicated to the proposition that it is well worth learning about the knowledge and perspectives of the different groups involved in the technological issues of our times, for only with such understandings can decisions about the issues be made. We need to learn about the perspectives of those in industrial management, if at all possible, and how their world view is constructed. Just as we try to teach about the nature of science, so we should also strive to teach about the nature of industrial technology.

GAMES AND IMAGINED SIMULATIONS

Ever since STS first broke in upon the school curriculum in the late 1970s there have been calls to develop new and appropriate strategies for teaching. Several of the suggestions produced have involved gaming, and simulation. According to Ellington *et al.* (1981) exercises of this kind can fulfil objectives:

> *educating through science* – fostering interpersonal and communication skills, and
> *teaching about the nature of science and technology* – illustrating the making of political, social and economic decisions.

There is little doubt that the first of these objectives can be met by group discussions about industry or other matters, in science or in any other school subject; it will be considered in some detail in later sections. But the second objective becomes problematic if the political, social and economic decisions lie too far beyond the teacher's and the student's own experience.

A number of fairly light-hearted simulations of other countries' technological problems are available, which may deserve the name 'game' not just because they try to amuse students, but because their names and fact-sheets immediately show them to be thoroughly fictitious. Although much may be learned through fiction it is doubtful if STS, whose very basis is relevance to real social problems, can afford to use it. Early games such as 'Minerals in Buenafortuna' (1983) used just such fact-sheets and encouraged students to discuss the issues that had been invented in rather contrived and restricted situations. Students were working with circumscribed sets of information and soon found that the agenda was already set by the authors. Questions such as whether the country really wanted to develop its mineral resources were taken for granted. Although the authors stated that open-ended questions such as 'the consequences in terms of pollution, noise and the disruption of the local community' can be put to the group, the 'only problem of any importance', they admitted, was predetermined by the game-makers.

The word 'game' is bound to be misleading in a context where a simulation of reality is intended. It is possible to buy many of these, ranging from simple snakes-and-ladders to complex role-plays about newspaper reporting of a health hazard in the Third World. In the early 1980s there was even a dice and card game about subsistence farming published by Oxfam, in which participants picked up cards announcing that they were suffering from severe malnutrition, life-threatening diseases, or even death. It was called, with quite startling ineptitude, 'The Poverty Game'! It has now been re-named 'The Farming Game'. Although it almost always caused hilarity in totally inappropriate places, this game did serve one purpose for which it would be hard to find its equal. When the players reached a stage at which their village was so deeply sunk into poverty that at long last they were permitted, by the rules of the game, to pick up a 'Help' card from the pack, there were occasional rebuffs when the legend on the back stated starkly 'Western governments do not like the politics of your country – NO AID'. The students' disappointment and muttered comments of 'not fair' made a brief but instructive point.

What these imaginary scenarios were really attempting was (a) a simulation of a *nearly* real situation and (b) a role-play by students. The students were asked to act out particular roles in order 'to appreciate hard decisions made by others' (Ellington *et al.* 1981). This created three serious problems:

1 The first was that most students would be making their own difficult future decisions as citizens rather than as technocrats so the activity missed that immediate relevance for which STS education aims.
2 Second, in so far as the situation called for role-play of characters whose background knowledge and skills were largely unknown to the students, in practice it produced enormous difficulties.
3 The third problem was that acted parts call for artificial opinions. Participants who already had formed clear, and even passionate, ideas on the public issue in question, might be precluded by their given role from expressing what they really believed.

Much has been learned about simulations and other classroom activities since those comparatively early attempts. Nevertheless some of the problems of designing and using simulations still remain, most noticeably those relating to industrial understanding.

TEACHING ABOUT TECHNOLOGY, ECONOMICS AND INDUSTRY

Economics is a popular subject in the sixth form with ever-increasing enrolment. It also has a part to play, at this level, in STS courses, but not as a dry clear-cut mathematical or theoretical discipline with complex modelling and a right answer which relates more to industrial growth than to quality of life. Nor is it of very great value just to burden all the students with endless graphs of imports and exports related to some technological innovation. We shall, of course, want all our students to be numerically literate to the extent of being able to scan information from graphs and charts of various kinds, with ease. However, it is the use to which such information is put which distinguishes STS from economics for its own sake.

Economics, like science, is just one part of the social dimensions of technology with which our courses will be concerned. It is a weighty factor for industrial bosses to take into account when they make decisions. Although teaching about technology within industry has been considered here, alongside simulations and role-play, it is by no means certain that these are the only ways, or indeed the best ways in which it can be taught.

Stories of past innovations are an excellent way to illustrate important points as well as being very inspiring to some types of student (e.g. Goodyear and the vulcanisation of rubber, or Russell Marker's explorations for making an oral contraceptive). From these stories, so long as they do not amount to any more than heroic legends, the following general points should emerge:

- Scientific knowledge is not always essential for invention, but it will accelerate its later stages.
- Chance plays a part in invention, but events still have to be noticed and exploited by the inventor.
- War often triggers and accelerates innovation.
- Discoveries may be made by several inventors at the same time because of market drive.
- New technologies change people's ways of living in both expected and unexpected ways.

Other aspects of technology also need teaching. We shall want our students to learn about cultural differences in the technologies appropriate for different countries, and the economic constraints which operate there. Closer to home they will need to learn a little about the role of technology in modern industry, which is substantially different from the tales of individual inventors mentioned in the previous paragraph. This will involve some practical economics related to the costs of R&D (Research & Development), competition after the first phase of innovation which is protected by patent, and military spin-off into civil use. It is here that simulations of what it might be like to make decisions within industry may be able to breathe some life into these rather dry and esoteric notions.

INDUSTRIAL SIMULATIONS

Most teachers find industrial simulations extraordinarily difficult to run in class, not just because they themselves have little grasp of economics, but because they have so little feel for the human context which they are trying to simulate. This becomes most apparent when they need to show their classes what kinds of argument would win the day when rival projects jostle for funding within an industrial firm. Some teachers have found an excellent local solution to their problems.

One very experienced STS teacher told me how she had once set up a hospital scenario where she and her students could study the decision-making concerned with priorities for operations such as kidney transplants and hip replacements. She had selected the problem from some resource materials. The students, using costings from the printed example, had already spent about a week trying to decide what treatments and operations they would put money into. Then she invited someone from the management team in the local NHS hospital to come in. Given the same problem she asked him to tell her class how he would have allocated the money. 'And, do you know', she said 'it was *totally* different from anything that they or I had come up with!' But when the manager made his presentation and went through his reasons it had all seemed completely valid to both teacher and students. They could immediately see why he had made his decision.

> It was fascinating. I could not have done that sort of exercise and given that kind of reply myself. Economic and industrial awareness are important because they influence decisions which directly affect society. I get the impression that decisions are made as to whether or not a particular product will have R&D money put into it for reasons I would never have imagined. It goes ahead for important internal reasons, not just as a result of simple market research.
>
> I have never found role-play very successful in my classes unless I've already got some familiarity with the background. Role-play in industry is particularly difficult. For GCSE courses I can make do with a computer program showing, for example, the costs of metal extraction, or the advantages of one site over another. But for more advanced work you do need to have a proper science and technological link. I think that most

areas have them now. In my area the 'neighbourhood engineer' is from the polymer industry, and he has always been very keen to come in and talk, not about the science involved because I can do that, but about the decision-making processes within industry – and that's exactly what I need.

Other STS teachers and resources designers have held similar views on the need for knowledge about industrial decision-making. New course materials (e.g. SATIS 16–19 (1991)) are appearing for the sixth-form age group but it seems possible to discern the same kinds of problems in most of the units which aim at industrial simulation.

One simulation (Unit 4), 'R&D at MUPCorp' (from SATIS 16–19), is said to explore 'the various decisions which must be taken after the initial scientific discovery of a product or process, up to the point at which it might become a commercial product'. This seems ambitious but it leads to a short and well-devised activity. The students take up roles as Project Managers with the task of deciding which of a number of 'promising' research projects should be explored further with a view to future investment. For each project they have to consider at the very least:

– whether it will work on a larger scale
– what uses it may have
– how big the market might be
– how it fits in with the firm's existing expertise
– social effects
– scale of manufacturing plant
– promotional ideas for advertising

The printed list is much longer and the tasks seem to be demanding.

There are ten new scientific research projects to be considered; all of them are comprehensible, at least in general terms, to a lay person, and most are thought-provoking and even amusing. The activity was written by a science teacher, vetted by some industrial scientists, and shows every sign of being fun to do in the classroom, with groups of students extolling the virtues of their particular product with the 'added spice' of a threat of redundancy if they fail to convince the Board!

The author of that activity adds a note from his own experience, and those of others, that 'it is important that students should not get "hung up" on the nature of the product. Scientific licence is allowed in advocating the merits of proposals which seem outlandish.' This point is thought-provoking. The purpose of this simulation, and others like it, is to experience some of the problems of industrial decision-making from an internal standpoint. From what has been discussed earlier it is clear that the gaming aspect of the activity could easily outweigh the relevant industrial aspects. Here again the presence of a 'neighbourhood engineer' might well be very valuable in turning the balance towards reality.

Another simulation (Unit 56), 'Planning a new edible-fats factory' illustrates an alternative approach, which would seem to ensure validity, by inviting industrialists to write the simulation themselves. (Several of this kind of exercise already exist but, in the experience of some teachers have not been easy to use.) This example, which runs to many pages of close script, is based on a real case study which is used in industry as a training exercise. Once again the students work in groups but, instead of taking on roles of scientific entrepreneurs, they have to become 'management consultants' who make detailed presentations about the best site for a new factory making edible fats, or 'specialist subcontractors' who give, or sell, specialist advice to the contractors.

This exercise has not only traded fun for reality and made a convincing simulation of a real situation, it has also asked the students to adopt specialised professional roles. Now the printed suggestions for running the simulation specifically include inviting a 'visitor from industry' to take part. This is clearly an essential ingredient if there is to be any chance of making such a difficult activity come to life in a school classroom. Teachers who have succeeded with this sort of simulation have often involved the whole of the sixth form for a complete day of 'industrial awareness' activity.

FROM INSIDE INDUSTRY OR FROM OUTSIDE?

Even if all the practical difficulties are overcome the simulation of industrial decision-making may still miss most of the central concerns of STS. (One teacher even commented that, in the previous industrial simulation, the basic STS question – 'Do we really *need* another factory?' – could only be treated after the activity is over.) Although all our students do need some understanding of the economics of innovation, most teachers in schools with a mixed intake will want to spend more time considering the point of view of the workers or the general public. Here it will be the student's values which suggest priorities, and not the rules and roles of the simulation.

This externalist approach would teach from the perspective of active and concerned citizenship. The students would be learning, for example, to value moral and civic reactions to the act of pollution. The following extract comes from the experience of an enthusiastic STS teacher from a working-class area in London, who is talking about the work he does on industrial hazards with Year 11 pupils. The strategy, of course, can be neither simulation nor role-play if the outcome is to concern real social action. Instead he weaves STS into his school coursework, teaching about industrial controls in this country, and then contrasting it with what happens abroad.

We do a lot about hazards and the transportation of dangerous chemicals – how to deal with spillages, and controls in the chemical industry. We were talking about hazard signs and the kids were working out how to recognise the dangerous chemicals, and it seemed that everything was wonderful – the signs were clear and the fireservice well organised.

Then I said 'How would you feel if there was a chemical spillage and ten thousand people died?' You know, they just laughed, and said, 'No. It couldn't happen.' Of course over here it couldn't happen, but I was leading up to talking about the tragedy at Bhopal, and conditions in the chemical industries in the developing countries. This really took off. We have a lot of Asian children here at this school, boys and girls, and they knew nothing about it. They listened. All these people still dying in Bhopal. You should have heard how they listened!

It would be difficult to deal with issues as emotive as this through simulation and role-play. The aims would be completely different to those in industrial simulations which study the internal processes of decision-making. Now the students would need to have freedom in constructing the roles that they *want* to play, since the objective would no longer be to 'feel your way into someone else's shoes'. The new objective will be to work out what their own sense of justice and compassion demands in the kinds of circumstances where ordinary people may confront risk or disaster. The rationale for setting this kind of teaching in a simulation is that there is something in the procedures being simulated which could be especially valuable to the students as citizens.

SIMULATION FOR UNDERSTANDING SOCIAL DECISION-MAKING

One arena for decision-making, that of public inquiries, has certainly not been ignored by the writers of simulation resources. Usually they dissect the problem, which might be the siting of some potentially hazardous plant, in terms of the arguments which might be presented by different interest groups. Thus it falls neatly into a kind of team game in the classroom. The great advantage of this is that several important points of view are presented to the students, and information for the various teams can be provided. Once again, however, the criticisms which have been levelled against other simulations cannot be avoided. The students are marshalled into predetermined camps, the agenda is set, and committed students may find no way to express their own beliefs.

It is difficult, although not impossible, to avoid these traps while keeping to the simulation format. Simulations about current concerns are particularly successful. They both catch the students' interests and ensure that the fictitious 'gaming' aspect is avoided. It is also very valuable to simulate a procedure – inquiry, court of law, or inquest – at the time when public attention is focused upon it. The organisational problems include providing information (not difficult if there is plenty of newspaper and television coverage) and allowing space for individual, and possibly emotive, points of view which may be less easy.

SUMMARY

This chapter has produced an odd assortment of evidence about simulations. Some of the examples have been given in the words of those who carried them out because there is a strong personal element in the choice of strategy. Teachers vary enormously in their attitudes towards any sort of 'acting' in the classroom; some love it, others are frankly scared. If the context is unfamiliar to the class, the teachers' misgivings about the activity may be justified.

The internal dynamics and decisions of the industrial boardroom are by no means central to STS, although they can be instructive if well done. Civic contexts for decision-making, such as courts of law and public inquiries are closer to the citizen and may produce rewarding simulations. The best of these strategies which (a) use a valuable context for the simulation, (b) which is adequately familiar, and (c) allows for the expression of individual views, can be quite excellent.

REFERENCES

Ellington, H., Addinall, E. and Percival, F. (1981) *Games and Simulation in Science Education*, London, Kogan Page.

McConnell, M. (1982) 'Teaching about science technology and society at the secondary level in the United States. An educational dilemma for the 1980s', *Studies in Science Education* 9, 1–32.

SATIS 16–19 (1991) *The Framework Units* (edited by A. Hunt and J. Solomon), Association for Science Education, Hatfield.

Chapter 16

Assessment of design and technology[1]

Richard Kimbell

In reviewing the development of assessment techniques in design and technology, Richard Kimbell shows how the lessons learnt from experience give guidance to good practice.

INTRODUCTION

There are three central arguments in this chapter

1 Assessment policy and practice in design and technology has become – over the last twenty years – increasingly concerned with details and specifics and less concerned with broad judgments. The emergence of a reductionist approach to criterion referenced assessment will be illustrated through three brief case studies.

2 The progressive atomisation of assessment – ultimately exemplified in the national curriculum (hereafter NC) – appears to demand practices that are inappropriate and cumbersome, lacking validity in terms of the established principles of the discipline, lacking reliability (judging by the evidence from research) and lacking manageability (any teacher will tell you).

3 To avoid these pitfalls, it is important that teachers incorporate holistic and judgmental approaches into their NC assessment practice. Approaches have been developed that capitalise on the benefits of detailed diagnostic assessment within the context of a holistic overview.

THE PROGRESSIVE ATOMISATION OF ASSESSMENT

My first case study is drawn from a pioneering CSE course in the early 1970s,[2] and was the first course explicitly to identify the *process of designing* as the basis for assessment. It created a seven-stage process that began with a general investigation of the context from within which a design brief might emerge, and ended with an evaluation of the outcome of the design and development process. This staged process was converted into an assessment scheme within which all the stages became – in turn – the focus of explicit

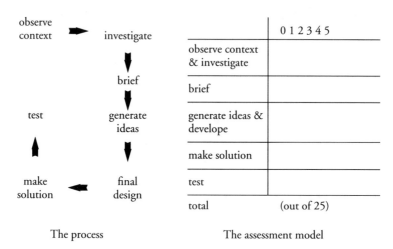

The process   The assessment model

Figure 16.1 Process and assessment model for a CSE design studies course

assessment. For the first time, the whole of the design and technological activity was being assessed instead of simply the practical outcome of it.

The stages of the process were assessed on a sliding scale from 0 (no real attempt) to 5 (comprehensive grasp of the capability). The final mark out of 25 was therefore seen as a measure of whole capability. It was in fact a fine example of norm referenced assessment, for the practice of teachers was typically to rank-order their pupils and then distribute the order across the mark range on the assumption that the best pupils should get top marks and the worst should get the bottom marks. This tendency to distribute pupils around a norm was reinforced by the paperwork that described 3 as being 'average' with 2 and 4 being respectively below and above average. The marking was of necessity qualitative, with very few guidelines to inform the process of setting standards.

My second case study is from the first generation of national criteria GCSE syllabuses in 1986–87.[3] The lineage of the assessment scheme is quite obvious; the stages of the design process once again being the basic structure of assessment. However, one of the fundamental tenets in the development of the GCSE was that norm referencing of the sort that was commonplace in the old GCE and CSE examinations was unhelpful because it did not identify in clear and positive terms *what pupils were capable of doing*. By contrast, the *GCSE General Criteria* were specific in requiring examinations that ensured proper discrimination and provided opportunities for pupils, 'to show what they know, understand, and can do' (DES/WO 1985: para. 16).

Here was a clear imperative to draw up a set of criteria that would enable us to remove for ever the concept of 'average' performance. Rather, the quality of capability that was to be assessed was *defined* at different levels of excellence, and pupils could then be assessed by the teacher identifying which descriptor applied to each pupil. If a pupil got 4 out of 5 for 'evaluating' it was not simply because she was nearly (but not quite) at the top of a rank order of other pupils, but rather because she was capable of doing the defined requirement of 4-ness.

> the performance required to achieve a particular mark is therefore specified in advance in the list of criteria on the form. It is therefore both more precise and more useful in a situation in which it is impossible for one teacher to know exactly what norms will be used by another teacher . . . the norms are encapsulated in the criteria.
>
> (SEC 1986: 38)

Looking back at the CSE example we can see that this GCSE equivalent of the assessment of a pupil's 'evaluation' has – once again – a five-point scale, but that this time each point on the scale is identified through a unique descriptor.

The candidate's evaluation:

0	– has not been attemped;
1	– is irrelevant;
2	– is relevant but superficial;
3	– represents an honest attempt to appraise his or her work but lacks objectivity and is either incomplete or not altogether relevant
4	– is complete and largely relevant but lacking in objectivity
5	– is thorough, objective, relevant and concise; it would provide a useful source of reference for later material

Figure 16.2 Assessment scheme for a GCSE CDT: design and communication course

Clearly, these descriptors were intended to aid the teacher in deciding at which level to place the pupil, and also to serve as a focus for discussion in the moderation process. In theory, the criteria attempted to embody the received wisdom of what excellence entailed, thereby supporting the process of assessment. In practice, however, they represented little more than the best guess of what the chief examiner thought might be important. They were often arbitrary, ill-informed or little more than normative statements – like 'thorough', for 5 marks in Figure 16.2.

In November 1989 the national curriculum Order for technology for

England and Wales was finally ratified as a foundation subject in the national curriculum, and it provides my third example (see DES 1989). The Statutory Order seeks to lay out – for the first time – a comprehensive description of the progression of capability that is required between ages 5 and 16 both in terms of the *Programmes of Study* (PoS) that teachers will use in school courses and the *Statements of Attainment* (SoA) that pupils should seek to achieve through those programmes.

The four *Attainment Targets* (ATs)[4] again reflect the process of design and development and the SoAs are intended to provide a comprehensive criterion referenced assessment scheme within those ATs. It is interesting to note that there are 118 such SoAs, each intended to describe a specific quality at a particular level. The simple (1970) sliding scale (0–5) has become a mass of 'can do' assessment statements to which the teacher has merely to say yes or no. The NC has in effect created a digital assessment scheme in place of the former analogue approach.

For the purposes of comparing the three case studies, it is interesting to contrast the 1990 NC SoA for 'evaluating' (AT4) with the assessment criteria for the same quality under the former (CSE and GCSE) arrangements. The national curriculum levels that are equivalent to GCSE are levels 5 to 10 and – just for AT4 (evaluating) – there are fourteen separate descriptors.

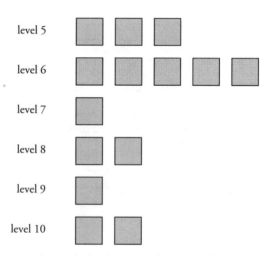

Figure 16.3 Elements of assessment for the national curriculum (England and Wales 1990), attainment target 4 'Evaluating'

To place a pupil in one of these six levels (5–10) the teacher has to make fourteen individual yes/no judgments against the SoAs. We have gone from (in 1972) one single judgment of capability in evaluating, to (in 1986) a choice of one 'best fit' descriptor from five possibles, to (in 1989) a series of fourteen independent yes/no decisions that are then processed into an answer. In order to achieve clarity in measuring pupils' work, the units of assessment have become smaller and smaller and they have been reduced (like the Grand Old Duke of York) to one of two states – up or down, yes or no.

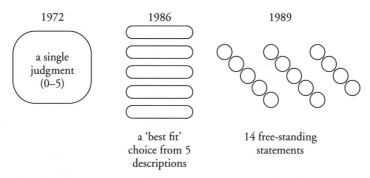

Figure 16.4 The progressive atomisation of assessment over twenty years

These three case studies are by no means the only ones (or even the most extreme ones) that I could have chosen to illustrate the trend towards detailed – atomised – assessment. Significantly more extreme versions exist. The Graded Assessment scheme for CDT, for example, maps out hundreds of assessment boxes to be ticked when single or multiple skills have been demonstrated by pupils.

The big question of course is whether it is a better (fairer, more reliable, more informative) system? It is tempting to believe that converting complex judgments into digital (yes/no) classifications will produce the same crispness and clarity in assessment that it achieves with the digital processor in my amplifier. But let us examine for a moment the problems involved.

THE LIMITATIONS OF ATOMISED ASSESSMENT

The first difficulty centres on the problem of losing sight of the wood while we are trying to count the trees. It's a bit like doing a jigsaw. If you pick up a single piece of the puzzle it tells you very little about the whole picture and even less about the *quality* of that picture. Small, individual judgments make sense only if they are contextualised by a wider field of vision.

A second difficulty lies in the fact that in these categorical (yes/no) assessments, it is by no means obvious how to distinguish between a yes and a no. It involves a calibration exercise to decide the quality threshold at which a no becomes a yes. In a recent sub-aqua examination I had to demonstrate that I could tread water for one minute with my arms above my head. The instructor tells me that the results of this test are usually clear, you sink or you don't sink. It is (generally) good digital data. But few school-based assessments are so clear-cut.

The following statement is from the 1989 NC Order and requires that pupils be able to 'use specialist modelling techniques to develop design proposals'. How do we calibrate the achievement threshold for such a statement? At what level of capability does a 'no' become a 'yes'? Does it refer to a 5-year-old squeezing out some plasticine, or to an 8-year-old experimenting with a lego mechanism, or to a 15-year-old modelling a stage set? In reality, of course, designing *at all levels of capability* involves a degree of modelling. But a digital, categorical assessment system requires that all pupils be put into one of two camps – the modellers and the non-modellers. Any decision here will not only be arbitrary it will be misleading. It will imply that the 'non-modellers' cannot model their ideas, when in reality it will mean that their modelling facility has not reached the arbitrary threshold level.

A third difficulty is amply demonstrated in my three examples simply by noting the *number* of assessments that need to be made. It follows that, as the units of assessment get smaller and (supposedly) more precise, they have also to get more numerous in order to cover the same ground. The price of atomisation is proliferation and an interesting parallel can be found in the engineering toolbox.

The go/no-go gauge is a precisely ground instrument that gives a clear (yes/no) answer to a simple question, 'Is this bar 20 mm in diameter?' If the gauge fits snugly on the bar the answer is 'yes'; if it does not then the answer is 'no'. It is a very limited instrument that is only capable of supporting that one single decision. For effective engineering therefore you need a great store full of them, all of slightly different sizes. Go/no-go gauges are therefore not measuring devices at all, but are really *checking* devices. The 20 mm diameter gauge is not used to measure whether a bar is 10, 15, 20 or 25 mm in diameter, it is used as a precision check exclusively on bars that are known to be (or supposed to be) 20 mm diameter. Effective use of go/no-go gauges therefore depends on a prior *judgment* about the size of the bar. A skilled fitter could make far more efficient use of these gauges than an unskilled one.[5]

The point of the story is merely to indicate that a system based on atomised, categorical assessment can only sensibly work if the operator (teacher) is able to make a prior overview judgment and hence select the appropriate criteria of validation.

A fourth difficulty concerns the extent to which individual judgments necessarily interact in the assessment of capability. It's a bit like judging the quality of an omelette. However good the eggs are – and the herbs, and the butter, and perhaps the cheese – the key question is how well they are blended to work together and enhance each other. To treat the judgments as independent points to be scored is seriously to misjudge the interdependence of the elements that go to make up technological capability. Do we not know when we have eaten an exquisite omelette?

MAKING JUDGMENT MANAGEABLE

In examining these difficulties arising from the progressively more atomistic assessment in the case studies, it is interesting to reflect on the level at which *judgment* is being exercised by the teacher.

In the CSE example, teachers had to make judgments in relation to five general categories of performance, e.g. a pupil's 'evaluation'. They did this by considering a *range* of evidence from all aspects of the pupil's work; the folio, their product/outcome, and in relation to any discussions or informal exchanges that gave the teacher insights into the pupil's level of performance. Each of the five judgments required the assimilation and cross-referencing of evidence, and any disparity in the evidence had to be reconciled in the judgments. Subsequently, the five judgments were amalgamated to arrive at a single score. By far the most critical part of the assessment process was the five judgments that the teacher made. Moreover – as I argued above – the many qualities of capability that overlap and affect each other can be taken account of in the reconciliation and cross-referencing process.

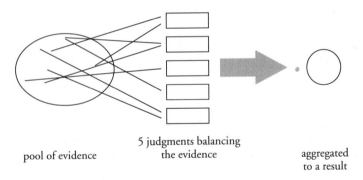

pool of evidence   5 judgments balancing the evidence   aggregated to a result

Figure 16.5 Assessment procedure for CSE

By contrast in the NC 1990 example, the teacher is required to look for evidence of a series of discrete and specific qualities, and in the GCSE equivalent range of levels (6–10) there are fifty-six such judgments to be made.

National curriculum assessment requires numerous free-standing judgments, which are then manipulated mathematically to arrive at a score. The judgments have necessarily to be small-scale and independent, and the subsequent score is controlled as much by the double layer of aggregation rules as it is by the judgments themselves. The final result is not a gestalt

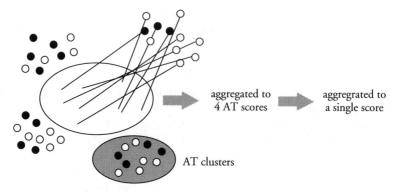

Figure 16.6 Assessment procedure for 1990 national curriculum

overview of a pupil's performance and capability, it is rather a formulaic 'answer'.

It is highly revealing talking to teachers who have been through this NC assessment exercise. Time and again I have been told of the situation where the process has been exhaustively (and exhaustingly) carried through to the 'answer' only for the teachers to say to themselves 'No that can't be right – Ali is not level 5 and she is certainly not better than Jo.' But being unable to balance the judgments, they do the only thing they are allowed to do to make the judgment 'right' in their eyes; they change some of the no's to yes's or some of the yes's to no's until such time as the arithmetic gives them the 'right' result.

Is this blatant cheating – is it defrauding the system – or is it the responsible use of judgment on the part of the teacher? Whichever view is held, it speaks volumes about the supposed objectivity of criterion referenced assessment. And, more fundamentally, it raises the very interesting question of the reliability of such digital assessment systems in technology.

RELIABLE ASSESSMENT – THE EVIDENCE FROM RESEARCH

The reliability of assessments in technology was a central concern of the survey by the Assessment of Performance Unit (1985–91). The survey involved tests on more than 10,000 pupils in 700 schools using three kinds of technological test: (a) extended project activity; (b) 90-min. paper and pencil tests; and (c) modelling tests (see SEAC/EMU 1991). A common assessment framework was used for all three approaches to testing and critically – for this discussion – it involved both holistic judgments of capability *and* atomised assessment of discrete qualities. The holistic judgment was on a six-point scale (0–5) the zero representing effectively a non-response and the five representing outstanding work. One hundred and twenty practising teachers were trained for the assessment of pupil work (both holistic and atomistic), and several mark/re-mark studies of marker reliability conducted. Every teacher was required to undertake one of these re-marking studies, which typically involved them in pairs, independently cross-marking a set of 200 pieces of work. We subsequently compared the rank order of pupils created by each teacher in the pair to get a measure of the consistency with which the assessments were being made.

The reliability statistics provide fascinating reading (SEAC/EMU 1991: 131–6). The holistic judgment provided correlations around a median of 0.74, a remarkably high figure. The detailed mini-judgments that were designed to illuminate these holistic judgments were typically recording correlations around 0.5–0.6, i.e. significantly less reliable than the holistic.

It seems that markers had a great deal more difficulty in coming to terms with these discrete judgments – and the evidence from marker questionnaires conducted after the exercise suggest that a large part of the difficulty lay in separating the qualities from each other.

Had we used the atomised judgments for the statistical analyses, by aggregating them up to an overall score for each pupil, these aggregated scores would have had a far lower inter-marker correlation than those that were achieved by direct holistic assessment by the markers. The holistic judgment allowed for the interaction of qualities and made it possible for markers to see how well the pupil was *making use* of their capability in one area to move the whole project forward. An individual strength – e.g. in communicating – is only a strength if it makes the pupil a better technologist. It is therefore not a judgment that can be made in isolation.

DEVELOPING RELIABLE, DIAGNOSTIC AND APPROPRIATE ASSESSMENT

The central thrust of my argument is that in assessing technological capability, the requirement to operate exclusively on the basis of detailed, itemised criteria (SoAs), is fundamentally unsound. It creates a superficially simple (tick-box) system, but its crude reductionist methodology creates enormous problems for the assessment of an integrated capability. In practice, therefore, it was bound to be (and has been shown to be) unhelpful and unmanageable as well as unreliable.[6]

It is nonetheless something with which teachers have to come to terms, so we have to find a way of making sense of the plainly dotty and to this end I offer the following approach.

MAKING ASSESSMENT MANAGEABLE

There are two appropriate uses for the detailed SoAs, but their use must be premised on an alternative way of looking at NC assessment. The process

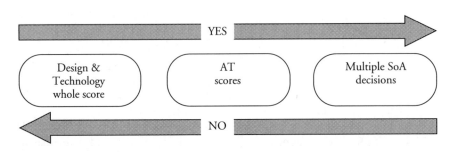

Figure 16.7 Procedure for making assessment manageable

must start with whole judgments and work towards detail. It must not start with detail and work towards the holistic.

Remember the go/no-go gauges. In order to make effective use of them, a prior judgment needs to be made about approximately which ones to try. So too with SoAs, there is no point in selecting ones that are quite inappropriate. Teachers need to develop a sense of levelness; what level 4 looks like – as a whole – what level 2 and level 6 look like – as a whole. The primary judgment then is to decide what level you believe a pupil to be at. Thereafter this can be teased apart into AT judgments,[7] identifying broad strengths and weaknesses. Then it is appropriate to look to the SoAs as a detailed cross-check. It then becomes a somewhat iterative process. If in looking at the detail it does not seem to fit, then it might be a cause for modifying the initial judgment, in any event this process is informed by decisions at both ends of the process – it is emphatically not a simple mechanical aggregation from the minuscule up to the whole. So one good use of SoA is as a checking/validating tool - to help confirm judgments that have been made.

Their second use is in informing the nature of the levels *as a whole*. The level 2 SoA may be regarded – collectively – as a basket of descriptors that, taken together, help to define 2-ness. This is after all how they were written by the original working group. There are other helpful guides in 'getting a feel' for level 2. It is – according to TGAT (DES/WO 1988) – the normal performance expected of 7-year olds, as is level 4 for 11-year-olds, level 5/6 for 14-year-olds and level 6/7 for 16-year-olds. Whilst assiduously avoiding any mention of norm referencing, TGAT helpfully provides normative guides for us! Level 2 therefore has to be seen predominantly through seven-year-old spectacles.

It is difficult to overstate the importance of teachers developing a sense of the quality of work that is appropriate at different levels – not by reference to tick lists, but by a broader recognition of quality. Quality as a whole at each level and quality within ATs at each level. It will progressively emerge – and can be deliberately developed – through moderation processes in which teachers debate the strengths and weaknesses in particular pieces of work and in relation to the whole basket of SoA descriptors. A helpful and manageable assessment challenge would be to construct – for each pupil and in every project a small profile of marks. Starting with the whole and teasing out strengths and weaknesses in the ATs.

This is already an informative picture of pupil performance which can be checked against individual SoAs if necessary. It is also a manageable assessment and recording burden and interestingly all that is legally required in the formal Assessment Order for Technology. In fifty pages of tightly packed legal text (Statutory Instrument and Education Order 1992, see DES 1992) there is not a single mention of SoAs.

An approach of this kind would be entirely within the spirit of NC technology in that it would enable teachers to reconcile its contradictions. It was constructed upon a view of technology as a whole capability (DES 1988: Ch. 1), and yet (apparently) it is to be assessed through the most atomised and disintegrated system imaginable. Teachers have it within their power to create a more balanced and iterative view of the assessment process weighing the evidence both as a whole and in diagnostic detail.

Professional judgment lies – as ever – at the heart of this debate.

NOTES

1 The material contained in this chapter has been selected and reorganised from two 'in press' publications by the author. See Kimbell (in press) (a) and (b). These publications expand on this chapter and may be used to explore some of the issues in greater depth.
2 A design studies syllabus developed through the North Western CSE Examination Board.
3 The Northern Examination Association syllabus for CDT: design and communication.
4 The 1989 attainment targets were, identifying needs and opportunities, generating a design, planning and making, and evaluating. In 1992 the attainment targets, statements of attainment and programmes of study were all redrafted, partly because of the genuine difficulties that teachers reported in working with the original version, and partly through the lobbying of special interest groups like the Engineering Council who disliked the dominantly procedural nature of the Order and who wanted a tighter prescription of the content to be taught.
5 It is interesting to reflect on the fact that as the engineering workforce became more educated (or at least more literate and numerate) the extremely limited go/no-go gauges disappeared in favour of more flexible measuring devices (vernier gauges and micrometers) that adapt to the size of the bar and yet render just as much precision.
6 One of the minor tragedies of the last four years is that the humane model of technology reflected in the 1989 Order got all the blame for the problems that resulted for teachers, when in reality it was significantly the fault of the assessment system itself – which had nothing to do with the definition of technology.
7 Two AT judgments proposed in the 1992 revised order, one in the order for Northern Ireland.

REFERENCES

DES/WO (Department of Education and Science/Welsh Office) (1985) *General Certificate of Secondary Education: General Criteria*, HMSO.

DES/WO (Department of Education and Science/Welsh Office) (1988) *Task Group on Assessment and Testing – A Report*, DES.

DES (Department of Education and Science) (1988) *Interim Report of the Design and Technology Working Group*, HMSO.

DES (Department of Education and Science) (1989) *Technology in the National Curriculum*, HMSO.

DES (Department of Education and Science) (1992) *The Education (NC) (Assessment Arrangements for English Mathematics, Science and Technology) (Key Stage 3) Order 1992*, DES.

Kimbell, R.A. (in press a) 'Assessing technological capability', in the *Proceedings of the INCOTE 92*, Weimar, Germany.

Kimbell, R.A. (in press b) 'Progression in learning and the assessment of pupil attainment', in *Innovations in Science and Technology Education*, Paris, UNESCO.

NW Secondary School Examination Board (1971) *Certificate of Secondary Education: Studies in Design*.

SEC (1986) *Craft, Design and Technology GCSE: A Guide for Teachers*, Milton Keynes, Open University Press.

SEAC/EMU (1991) *The Assessment of Performance in Design and Technology – The Final Report of the APU Design and Technology Project 1985–91*, London, School Examinations and Assessment Council/Evaluation and Monitoring Unit.

Chapter 17

'One in five'

Design and technology and pupils with special educational needs

Curriculum Council for Wales

This teacher support material was written by a group of practising teachers and advisory teachers as part of the CCW Teacher Support Programme.

WHO ARE THE 'ONE IN FIVE'?

It is estimated that 20 per cent (one in five) of pupils will have special educational needs at some time during their school life.

Pupils are said to have special educational needs if they have significantly greater difficulty in coping with their schoolwork, compared with other pupils of a similar age range. They are in need of some form of extra help to try to raise their levels of achievement.

These pupils may have difficulties which are:

- of a physical or intellectual nature;
- connected with a sight, hearing or speech impairment;
- emotional or behavioural;
- specifically related to aspects od communication and language;
- more general, covering some or all aspects of school work.

The usual definition of special educational needs come from the 1981 Act and refers to pupils with disabilities and learning difficulties. Some schools also include gifted pupils and those for whom English is not their first language; this chapter does not attempt to address the needs of these pupils.

As indicated above the term 'special educational need' covers a wide range of learning difficulties. Many pupils have special needs which are only temporary and so the actual percentage of pupils with a special need at any one time is probably nearer 16 per cent than the 20 per cent quoted (figures taken from *Getting in on the Act*, DfE 1990). Of this number approximately 2 per cent have statements of special educational need.

ASPECTS OF DESIGN AND TECHNOLOGY SPECIFIC TO CERTAIN PUPILS WITH SEN

Many schools will have established within their curriculum development plan and subject policies a coherent and detailed curriculum for pupils of all abilities. For some pupils with special educational needs this may mean that they are taught PoS material specific to levels outside the range specified for their particular age and key stage.

In special cases there is provision within the Education Reform Act for temporary exemptions by headteachers, or more permanent disapplication by an LEA through an amendment to a statement of special educational need.

The following two statements from the Order for technology (DES/WO 1990) apply to certain pupils with special educational needs. In relation to the attainment targets: 'Pupils unable to communicate by speech, writing or drawing may use other means including the use of technology or symbols as alternatives.' In relation to the programmes of study: 'A pupil who, because of disability, is unable to undertake a practical activity required under the programmes of study, may undertake an alternative activity which closely matches that activity.'

What are the practical implications of these two statements?

The first statement is about *communication difficulties*, and suggests alternatives to assist communication which could include the use of:

- computer programs and hardware such as concept keyboards;
- a scribe or mentor who is familiar with the difficulty;
- prepared cards containing symbols, phrases, messages or prompts;
- acquired alternative methods such as sign language, lip-reading or touch;
- audio/video tapes and recording to provide the pupil with appropriate information and to enable the pupil to record him or herself.

The second statement is about *carrying out practical work* and could mean in practice that:

- a pupil unable to prepare hot food products using an electric or gas cooker, for safety or other reasons, could use a microwave oven, be helped by a friend or teacher or even work with cold ingredients;
- a pupil unable to co-ordinate or control certain tools or machines to cut, shape or form materials could use pre-cut or prepared pieces and/or be assisted considerably.

Structuring the depth of focus in a design and technology activity or task

When devising design and technology activities for pupils, teachers should consider the appropriateness and depth of focus, or level, at which the activity is pitched. For example, is it appropriate to introduce a design and technology task relating to 'transport' at the same depth of focus for all abilities and needs? In this case, could all the pupils begin successfully if the tasks asks them to 'design a model vehicle and devise a way of moving it using stored energy'? In many instances there is a scope or flexibility available for the teacher to structure different layers within the activity and guide particular pupils to an appropriate, achievable yet challenging task.

The two examples in Figure 17.1 and Figure 17.2 show how this might be done. Both these examples help illustrate not only flexibility and opportunities for different abilities, but also how planning the task in this way can help the teacher to manage the activity and provide an element of progression as pupils take on more open tasks toward the top of the diagram.

Flexibility in design and technology processes

The design and technology processes indicated by the attainment targets do not always form a linear or mechanical route through a design and technology activity and should not be viewed or taught as rigid steps or stages.

Design and technology activities involve, in differing intensities and to different extents, a complex interplay of exploring and clarifying the task; generating, developing and communicating ideas; evaluating; planning; making artefacts and products; and testing.

In relation to these processes pupils with special educational needs will have particular gifts and abilities in particular types of work. Because these design and technology processes can and will vary from one design and technology activity to another, it is possible for teachers to devise activities for some pupils on the basis of their strengths and successes. When teaching may pupils with SEN this will mean directing design and technology activities around *making* and letting the other important processes be incorporated through and around *making*.

Centring design and technology on making artefacts and products does not mean that other processes should be neglected. Indeed, pupils will need to have access to these other design and technology processes to provide balance in their programme over a whole key stage, and of course to provide assessment opportunities for the SoAs within the attainment targets.

From time to time teachers will need to devise short design and technology activities which provide a particular emphasis and opportunity for pupils to achieve success in one or more design and technology processes.

For example, a focused task where pupils cut, shape, form and test strips

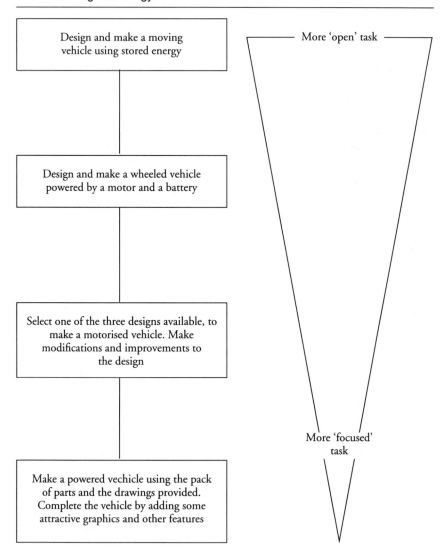

Figure 17.1 'Adjusting the depth of focus' in a control technology task

of different materials provides excellent opportunities, through discussion and recording of comments, to assess aspects of evaluation, materials awareness and knowledge. This can also provide opportunities to identify uses and possible projects in which these materials could be used.

Likewise, by providing a range of outline ideas for solutions to a 'design and make' activity, the teacher will be able to support the pupils and provide a good start for them to begin generating, developing and communicating their own ideas based around these beginnings. Again this would provide

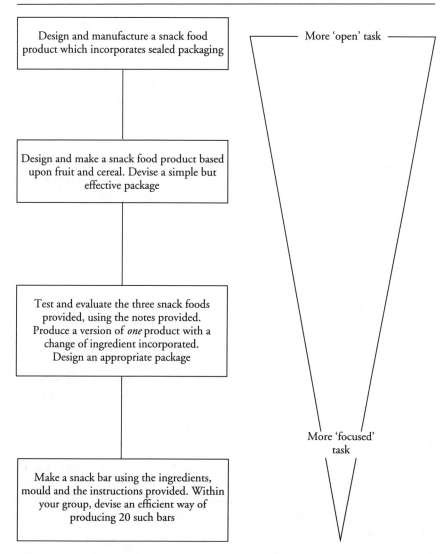

Figure 17.2 'Adjusting the depth of focus' in a food technology task

opportunities for assessing particular successes in particular statements of attainment.

Devising short 'extending tasks' in design and technology

For some pupils with special educational needs the nature of their difficulty may not unduly affect their working and achievement in design and technology. For example, a pupil with a slight hearing impairment can probably cope well with most design and technology work, given appropriate aid and any necessary support.

For other pupils with special educational needs the nature of their learning difficulty can greatly affect success in design and technology. Many of these pupils can gain success and achieve progress by being involved in fairly short 'extending tasks'. Short time-span projects which are devised to promote and provide small elements of success are not only very rewarding for the pupil but also provide opportunity for that success to be assessed.

The accumulation of success and achievement in this way can be structured so that a gradual move towards a statement of attainment or level of attainment can be achieved. Without this structure a pupil may remain between two national curriculum levels of attainment for months or even years.

An example of a short 'extending task'

The example of a short extending task given below could be devised to support progress and achievement in, for example, a pupil's communication skills in drawing. The task might follow the pattern outlined below:

1 pupil uses a light-box, tracing paper or grid paper to produce a copied drawing of a shape;
2 pupil follows faint guidelines or dotted lines to produce a drawn shape;
3 pupil produces own drawing of a shape alongside printed version on page, with key lines provided dotted;
4 pupil produces own drawing alongside printed version;
5 pupil produces own drawing of shape from observation.

In this example it is possible to trace the pupil's progress from being able to communicate by drawing with considerable help through to communication with little or no help and with intention. It should be noted, however, that such structuring and the devising of short extending tasks requires a great deal of teacher time and planning.

The support teacher

In some instances pupils with SEN will have the assistance of a support teacher in the classroom, and for working in design and technology. Support teachers have the experience, patience and expertise, in co-ordination with the class teacher, to provide a range of valuable services for the pupil. Such support work requires close collaboration and agreement on roles and responsibilities between teacher and support teacher. For many teachers the presence of another colleague in a teaching situation is a new and often unsettling experience. Figure 17.3 indicates some of the roles of a support

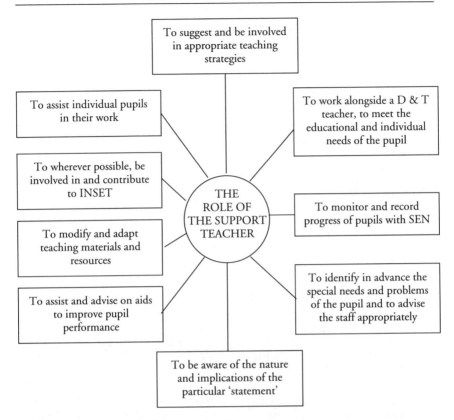

Figure 17.3 The role of the support teacher

teacher and could be used by teachers and support teachers to help formulate and agree upon responsibilities.

DESIGN AND TECHNOLOGY PROCESSES: SOME POSSIBLE PROBLEMS AND SOLUTIONS FOR SOME PUPILS WITH SEN

Depending on the nature of their special educational needs pupils may experience problems relating to certain design and technology processes, for example when generating their own ideas. Such pupils might achieve more success in other aspects of design and technology work. The following provides guidance for teachers on some of these problems, and offers some possible solutions. For convenience this guidance is presented under the three types or groups of 'learning difficulty', namely:

– physical and sensory difficulties;
– intellectual difficulties;
– emotional and behavioural difficulties.

Within each type or group of learning difficulties the design and technology processes central to national curriculum design and technology are also grouped. These processes, which are interwoven when pupils undertake designing and making, are described as:

– exploring opportunities and clarifying the task;
– generating, developing and communicating design ideas and proposals;
– planning and making;
– testing, evaluating and modifying.

Table 17.1 Some possible problems and solutions for certain pupils with physical and sensory difficulties

Possible problems	Possible solutions
Exploring opportunities and clarifying the task	
Certain project titles could be inappropriate.	Consider project areas carefully and incorporate pupil interests and experiences if possible.
Difficulties may directly restrict access to resources and situations, e.g. a visit.	Plan for provision and access. Provide alternatives where necessary.
Speech or other impairment could limit ability to communicate and approach the task.	Provide alternatives for communication such as scribe or concept keyboard.
Pupil lacks appreciation of likely problems their learning difficulty may bring to bear on later design and technology processes for example when *making*.	Highlight the positive and achievable aspects. Provide alternatives to assist situation, e.g. some pre-cut parts for making.
Generating, developing and communicating design ideas and proposals	
Clumsiness or difficulties in expressing ideas and in producing drawings.	Use a scribe to help record ideas and provide drawing aids.
Pupil has very limited range of ideas and experiences.	Provide plenty of appropriate resources, stimuli and ideas.
Difficulty in relating needs and concepts of task to ideas and solutions.	Provide a range of achievable though challenging ideas and solutions for pupils to develop.
Frustration and failure caused by restricted methods of communication imposed.	Teacher needs to value and make provision for a range of communication, e.g. talk or ideas communicated directly by working materials.

Table 17.1 cont.

Possible problems	Possible solutions
Planning and making	
Manipulation and co-ordination problems.	Direct practical support. Adapted tools and equipment. Use of jigs and devices.
Preparation and making lacks accuracy and quality.	Use of templates, jigs, some pre-cut parts. Tactful inputs by the teacher.
Unfair dependence on other pupils in the class or group.	Provide more support. Provide some additional time for pupils. Share support around class. Increase independence.
Lack of time to consolidate and practise skills and processes demotivates the pupil.	Provide extra time if possible. Less complex tasks. Shorter tasks.
Frustration and demotivation.	Reward all forms of progress. Devise short extending tasks. Relate activities to pupil interests.
Testing, evaluating and modifying	
Expectations of failure if comparisons are made with high achievers.	Ensure comparisons with peers. Hightlight progress as an individual.
Difficulties in recording and communicating thoughts and information.	Use of scribe or IT applications.
Low levels of evaluation and testing, e.g. 'I like it' or 'It doesn't work'.	Provide check-lists of considerations, questions, options.
Pupil has little interest in improving or modifying work done, wants to finish quickly.	Make the improvements with the pupil and highlight the increased value. Reward slower working.

Table 17.2 Some possible problems and solutions for certain pupils with intellectual difficulties

Possible problems	Possible solutions
Exploring opportunities and clarifying the task	
Inability to see value or point of the design and technology task.	Is the task appropriate? Teacher leads and feeds ideas including the showing of some finished examples.
Lack of confidence and inability to grasp or start the activity. Task is too 'open' and demanding.	Lower the level of expectation. Focus the task to suit ability and provide clear boundaries and sub-tasks.
Ideas developed are impractical.	Highlight any positive part of ideas. Explain why other pupils cannot realise some ideas.
Pupil has very limited ideas and experience to draw upon.	Provide a range of appropriate stimuli and/or some possible ideas for pupil to develop.

Table 17.2 cont.

Possible problems	Possible solutions
Generating, developing and communicating design ideas and proposals	
Inability or low interest to connect designing with making. 'Why design?'	Use product examples to illustrate the importance and enjoyment of designing. Design directly with materials.
Ideas are stereotypic and narrow.	Provide plenty of ideas and stimuli. Develop ideas with pupil.
Pupil only wants to 'make' something.	Devise short 'making' tasks having small and compulsory elements of designing.
Lack of confidence and pride in design work.	Praise small achievements. Pair up pupil with helpful and sympathetic pupil.
Planning and making	
Inability to retain instructions and to listen at length.	Provide regular reminders and/or information cards. Use shorter tasks and instructions.
Low levels of co-ordination accuracy and detailing.	Use of jigs, templates, patterns, pre-cut parts. Teacher contributions.
Health and safety problems. Low appreciation of potential dangers.	Take all reasonable precautions. Restrict access if necessary. Reward safe working. Provide clear rules.
Work is rushed and sloppy. Inability to transfer and repeat previous skills and knowledge.	Reward slower work. Provide short extending tasks. Repeat and practise skills. Teacher assists finishing.
Frustration and behavioural problems.	Set clear rules and expectations. Reward all progress. Short productive tasks. Build upon pupil interests.
Testing, evaluating and modifying	
Low levels of expectation and appreciation of quality.	Use examples to show value of improvements. Illustrate good and bad design in products.
Limited vocabulary and understanding of concepts.	Provide check-lists and plenty of group discussions. Help pupil to evaluate and discuss some favourite products.
Pupil sees little value in testing and evaluating. Wants to 'make it and take it home'.	Make testing and evaluating fun. Show how modifications can greatly improve product before taking it home.

Table 17.3 Some possible problems and solutions for certain pupils with emotional and behavioural difficulties

Possible problems	Possible solutions
Exploring opportunities and clarifying the task	
Low interest and concentration span.	Base activities around pupil interests and strengths. Short tasks. Provide choices.
Low standards of behaviour.	Provide clear and precise rules and methods of working.
Poor communication skills and low interest in forming own ideas.	Use of IT applications. Promote discussion of ideas. Reduce amount of writing and research.
Pupil withdraws and does not take part.	Trigger interest and involvement via pupil interests and previous successes in design and technology. Devise short tasks.
Generating, developing and communcating design ideas and proposals	
Ideas are unrealistic and do not match ability to 'make'.	Re-develop an idea generated by the pupil. Provide a range of ideas and solutions for pupil to adopt.
Pupil doesn't want to design and only wants to make.	Devise a 'make' task which will only work if some designing is done. Show importance of 'design' in pupil's favourite items.
Ideas are few and stereotypic.	Provide plenty of ideas, alternatives and stimuli.
Low level of communication.	Teacher acts as scribe for ideas. Plenty of discussion. Use of IT.
Planning and making	
Low level of patience. Wants to finish quickly.	Reward slow steady progress. Short tasks.
Pupil destroys or hides poor work or mistakes.	Highlight mistakes in the work of others. Show how many mistakes can be corrected. Remove fear of making errors. Teacher makes intentional mistake during a demonstration.
Pupil loses interest over long period of time.	Use short achievable tasks. Work on two tasks to provide variety and rotation. Include pupil interests.
Pupil is moody and stops unexpectedly.	Use friends in class to assist. Teacher patience. Discussion.

Table 17.3 cont.

Possible problems	Possible solutions
Testing, evaluating and modifying	
Processes regarded as irrelevant. Pupil wants to finish quickly.	Assist with some improvements to show value. Make testing and evaluating fun.
Pupil has fear of judging own work against higher achievers.	Discreet individual or peer group evaluation. Praise small amounts of success.
Pupil cannot associate these processes with the design and technology activity.	Explain reasons for testing, evaluating and modifying. Teacher undertakes processes to highlight the value.

SUGGESTIONS TO ASSIST PUPILS IN PRACTICAL CLASSROOM TASKS

This section provides some practical suggestions to help certain pupils with SEN in the classroom and is based upon the experiences and ideas of teachers. The list is not exhaustive and teachers should also endeavour to consider other methods of supporting pupils. Some of the suggestions relate to particular types of learning difficulty and to particular areas of design and technology, but many of them could benefit all pupils, for example the suggestion relating to the use of cutting guides. The suggestions are grouped as follows:

- communication;
- safety;
- organisation;
- tools, adaptations and alterations.

Communication

Using an audio tape or dictaphone

In many classes a tape recorder is used to record pupils' ideas, comments and evaluations. For many pupils this form of communication allows them to express their ideas and comments in a way that writing or drawing might not. A teacher can also use a recorder to store an explanation or the stages of a demonstration, so that some pupils can play back the information at their own pace and be reminded of ordering and detail.

Using a concept keyboard

A concept keyboard is a touch-sensitive electronic panel linked to a computer to provide pupils with an easy input facility. Overlay panels or sheets can be placed onto the concept keyboard to provide symbols or words which, when touched, trigger signals on the keyboard beneath, and thus to the computer. Plastic key-panels are also available which fit directly over the existing computer keyboard to simplify and enlarge the range and uses of keys. In design and technology activities a concept keyboard could be useful for some pupils as they undertake an evalutation exercise, for example.

Using grid papers

To assist pupils to draw particular shapes and forms on paper, a range of grid papers can be purchased. Some papers have lines at various angles to help pupils form 3-D drawings. Used in conjunction with a light-box, grid paper can be a very useful aid. Grid-printed card is now available for helping with card modelling and in trials this has proved successful with pupils of all abilities.

Using patterns, templates and guides

The provision of commercial and classroom-made templates and guides is essential for speedy and accurate work in design and technology. Professional designers, craftworkers, chefs and fashion designers, for example, all rely on such aids. For many pupils the assistance given by a pattern or similar aid can make the difference between success and failure.

Braille and large-print rulers

For pupils having visual difficulties, a range of Braille and large-print rulers, measures and other devices are available from specialist suppliers.

Using coloured overlays

Research has shown advantages in using colour-tinted clear plastic overlay sheets (OHP sheets) with pupils who experience difficulties with reading and with remembering key words. This method could be used to highlight particular words, stages and instructions in design and technology work. For example, some key words or parts of a diagram, relating to safety or hygiene, could be overlayed in red when using an overhead projector.

Making storyboards

Although time-consuming to produce, storyboards can provide an excellent reminder and visual tutor for many pupils undertaking procedures and tasks in design and technology for the first and second time. A stage-by-stage description of an operation can be produced using suitable artwork, symbols, notes or signs.

Safety

Low-temperature electric glue-guns

Glue-guns are an excellent tool for the classroom, but can be quite danger-ous due to the high temperatures of the glue and their tendency to suddenly spurt out quantities of hot glue. A number of suppliers now stock low-temperature glue-guns which are much safer and still provide the quick-joint facility.

A sewing-machine-foot needle guard

When using an electric sewing machine the curved front edge of the foot not only directs the fabric correctly towards the needle but can easily draw in fingers too. A small and low-cost simple-to-fit attachment is available, which is essentially designed to protect the needle during transportation, but can be used to reduce the hazards of machine use with some pupils.

Safety rulers and cutting guides

The use of modelling knives for design and technology activities and art work has increased in recent years. A traditional 'M' section finger-profile safety ruler is essential when a teacher allows craft knives to be used to cut straight lines.

One other version, and probable improvement on this design, is the home-made 'T-Shape' safety ruler. The inverted 'T' provides a good straight cutting edge and keeps the holding fingers behind a protective ledge. 'T' rulers can be made from old aluminium window-frame strips or from extruded 'T-shape' aluminium available in lengths from some DIY stores and bulders' suppliers.

A 'safe-cut' electric modelling saw

Reasonably priced electric saws are available which cut using the principle of a vibrating rather than rotating or sliding blade. The fine cutting blade vibrates and hums and will cut only rigid materials such as wood, plastic and card. If skin accidently touches the small blade, it will vibrate at the same frequency as the blade and so no damage will occur.

Under supervision, these saws can be used by a wide age and ability range and are excellent for model-making and for the cutting out of curved profiles and templates.

Using low-voltage and rechargeable power tools

Many manufacturers supply low-voltage power tools and transformers for use in schools and industry, thus cutting down the risks of electrical injuries and accidents. A range of rechargeable power tools is also now available; these can be of excellent benefit for working in design and technology by cutting down the number of trailing electric leads and in some cases the potential power available within the tool.

Rotary guillotines for cutting sheets of paper, card and plastic

Although all guillotines of the pull-down type are now fitted with blade-guards, they can be difficult to use as vision is reduced by the protective shielding. A number of roller, wheel or rotary-cutting guillotines are available which provide easy action with safety, in situations where the teacher allows use of a guillotine. Very often the risks in using rotary guillotines can be far less than in letting some pupils use scissors.

Organisation

Large labels on equipment, tools, racks and cupboards

Putting large and clear name labels on equipment, tools, racks and cupboards will greatly assist all pupils as they learn about equipment and its location. For pupils with severe visual impairment other strategies will need to be used, for example braille and/or raised silhouettes.

The positioning of pupils

Through experience most teachers know the best places to position pupils with particular needs when undertaking a demonstration or lesson. It is easy to forget that many of the children are seeing and following the operation from an upside-down view. It takes little planning to ensure that pupils with learning difficulties are positioned on the same side as the teacher if that will help, or that the teacher adapts the explanation or demonstration to cater for particular pupils.

Tools, adaptations and alterations

Using sticky pads and tape

A range of tapes, sticky pads and rubber feet are available in stores and from suppliers. Products such as these, which help pupils to hold things still, are of great benefit in improving their co-ordination and manual control. As adults we often forget that our own strength and co-ordination overcomes many of the problems that children experience when trying to hold something still.

A hand-drill stand

Using a hand-drill properly is quite a difficult operation for many pupils. When analysed it is apparent that there are five or six physical and mental actions involved in using a hand-drill. A stand or holding jig can be purchased or made which clamps the drill in a vertical position, thereby releasing the hands to assist the drilling and removing some of the complexity of use.

Adjusting work-table or chair heights

A range of school furniture is available which has height adjusters on the legs and feet. Attachments can also be purchased to fix to existing furniture so that height adjustments can be made. Adapting working heights is essential for many younger pupils and those requiring wheelchair access, for example.

Using a light-box

A light-box is a worktop or unit which has a clear or translucent top, under which is fitted a fluorescent light. The upward shining light will penetrate a few layers of paper and thus allow pupils to make successful tracings, copies and drawings.

A light-box can be made by replacing the lid of an old school desk with a clear plastic top, and mounting a neon striplight within the desk space. Aluminium foil can be used to line the inside of the desk to help reflect light upwards. *Warning: do not use a standard light bulb because of the heat generated. Have your unit checked by a qualified electrician and a safety officer.*

Modified handles and knobs

For pupils who have difficulties in gripping, holding and manipulating the smaller knobs and handles on some classroom equipment, one idea is to slit a tennis ball, or other suitable ball, and slip it over the problematic knob or handle. This provides a useful temporary adaptation where necessary.

In some cases, the reshaping or enlarging of a handle can prove to be a valuable modification to a tool or appliance. One way of doing this is to surround the existing handle with car-body filler and then for the pupil to grip the soft filler whilst wearing a rubber glove or a covering of clingfilm.

The filler will quickly set after the hand is removed. *Some fillers produce heat when hardening, so care is needed.*

A jig for sanding wheels and discs

Accurately making and shaping a model wheel or disc can be quite difficult. If a classroom is equipped with an electric rotating sander, then a simple jig can be made to fit onto the machine to help produce accurate discs.

The rough-cut disc or wheel is temporarily fixed by a nail or screw to rotate on a base-board, which is clamped in front of the sanding surface. Slight forward pressure into the sander is applied whilst the disc is rotated by hand on the nail or screw. Quick and accurate discs can be produced in this way, and this jig is especially useful when large quantities are required. *Use of such a jig by pupils is the responsibility of the teacher in charge.*

A measuring board and stick

There are many ways of helping pupils to measure and mark sizes onto materials. One such method is as follows. A stepped board is made with standard or required distances clearly marked or coded with colours. Different sections of material can be placed against the appropriate step and the length marked off at a common edge. Such a device can be incorporated into a sawing block or bench hook.

Similar assistance can be provided by using a stick or strip of card. A plain piece of wood-strip or card can be marked off with appropriate distances and/or symbols for a particular project. Pupils then only have to deal with a few marks on the stick, as opposed to the many on a standard ruler, and distances can be easily transferred onto the materials being used.

Such simple aids are also useful for all abilities, for example when pupils need to quickly check dimensions of products on a small production-line project.

A hint to help with nailing

Holding nails in position whilst hammering them in is often a difficult and painful experience no matter what one's age or ability. One useful tip is to first push the nail into the end of a strip of thin card or foam. The nailing is then started by sliding the card into position and hammering with the fingers well back. The card or foam can be pulled away as the nail is driven in. As well as saving the fingers, this tip is valuable when trying to hold and start a nail in a difficult corner or position.

An 'extra hand' when using scissors, cutters and snips

Mastering the use of a pair of scissors, snips or general-purpose cutters can be difficult for some pupils, especially for some of those with physical difficulties, when cutting complicated shapes from tougher materials. A hint is to carefully clamp one of the handles into a vice or fix it to the edge of an old worktable. This leaves just one handle to be operated and provides an easy-to-use fixed guillotine or shears.

Co-ordination and accuracy can improve quickly and downward pressure on the one free handle increases cutting efficiency. Please note that scissors handles do not last long if over-tightened regularly in a vice. Also *remember to remove the tool or cover the blades when not in use*.

REFERENCES

DES/WO (Department of Education and Science and the Welsh Office) (1990) *Technology in the National Curriculum*, London, HMSO.
DfE (Department for Education) (1990) *Getting in on the Act*, London, HMSO.

Chapter 18

Craft, design and technology and the gifted child

Ron Lewin

This chapter examines the general characteristics of gifted children, the perceptions and attitudes of society towards them, and possible ways to offer them help. It is proposed that in the area of design and technology there should be a similar approach to that adopted for talented musicians where the students go to normal schools during the week but receive special tuition and meet with similar children during the weekend.

ANECDOTE

'Knowing of your interest in technology perhaps you would look in one Saturday afternoon', said the lady from the National Association for Gifted Children. Dutifully I went along and there in the classroom were children from 6 to 11 years of age playing with board games and computers and enjoying each other's company. My eye caught a young boy intently working away in the corner on some electronic circuitry whose complexity did not seem to fit with his age. 'That looks interesting', I proffered. David looked up and instantly replied 'Do you know anything about electronics?' I mentioned that I had some small knowledge of the subject which gave rise to an unexpected response which surprised me. He proceeded to engage me in a high level discussion about the circuitry more appropriate to a member of a University Research Department. His manner was eager but matter of fact; he was not out to impress me but simply to ask if I would explain why the circuit he had developed when connected into his television at home received signals from Europe!

OUR FIRST EXPERIENCES

I next met David at an Explorer's Summer School when running a course on craft, design and technology. During the week the children between 9 and 11 years of age were introduced to materials, structures, energy, control and the design process. The course was staffed by CDT teachers who, without exception, were impressed by their experience. The young people showed an exceptional level of curiosity combined with practical ability; they demonstrated a knowledge of science and technology expected in pupils many years their senior; they had a sharp sense of humour and often saw ordinary situations in an unusual or novel way.

There was, however, another side to the story. As we learned more about these children we found that several did not find their home and school particularly happy environments. Their parents often perceived them as naughty while their school friends did not understand them; some were often lonely and had developed special ways to protect themselves against both mental and physical attack by others. By the end of the week the children were more self-confident and starting to deliver some of their latent potential by finding that there were other young people like themselves and there were adults who understood and shared their fascination with craft, design and technology.

At that time I was Project Director of the Fulmer Industry Education Project the aim of which was to develop ways to introduce science and technology into schools. As professional scientists and engineers, we recognised that these young people had that special mix of qualities needed to push the boundaries of technology forward into the next generation. This message was understood by the Industry Education Unit of the DTI which provided funds for us to raise an awareness in parents and teachers as to the value of these children in our society and, probably more importantly, for these children to realise their own self-worth.

As we pursued our investigations we first found that society in general had little interest in talented children. A typical response was 'If she is that bright she ought to be able to help herself'. There is a feeling that gifted children have an immediate advantage over others and can be successful without any help; to give them special attention is both élitist and an affront to our educational system. Even a short encounter with these children shows this to be far from the truth; they have special needs just as much as the physically or mentally handicapped. We saw that with the right encouragement children with these qualities could make a tremendous contribution to our society. Without any help they can become anti-social and present behavioural problems which could eventually cost society a great deal of time and money.

The following poem written by such an 11-year-old child is most evocative:

'The Wall'

They laughed at me.
They laughed at me and called me names,
They wouldn't let me join their games.
I couldn't understand.
I spent most playtimes on my own,

Everywhere I was alone,
I couldn't understand.

Teachers told me I was rude,
Bumptious, overbearing, shrewd,
Some of the things they said were crude.
I couldn't understand.
And so I built myself a wall,
Strong, and solid, ten foot tall,
With bricks you couldn't see at all,
So I could understand.

And then came Sir,
A jovial, beaming, kindly man,
Saw through my wall and took my hand,
And the bricks came tumbling down,
For he could understand.

There are several well-established myths concerning children with talent, which give rise to attitudes of indifference and even hostility. For example,

False	True
1 They will succeed by themselves.	They will fail to be motivated and will not succeed if neglected.
2 They need a greater quantity of work to keep them occupied.	They need a different quality of work to extend them.
3 They are self-centred 'clever dicks'.	They often have a poor self-image and may well be insecure.
4 They are keen on school work.	They often dislike traditional school work.
5 Most talented children are easily identified.	Many talented children are never spotted.
6 Talented children come from middle-class backgrounds.	Talented children are found in all social classes.
7 All teachers are sympathetic towards the needs of talented children.	Some teachers are indifferent, hostile or sarcastic.
8 Talented children are popular with other children.	They are often unpopular and not accepted: to be accepted they may deliberately under-achieve or be naughty.

Perceptive parents with talented children start to sense that their child is different from the average well before they go to primary school. Some exhibit a high level of curiosity, an advanced vocabulary, ask lots of questions, retain information and have good recall. Others have a good imagination, can grasp concepts and show links between them. Some like collecting things and have a wide range of interests. They can also be very frustrating to others, often appearing aimless, uninterested, self-centred and having an intense interest in certain subjects. Their sense of humour is often very sophisticated. These characteristics can be observed to a greater or lesser degree by children in a broad spectrum of talent but those with a particular flair in the subjects of craft, design and technology reflect the nature of the subject.

Before describing the qualities seen in the boys and girls that we have studied it is necessary to mention the essential components of craft, design and technology. I believe each element in that title is important and it would be a sad day if we were ever to lose the craft end of craft, design and technology at the expense of high technology.

Essentially, craft, design and technology is to do with production of man-made products which reflect functional and aesthetic values, using our knowledge of materials, structures, energy and control. Successful products need to be made purposefully and require people with a wide range of abilities and skills to work as a team.

CDT is the fusion of three qualities, namely those of the head, hand and heart. In other words, successful products contain a balance between intellectual, practical and aesthetic dimensions. Remember these three words when you next visit, say, Paddington Station and look at the great structure produced by Brunel. Imagine the intellect that went into the design of the structure, the manufacture of arches and pillars from cast iron and lastly the beauty encapsulated in the finished product.

In the group of boys and girls that we have studied the following characteristics predominate. They are particularly interested in man-made artefacts and enjoy designing and making things from different materials; they like to know how things work and are keen on constructional kits; they have a fascination for science, mathematics and computers; they are good at practical problem-solving and can use their hands and like making things well; they often think through diagrams and drawings and have a good spatial understanding. And as you might expect they are interested in inventors and inventing.

HOW CAN WE HELP THESE CHILDREN?

One possibility is to have a full-time special school for children with technological talent. Such a suggestion is poorly received in the United Kingdom. Quite apart from the élitist argument it must be recognised that technological achievement requires teamwork and the need for people of different abilities and backgrounds to work together. Educating a group of talented young technologists with little contact with the rest of the population would create major problems when the children came to maturity.

A second suggestion is to do nothing and hope that their natural talent will be recognised in due course. Our experience is that this will not necessarily happen, particularly if the child comes from a disadvantaged background.

The solution probably lies somewhere in between these two extremes and has been adopted in the subject area of music. Here, talented musicians go to normal school but at the weekend meet with people of similar ability; the weekend school includes individual tuition, group work and social activities. The children rehearse and perform public concerts, attend summer schools and masterclasses. Parents and professional musicians make a major input and music-making at the highest standard can become part of a normal way of life. Such activities can find their counterpart for children with a talent for craft, design and technology.

In Berkshire, we believe that as far as possible facilities for gifted children in any area of the curriculum should operate within the comprehensive system. Supplementary help should be given where intellectual and emotional considerations indicate that it is needed. In terms of CDT, primary teachers are made aware of children with exceptional ability during INSET courses and through the film and associated book *A Talent for Technology* (Lewin, 1986) which offers extension projects for use by teachers and parents. Further, children are encouraged to enter for our primary technology fairs when they have the opportunity to demonstrate their abilities in the areas of craft, design and technology. Other children attend summer schools such as those run by the Potential Trust. In these ways and others, such as the educational psychologist or the class teacher, we are put in touch with children who need help. One example is an Asian boy of 9 who has quite exceptional talent. His headteacher contacted me and I arranged to meet the boy. This child stood out from the rest in terms of his technical knowledge, enthusiasm and creativity. This Christmas he sent me plans for a helicopter; the spelling was terrible but both the three-dimensional and engineering drawings showed a remarkable vision and command of design, creativity and spatial awareness. Another example was a young girl who designed a way of keeping lollies on their sticks by drilling holes in the wooden handles thus allowing the ice crystals to lock the lolly in place. Another was a young lady who suggested designing pencils so that there was no lead in the last 2 inches, thus saving money for the company.

At the secondary level where such a talent might manifest itself in the CDT class we have a Saturday morning Engineering Club linked to a local engineering industry training group. As a result of contacts with the schools, teachers are invited to send selected candidates to the Club. As with the musical counterpart, the sessions include theory and practice; the project work is carried out in teams and the young people enter for local and national competitions. Visits are arranged to museums, laboratories and companies; speakers come from education and industry. Time is given for the students to meet each other and share common interests.

Unlike talented musicians, we have not asked them to show a level of competence before joining the club but rely on the judgment of the teachers and the young person's own enthusiasm. We have developed some tests which are a very rough indication of ability in craft, design and technology but the whole subject is very complex due to the breadth of qualities demanded.

Our interest is not to test talent but to liberate it for the benefit of the child and eventually society. As we work with children in our schools we see ample signs of this country's future creative resource, essential to develop the products needed to take us into the next century.

The question is whether the UK should adopt a more structured approach to encouraging these young people to develop their talents.

REFERENCES

Lewin, R.H. (1985) *Primary Craft, Design and Technology – Let's make it work*, Berkshire LEA.
Lewin, R.H. (1986) *A Talent for Technology*, Berkshire LEA.

Part IV

Current issues in technology education

Chapter 19

Vocational education, general education and the place of technology

Frank Banks

The final part of the reader is concerned with broad issues and Frank Banks begins this with an analysis of the wider purposes of technology education for all.

INTRODUCTION

The development of technology education in recent years has been extremely rapid. All pupils now study technology to the age of 16, yet some subjects with a much longer curriculum history, such as science, have only recently achieved this status. In this chapter the reasons for studying technology will be examined in the light of the political thrust behind its encouragement, the educational ideology which has nurtured its growth and, briefly, the curriculum history which has provided its roots. By clarifying the general aims of why we require all children to study technology, we can have increased confidence that the learning experiences we provide are relevant, interesting and worthwhile.

THE GREAT DEBATE

Prime Minister James Callaghan's speech at Ruskin College Oxford in October 1976 voiced a number of general concerns about the purpose and direction of the British education system three decades after the introduction of the 1944 Education Act which brought secondary education to all. It was the catalyst for a 'Great Debate' in education that eventually paved the way to many of the 1988 reforms which, amongst other things, brought in the national curriculum. Callaghan was warned not to make his speech as such topics were not the province of politicians. This was the prevailing view at the time; the professionals knew best. Sir David Eccles, a Minister for Education in the 1960s made reference to the 'secret garden of the curriculum' and the head of William Tyndale school who had recently been in dispute over teaching methods in his primary school is reported to have said, 'Don't talk to me about parents, teachers are the pros here!' (reported by

Marland 1992). In the 1990s such attitudes seem extraordinary as much legislation has encouraged parents, governors and industrialists to voice an opinion on the goals of education.

Before 1988 the Head, Governors and LEA, but in practice very often an individual classroom teacher, was responsible for the content of the curriculum. LEAs could, and sometimes did, intervene in curriculum issues by virtue of having control of finance but, in general, a school staff were very much their own people. It is remarkable, therefore, that the day-to-day lives of different schools were so similar. This can to some degree be explained by external examinations and their backwash effects dominating much of what happened in post-primary education. Likewise the selection examination at 11+, or the collective memory of its demands, helped to determine the primary curriculum. But there is a stronger driving force than the demands of external assessment. Schools were, and because of the structure of the national curriculum still are, dominated by the idea of subjects as intellectual disciplines. The prevailing culture in many schools is that of providing a 'general education' within a 'liberal humanist' tradition.

WHAT IS LIBERAL EDUCATION?

Anyone who has been through an educational experience has explicitly or tacitly adopted an educational ideology. Teachers, like anyone else, assume a point of view on the learner, the subject matter being taught, the society for which pupils are being prepared and the way schools and other educational institutions should be run and who has a right to exert an influence on them. The ideology known as 'liberal humanism' may be described as the cultivation of the intellect, and the purpose of such an education is attaining intellectual excellence. It takes a view of knowledge as being active and interconnected, more than simple recall of facts. To be educated in this tradition is to develop certain fundamental concepts and also to know how to find out and research. The intellectual challenge which this requires of an individual is formidable and justification in itself for its value. It initiates an individual into the culture of those who share that subject-culture and justification by criteria set outside the subject itself is considered irrelevant. The reverence for the activity of the mind was responsible for the establishment of a hierarchy of subjects in schools which tended to place cerebral subjects such as Latin, physics, mathematics and history above practical subjects such as craft, home economics and art. Such a view of the worth of academic excellence over the practical was adopted by almost all grammar and independent schools and tacitly underlies the concern over maintaining standards by such groups as the Centre for Policy Studies.

A strong 'liberal-humanist' ideology can lead schools (and other places of learning such as universities) to consider themselves places apart, divorced from 'the world of work' or any notion of immediate usefulness, being in control of their own destiny as they alone perceive themselves as being best equipped to judge what is of worth. Someone educated in this tradition would be assumed to have a general knowledge applicable to a range of contexts. Technology is, therefore, more acceptable to proponents of the liberal tradition than is craft as they would value technology as an intellectual process applicable in everyday life and across contexts. However, some researchers (see Hennessy and McCormick, this volume p. 94) would question this.

WHAT IS INSTRUMENTALISM?

Just as there are many shades of opinion as to what might be called liberal education, so there is a spectrum in what is labelled 'instrumentalism' which is closely linked to vocational and pre-vocational education. Merson summarises some general features of instrumentalism as follows:

1 A belief that social and economic ends can be achieved through educational means, particularly when these ends are not utopian nor involve radical change. (Education serves society.)
2 An emphasis on the relevance and utility aspects of knowledge.
3 The dominant model of learning underlying educational arrangements is a simple mechanistic input–output model. (Particular skills for particular identified purposes.)
4 An implicit commitment to simple utilitarianism in economic terms, i.e. the justification of educational and social action lies in its ability to improve economic and industrial growth and this is realised through increased production and consumption, and thus brings about increased happiness.
5 A correlative of the above is that educational action and content are seen mainly as a means to ends outside itself. (No learning for learning's sake.)

(Merson 1980: 17)

One end of the instrumentalism spectrum is concerned with training for a specific job. At the other end is a pre-vocational education to 'equip young people with the knowledge, skills, competencies, qualifications and attitudes which they will need at work in a rapidly changing highly technological society' (Jones 1989: 351); on the face of it a 'training of the mind' which does not look so different from liberal humanism described above. But there are, in fact, two important differences. The first difference is in the educational purpose as seen by either the teacher or learner and the second is in the extent to which those other than teachers are able to judge what is of value.

Some who share this ideology see the purpose of technology as general preparation for employment. For them the content of technology is particularly important as it should reflect at least in broad terms the needs of the 'world of work'. Jephcote and Hendley (see p. 209 in this volume) catalogue the ways design and technology has been seen as a vehicle for economic and industrial understanding (EIU) by many employer organisations.

CONSEQUENCES OF THE 'GREAT DEBATE'

Pring (1992) has classified the criticisms articulated in the post-Ruskin debate into four areas; low attainment standards compared with both those of former years and with our nation's major competitors, a lack of relevance in the curriculum towards our country's economic needs, a lack of personal relevance for pupils resulting in low motivation and poor staying-on rates and, lastly, a failure to address the social concerns of pupils and the society in which they live.

All four of these concerns were addressed by the Technical and Vocational Education Initiative (TVEI) which was first introduced in 1983. It was aimed at the 14–18-year-olds who, it was felt, largely failed to jump the intellectual hurdles of GCE valued by the liberal tradition because its relevance was, for them, too vague and ill-defined. A focus on preparation for work and adult life, it was argued, would re-motivate them.

> For much of our previous history those young adults would in the main have been engaged in the working life of the community at that age. It is not, therefore, surprising to find that the interests of many of them are in things which are relevant, which bring a sense of achievement, which can be seen to relate to the world outside school.
>
> (Woolhouse 1984: 135)

A plea to re-orient the direction of the curriculum was made by Jones, (1989). It is unambiguous in its declaration of purpose for an instrumentalist curriculum, that it will benefit the economic well-being of the country and satisfy those who fear that Britain is becoming a low-skill, low-wage economy:

> As a nation we are desperately short of people with professional, managerial and technical skills, and over-supplied with unskilled workers. We need to raise the levels of achievement of all our students if they are to find work, and if we are to survive economically.
>
> (Jones 1989)

TVEI was not a curriculum as such, but a means of funding projects which satisfied certain criteria aimed at challenging the assumptions implicit in the liberal tradition. It encouraged certain subject areas, favoured particular teaching and learning strategies, and was aimed at all young people. It aimed to do this for the 16–19 age range by:

1 relating what is learnt in schools and colleges to the world of work;

2 improving skills and qualifications for all, in particular in science, technology, information technology and modern languages;
3 providing young people with direct experience of the world of work
through real work experience;
4 enabling young people to be effective, enterprising and capable at work
through active and practical learning methods;
5 providing counselling, guidance, individual action plans, records of
achievement and opportunities to progress to higher levels of
achievement.

(TVEI 1990: 3)

As TVEI developed, its general vocational thrust was not lost but the
national curriculum picked up the issue of a broad and balanced education in
science and technology. The City and Guilds of London Institute arranged
accreditation of many facets of a pre-vocational curriculum with the
Certificate in Pre-vocational Education (CPVE) which developed into the
Diploma in Vocational Education (DVE). TVEI's directors became bolder
in suggesting industry and commerce should be involved in helping to shape
what was done in school and in ensuring 'that the whole curriculum is
related to the world of work' (Jones 1989).

WHY SHOULD WE TEACH TECHNOLOGY AND WHY
SHOULD EVERYONE LEARN IT?

The TVEI was introduced in 1983, the first CTC was set up in 1988, the
national curriculum in technology was introduced in 1990 and the first
designated technology schools in 1991. An inspection of the chronology of
these developments suggests that the ideology which has driven this move
towards a practical technology curriculum for all, and fuelled the political
will to make it happen, is 'instrumentalism'. But is this ideology shared by
classroom teachers and by those responsible for the day-to-day curriculum
organisation in schools? Can technology be considered a 'subject' in the
sense of an intellectual discipline which, in a liberal sense, has a content and a
methodology of intrinsic value? To a large extent this depends on what is
encompassed by the definition of 'technology education'. There are four
broad reasons for all children to study technology.

First, McCormick (1990: 5) has indeed made a case for technology's
'intrinsic worth'. He argues that two important aspects of learning which
challenge the intellect flow naturally from school technology; the solving of
real problems and the reflective thinking such problem-solving promotes,
and the synthesis of thought consequent on that process because real life
does not respect traditional subject boundaries.

Another reason for a technology curriculum for all is to ensure all people
are aware of an important part of our culture. Lawton, in an analysis of

cultural variables, noted 'Specialisation is inevitable, but schools have a function not simply to select for specialisation, but also to enable the young to have a general technological understanding despite the need for specialisation' (Lawton 1983: 16). This is a plea for the inclusion in the curriculum of an aspect of life which has a direct impact on us all, not just technical experts, and for which we as citizens should be empowered to express an informed opinion. They need to be 'technologically aware'.

The technology national curriculum for England and Wales introduced in 1990, and to a greater extent the curriculum for Northern Ireland and the 1992 proposed revision, has stressed technological capability. The tradition of liberal-humanism in schools which for so long denigrated the practical was much criticised during Callaghan's 'Great Debate'. A need to educate people who could 'do' as well as 'know', who were 'technologically capable', was emphasised particularly by the 'Education for Capability' movement (see RSA 1984). This third reason for teaching technology is most clearly identified with instrumentalism but, as explained earlier, learning about the 'technological process' could also be seen as learning a 'transferable skill' and not specifically linked to vocational preparation.

Some teachers, initially hostile to their perceived aims of TVEI were won over to the initiative by its pupil-centred objectives such as individual target-setting and supported self-study. Vocational education that teachers originally treated with suspicion as simply producing 'factory fodder' was embraced as a more relevant and worthwhile curriculum for those pupils who had not found the values of an academic curriculum meaningful. The rhetoric of a technology curriculum for economic growth was accepted by pupils and parents as a clearer more relevant preparation for working life and many teachers share this rationale. The final reason for everyone learning technology, therefore, is that it is important in wealth creation.

WHAT SORT OF AN EDUCATED WORKFORCE DOES INDUSTRY WANT?

Technology education taken to encompass technological awareness and capability in its widest sense, taught by a problem-solving approach, sometimes seems to fit a number of different ideologies; or perhaps it fits none neatly.

There is a current confusion due to conflicting goals. On the one hand there is a national curriculum promoting separate subjects, there is a 'back to basics' rhetoric and a desire for maintenance of standards by end-of-course written papers which will exclude many. On the other hand there is a desire for a vocationally oriented curriculum promoting real-life problems, continual assessment by project work and records of achievement showing what all pupils can do. The confusion in 1992 about what school technology in England and Wales should be reflected the confusion in the direction of education policy. The emphasis is now on 'designing and making' and the practical realisation of 'high quality products' combined with work that is 'rigorous and intellectually demanding' (DFE/WO 1992: vi). This intellectual emphasis will help to justify its place within a national curriculum for all, but the key stage 4 provision is flexible to allow technology to be included in a 'vocational course' for some (DFE/WO 1992: 9). The new problem is a reconciliation of a technology education for all with a specialist technology curriculum for some.

So what sort of an educated workforce do commerce and industry want? International comparisons are always difficult as the conditions which give rise to differences are often complicated. Germany (usually the former Federal Republic (FRG)) is often held up as an example of best practice in vocational education and the bringing together of general education and technical education. The legal framework which encourages apprentice training and the conditions, both social and economic, which allow so many students to take advantage of the arrangements are too complex to explore fully here. Germany does, however, seem to have satisfied the major criticisms of pre-vocational courses in this country. In Britain such courses are criticised as being a second-class education further disadvantaging certain social groups and also unsuitable for a society suffering structural unemployment (see Atkins 1989: 137). In Germany unemployment is less severe and the economy stronger. It provides 20 per cent of the world's high 'value added' goods with less than 1 per cent of the world's population and 2 per cent of its land area (Banks and Jones 1991). Vocational training there is not perceived as being an inferior education. A British HMI evaluation of the German system found;

> There appear to be three reasons why well-qualified young Germans with the *Abitur* [high school leaving certificate] enter apprentice training. Firstly, some regard an apprenticeship as a valuable experience in its own right leading to a qualification which will always stand them in good stead. Secondly, the acquisition of a qualification in a classified occupation is seen as a protection against unemployment. Thirdly, there appears to be greater parity of esteem in the FRG between academic and vocational qualifications than is the case in the United Kingdom.
>
> (HMI/DES 1991: 7)

In Germany a greater time is devoted to general education within post-16 vocational courses than in the UK. Subjects such as German, politics and law are taught by the same teachers who have the skills and content knowledge to teach about the technical parts of the course. 'It was doubted whether general education would be valued and esteemed by students to the same extent if taught by staff who lacked specific vocational expertise and appeared culturally different by virtue of a more exclusively academic background' (ibid.: 28).

The dual system operated in Germany ensures a close link between the courses provided by colleges and the in-house work experiences of the students. The German communications firm SEL has moved to a vocational training course which is very similar to the content and methods found in technology courses in the UK. The practice in many UK schools, it seems, is ahead of that in German schools and more closely in tune with 'what employers want'.

Table 19.1 SEL training methods

Old	New
'Show and copy'	Projects
Fabrication of pre-prepared items	Work out what is needed to construct items
Superficial discussion	Simulation of construction including estimates of time and other costs
Teaching Styles	
Didactic	Learner centred
Respond to a brief	Respond to an identified need
Solitary learning	Cooperative Learning
Copy isolated tasks	Total process
Facts based	Processes important
Learning outcomes	
Facts, specialised knowledge	Facts, methods, social skills, evaluative skills and an ability to co-operate

Japan is another successful economy with quite a different vocational tradition. Unlike Germany, general education is much more popular than vocational education and has a strong theoretical bias. Technology is not taught in schools which lean heavily towards mathematics and science and away from creative subjects. Even in university engineering courses practical work is limited (Dore and Sako 1989).

The evidence that a strong economy is the product of a technology curriculum with a clear vocational bias, therefore, is weak. Japan's education system does not value the practical curriculum and Germany is attempting to train people with more transferable problem-solving skills.

ACADEMIC AND VOCATIONAL QUALIFICATIONS: PARITY OF ESTEEM

Friedrich Ebert, founder of the German Social Democratic Party once said: 'General education is the vocational education of the upper class; vocational education is the general education of the working class' (in Finegold *et al.* 1990: 3). University entrance has a long tradition of selection by examination and the GCE A level is a continuation of this. Practical skills have been regarded with suspicion by many admissions tutors, and woodwork and metalwork, for example, were never recognised as an acceptable entry qualification. This has long been a source of irritation for teachers. An HMI report in 1982 noted that engineering departments were 'on the one hand paying lip service to the need for design capability in students and on the other hand giving greater weight to the possession of an A level in pure science' (DES 1982).

Vocational qualifications such as those awarded by the Business and Technical Education Council (BTEC) have been an increasingly important source of recruitment to technology in higher education: 'In 1989, 12.5 per cent of all acceptances in engineering and technology in universities, and 33.0 per cent in polytechnics, were on the basis of vocational qualifications' (Smithers and Robinson 1992: 17).

A levels have been very resistant to change as they have been considered the 'gold standard' of academic excellence over the years, yet many consider them narrow and over-specialised. Vocational qualifications have generally been 'regarded as too job-specific, low level and ill-coordinated' (Finegold et al. 1990: 4). As a consequence there has been poor parity of esteem between the two. There have been many schemes suggested to help bridge the divide; a British Baccalaureat, a Technological Baccalaureat and common core skills between A and A/S level. Perhaps an Advanced Diploma to which A level, BTEC qualifications, General National Vocational Qualifications (GNVQs) and the occupationally specific National Vocational Qualifications (NVQs) could all contribute will gain acceptance during the 1990s rather than the more radical change needed by adopting a 'Baccalaureat' system.

TECHNOLOGY IN THE 1990s

As the previous discussion has shown, technology education has suffered from a lack of clarity of purpose which must be rectified if teachers are to know what they are trying to achieve and pupils are to be motivated to learn. Technology will be a major contributory subject to the changes in general and vocational education which will characterise the middle 1990s. The differing focuses between a 'liberal' or 'instrumental' education should not be allowed to prevent pupils passing successfully from the national curriculum to higher education and employment. It is, therefore, important that teachers have a clear view as to why their pupils are involved in the study of the subject, and how the subject makes pupils capable of contributing to modern society and aware of its impact on that society. To quote Callaghan:

> The goals of our education, from nursery school through to adult education are clear enough. They are to equip children to the best of their

ability for a lively, constructive place in society and also to fit them to do a job of work. Not one or the other, but both.

(Callaghan 1976: 332)

REFERENCES

Atkins, M.J. (1989) 'The pre-vocational curriculum: a review of the issues involved', in P. Murphy and B. Moon (eds) *Developments in Learning and Assessment*, London, Hodder & Stoughton.

Banks, F. and Jones, H. (1991) *A Comparative Study of Apprentice Training in South Wales and Germany*, Swansea, University College of Swansea.

Callaghan, J. (1976) 'Towards a national debate', reprinted in *Education*, 22 October: 332–3.

DES (1982) *Technology in Schools*, London, HMSO.

DFE/WO (1992) *Technology for Ages 5 to 16 (1992): Proposals of the Secretary of State for Education and Secretary of State for Wales*, London, HMSO.

Dore, R.P. and Sako, M. (1989) *How the Japanese Learn to Work*, London, Routledge.

Finegold, D., Keep, E., Milibrand, D., Raffe, D., Spours, K. and Young, M. (1990) *A British 'Baccalaureat'*, London, Institute for Public Policy Research.

HMI/DES (1991) *Aspects of Vocational Education and Training in the FRG*, London, HMSO.

Jones, A. (1989) 'The real aims of TVEI', *Education*, 14 April: 351–2.

Lawton, D. (1983) 'Culture and the curriculum', Unit 3 of E204 *Purpose and Planning in the Curriculum*, Milton Keynes, Open University Press.

Marland, M. (1992) Interviewed on the *Analysis* programme 'Hard words in the classroom', BBC Radio 4,10 December.

McCormick, R. (1990) Paper given at the NATO Advanced Research Workshop: Integrating Advanced Technology into Technology Education, 8–12 October, Eindhoven, The Netherlands.

Merson, M. (1980) E203 *Curriculum Design and Development*, supplementary item *Curriculum Issues and the Technicians' Education Council*, Milton Keynes, Open University Press.

Pring, R. (1992) 'Liberal education and vocational preparation', in M. Williams, R. Daugherty and F. Banks (eds) *Continuing the Education Debate*, London, Cassell.

RSA (Royal Society for Arts) (1984) 'Manifesto of education for capability', *RSA Newsletter*, Spring.

Smithers, A. and Robinson, P. (1992) *Technology at A Level: Getting it Right*, London, The Engineering Council.

TVEI (1990) *Guidance for Preparing TVEI Extension Proposals for the 16–18 Phase*, London, Training Agency.

Woolhouse, J. (1984) 'The Technical and Vocational Education Initiative' in D. Layton (ed.) *The Alternative Road*, Leeds, University of Leeds.

Chapter 20

How design and technology can contribute to the development of pupils' economic and industrial understanding

Martin Jephcote and David Hendley

This chapter specifically asks how design and technology can contribute to the development of pupils' economic understanding. Most interpretations of economic understanding have placed it within a business and industry context. The authors acknowledge this but argue that a narrow interpretation, which ignores other contexts, will not provide opportunities for economic understanding to develop on a wider front and will essentially deny pupils access to a broader and more critical understanding. They suggest that the relationship between economic understanding and design and technology which promotes this critical understanding can be achieved by giving a central place to values. Economic 'solutions' and technological 'solutions' both must be subjected to critical review and this process of review will be influenced by the values, attitudes and beliefs held by individuals and groups.

BACKGROUND TO ECONOMIC UNDERSTANDING

Recent years have witnessed an emerging number of terms and definitions, among them:

- *economic literacy* which had the aim of giving pupils a tool kit of economic terms and skills of analysis which they could apply to economic problems;
- *economic understanding* which was seen as preparation for the roles of producer, consumer or citizen;
- *economic awareness*, seen as a way of drawing from a range of subject disciplines in order to analyse the economic system, and help solve economic problems;
- and more recently *economic and industrial understanding* (EIU) as a cross-curricular theme within the national curriculum, emphasising the importance of business, industry and enterprise as areas which can contribute to education.

These developments have been a response to an evolving partnership between education, industry, central government and LEAs, and have depended on the support of a vast number of organisations and agencies such as Economic Awareness and Teacher Training (EcATT), Schools Council Industry Project (SCIP), Science and Technology Regional Organisations (SATRO), Understanding British Industry (UBI), Careers Research Advisory Council (CRAC) and others including the Economics Association, Department of Trade and Industry, Department of Employment and the Department of Education and Science (DES). These developments have been a feature of the education debate over the last fifteen years: spurred on by key statements made by Callaghan and Joseph; reflected in DES and HMI statements; picked up as a key strand of the Technical and Vocational Education Initiative (TVEI); and now having separate non-statutory guidance for EIU in England and Wales. Given the breadth of this partnership it is not surprising that there are areas of conflict, for example, in the definition of economic understanding and how best to develop it as a curriculum entitlement for pupils.

There is, at a school level, a growing amount of work taking place with the aim of developing and extending some form of economic understanding in pupils. That task has, hitherto, been undertaken in a number of ways including work experience programmes, industrial links, enterprise activities and through modules in personal and social education. However, given the structure of the national curriculum and the emphasis on a subject-based curriculum, attention is now being given to how core and foundation subjects can contribute to the development and extension of pupils' economic understanding. This chapter considers that question in relation to design and technology – a subject which now has the opportunity to contribute to the learning of every pupil and, therefore, to their economic understanding.

WHAT IS ECONOMIC UNDERSTANDING?

It is to be made clear from the outset that although the acronym 'EIU' is widely adopted, there is certainly not a shared common understanding of this or any other phrase. A recent HMI report on *Economic and Industrial Understanding 5–16* (1992) makes the point that there is no single and widely accepted definition. They note that EIU is to do with preparing pupils to make economic decisions but this leaves much room for interpretation.

At its narrowest EIU is seen as providing pupils with the necessary skills and competences as a preparation for work; providing an understanding of the workings of business and the economy. A broader view sets EIU in the context of contributing to a general education, helping prepare pupils for adult life. There is now common agreement that EIU is a cross-curricular theme and not a separate subject and, moreover, that it should be part of an entitlement curriculum for all pupils.

Davies (1991) analysed five HMI reports which looked into aspects of economic awareness and economic understanding (including work experience and mini-enterprise). He concludes:

'Reviewing personal experience of the economy'; 'developing a critical ability in relation to evidence' and 'an awareness of personal and social values' are all mentioned in these reports. The notion that Economic Awareness is about learning economics, and that learning economics means learning particular economic ideas is, however, more prominent.

A later HMI discussion document (HMI 1990) indicates little change. Economic understanding, it states, is:

concerned with those concepts which underpin all human endeavour related to the creation and distribution of wealth. It is also concerned with an understanding of the institutional framework and those social structures which currently exist to further wealth generation and order its distribution.

The document recognises that a one-sided view should not be given and notes the importance of values, but generally it leaves the impression that pupils have to be aware that they live in a world where the die is cast, that they live in a business and economic society and need to learn about business. To gain an economic understanding they must grasp economic principles and concepts.

Curriculum Guidance 4 (NCC 1990a) makes the broad statement: 'Education for economic and industrial understanding involves controversial issues, such as the impact of economic activity on the environment.' This document further states that 'schools should ensure . . . where relevant . . . a balanced presentation of opposing views', but it does little to present such a view in its notes and examples. These emphasise another statement made in the introduction: 'Pupils need education for EIU to help them contribute to an industrialised, highly technological society. . . . To meet this challenge pupils need to understand enterprise and wealth creation and develop entrepreneurial skills.'

It was noted in an NUT discussion paper (NUT 1990) that the view put forward in *Curriculum Guidance 4* promotes economic understanding as a body of knowledge with concepts and attitudes to understand rather than challenge. The NUT quotes the suggestion made by NCC that in Key Stage 3 schools should teach pupils that 'Companies compete in business through innovation, price and advertising, aiming to increase their share of the market and sell more goods and services.' The NUT paper suggests that an alternative approach would be to 'encourage pupils to question and challenge the whole notion of competition in business and elsewhere'. The NUT goes on to state:

In terms of classroom practice this means that a 'knowledge' teacher would be in charge of 'the truth' and would help his/her pupils arrive there, while the 'critical awareness' teacher would confront the pupils with a range of views to be analysed and challenged.

Generally, for activities in design and technology, the focus and interpretation of EIU is on personal financial management, work and industry. Stress is placed on the importance of money values and profit. These interpretations do not constitute a cross-curricular theme, they are more like a simplified, uncritical and straightforward approach to business studies and they ignore any real consideration of how values, attitudes and beliefs lie at the heart of economic understanding.

We find the definition provided by the MSC (1987) a helpful one:

Individuals, industrial, commercial and other groups in a country, as well as national and international communities make decisions about the use of resources. Together their decisions create the institutions, habits, values and constraints which in turn influence individual and group behaviour and decisions which comprise the economic system. To understand how the economic system works – to be economically aware – means to be able to assess the implications of individual and group decisions and to evaluate them.

This description gives us a starting point from which to develop our own interpretation of economic understanding.

The society in which we live is created by the people who make up that society. Acting individually or in groups people make decisions about the use of the world's resources which affect the quality of life for members of that society. The process of design and technology – an integrated process of identifying needs, designing, making and evaluating – is one of developing and using skills, abilities and resources (including physical and mental effort) which brings about changes in peoples' lives and their environment. It is in part a decision-making process which involves comparing the available alternatives and making choices based on an assessment of their consequences.

Making such decisions as individuals, and to begin to appreciate the basis on which these decisions are taken – including knowledge, values, attitudes and beliefs – is to begin to develop economic understanding. To recognise how other individuals or groups such as communities, business and commercial organisations make decisions about the use of resources, is to further develop economic understanding.

Through design and technology pupils should confront three questions:

1 What type of society is it they want to live in now and in the future?
2 Which aspects of our society do they currently value and which do they seek to change?
3 How should society's resources be organised and distributed?

Specifically, we should consider how design and technology can help in causing pupils to reflect on such questions. Our own view of what developing economic understanding is about does not itself provide or invite pupils to provide single or simplistic answers to these questions. The economic society in which we live is complex and answers to these questions are bound to be controversial. Descriptions of economic understanding which reduce it to a mere statement of skills, competences or areas of experience are unlikely to give rise to a consideration of questions of this order.

THE IMPORTANCE OF A BROAD RANGE OF CONTEXTS

An assumption made by many is that within design and technology it is the business and industry context through which economic understanding will be developed. Contact with teachers in schools indicates this to be the case and, furthermore, some assume that economic understanding is an automatic by-product of doing any work in this context. The NCC *Non-Statutory Guidance for Design and Technology* (NCC 1990b) offers advice by stating:

> Pupils need experience of the technological needs and opportunities arising in business and industry, and of the judgements which must be made. Considerations such as:
>
> client and consumer satisfaction;
> the importance of quality;
> added value;
> business structure;
> production quantities;
> market size;
> environmental impact;
> finance and deadlines;
> health and safety;
>
> can arise naturally when technological activity is related to business and industrial contexts. Work-related activities can foster and demonstrate the value of personal qualities such as enterprise, self-discipline, persistence, social responsibility and ability to work with others, take initiatives, decisions and risks.

What we see is an emphasis on the business and industry context although there is an indication of the importance of the personal qualities which can come about, presumably because of the process-based nature of design and technology. *Curriculum Guidance 4* (NCC 1990a) is similar in its emphasis referring to pupils learning about – through design and technology – 'efficiency', 'productivity', 'investment', 'risk', 'marketing', 'supply and demand'. HMI in their discussion paper (1990) express the view that a narrow focus on marketing and costs provide 'only a partial coverage of the desirable educational agenda' and call for a balanced economics education which considers broader issues including those on a local, national and international level. However, HMI also express their concern that: 'Given the focus of technology and the amount of time likely to be allocated to it, the business and economic dimension is unlikely to expand beyond a basic interpretation of these requirements in most schools.'

We are less pessimistic, believing that the primary need is to make technology teachers aware of the broad range of contexts which can be used for developing economic understanding. At the same time teachers need to be persuaded to organise their classroom activities so that pupils' economic understanding can be explored and extended.

The emphasis on business and industry narrows the view of economic understanding and tends to limit the range of contexts and experiences through which it can be explored in technology. The economic system is complex and is made up of many participants. Economic understanding must embrace all aspects of economic activity, so just as people go to work or engage in business, it is necessary to include how people go about their daily lives and the paid or unpaid contribution which they make. In adopting a broader approach to economic understanding then, so too can a broader range of contexts and experiences be included. Indeed, just as design and technological contexts include the home, school, recreation, community, business and industry then economic understanding can be developed through them.

Without a broadening of the contexts to explore and develop economic understanding there is the possibility that a business view of the world is projected. Standards become business standards, and language affected – even taken for granted. Words such as 'profit', 'efficiency' and 'productivity' are adopted as part of everyday speech and are used in a variety of situations as if they had a single meaning. But we have to be clear. Knowing about businesses, how they operate, the constraints under which they work, and their contribution as producers and employers is important. The ability to question and critically appraise their activities is equally important: pupils need the opportunity to reflect on their experiences of business and economic activity.

The home as a context can provide the focus for questions like 'Is there adequate housing for everyone? Why is there homelessness? What can be done about it? How can we improve the environment in which we and others live?' The community can be used as a way of considering alternative means of provision of care and services, or be concerned with decision-making about the use of land for building or other purposes. Through recreation pupils could look into the provision of play areas, museums and other facilities, and school, too, can become a context for economic understanding without being limited to business-type activities.

Design and technology must also be seen in a global context. One concern with which technology has to deal, is the increasing interdependence of global societies, and their use of the world's resources. A second concern is that of the global environmental crisis caused by environmental degradation (witness, for example, acid rain, Chernobyl, the destruction of rainforests and depletion of the world's natural resources). These are areas which economic understanding has a great deal to offer technology.

When the concerns of global interdependence and environment are included as a context, technological responses to societies' problems have to be considered in a framework of economic understanding. If economic understanding is interpreted a narrow sense then it will ignore the key technological issues facing world society now and in the future.

If pupils are to consider what type of society they want to live in, the reality of global interdependence means this should include a world perspective; if they are to consider how the world's natural resources are to be organised and distributed, they must take into account what those resources are, where they are located and the consequences of using them. The sorts of questions which we should ask pupils to consider are: 'How should the world's resources be used?'; 'What are the consequences of these decisions on the people of the world and the environment?'; 'How can technology, based on economic understanding, inform our solutions to these problems?'

HOW SHOULD PUPILS RESPOND

Given the questions posed and based on what we see economic understanding to be, we would not expect there to be a predetermined set of outcomes or standard responses. How pupils respond to any task or problem – what they say, how they act, the solutions they produce – must be taken individually. Pupils must make clear the reasons for their actions and justify them. Opportunities should be provided for individuals to be questioned and challenged.

Consider, for example, the following questions:

> Is it 'better' to burn cheap fuels (based on hydrocarbons?) or renewable fuels? Is it better to have whiter than white (chlorine bleached) nappies or duller ones? Is it better to have motorways or the acres of open country they use up?
>
> (APU 1991)

The teacher is responsible for creating classroom activities which allow pupils to explore their own ideas, to compare their ideas with other pupils or ideas from other sources, and to reconcile the differences. Pupils will initially draw from their own experiences and are likely to base solutions on their own preconceptions, their notions of what is better and for whom. They need, therefore, to explore and develop their own values, attitudes and beliefs about the quality of society and need to be aware of the needs of others. This is a process of review and reflection which needs to be incorporated into the design and technology process.

One difficulty which faces teachers in the current arrangements for design and technology (based on the cycle of the four attainment targets in England and Wales) is that it has become a systematised process providing little opportunity for handling the values implicit in the economic dimension of technology. This has come about because of the apparent disembodiment of evaluation and, instead of being integral to the process, evaluation takes place after key decisions have been made and acted upon. The proposals stemming from the review of technology (DFE 1992) recommend just two attainment targets (designing and making) and offer some scope to correct this situation and emphasise the importance of evaluation during the process of designing and making. At first sight, the switch to judging the quality of a product made in design and technology by its fitness for its intended purpose, which includes asking such questions as 'Will it damage the environment?' gives grounds for optimism. We are, however, less optimistic regarding the programme of study section for business and industrial practices which includes EIU. The introduction to the report notes that no attempt has been made to cover the whole field, but it still chooses to focus on the need for pupils to consider the cost of materials and time and the concepts associated with market research, advertising and production. We would continue to encourage teachers to look for opportunities to develop pupils' economic understanding throughout the design and make task and across all elements of the programmes of study.

REFERENCES

APU (Assessment of Performance Unit) (1991) *Assessment of Performance in Design and Technology*, London, SEAC.

Davies. P. (1991) 'Review', *Economic Awareness* 3 (2).

DFE (Department for Education) (1992) *Technology for Ages 5–16 (1992)*, London, HMSO.

HMI (Her Majesty's Inspectorate) (1990) *Statement on Business and Economic Education 5–16*, unpublished.

HMI (Her Majesty's Inspectorate) (1992) *Economic and Industrial Understanding 5–16*, London, Department for Education.

MSC (1987) *Economic Awareness across the Curriculum*, TRIST Document of National Importance 1, Sheffield, Manpower Services Commission.

NCC (1990a) *Educating for Economic and Industrial Understanding, Curriculum Guidance 4*, York, National Curriculum Council.

NCC (1990b) *Non-Statutory Guidance for Design and Technology*, York, National Curriculum Council.

NUT (National Union of Teachers) (1990) 'Report from National Conference', in *Economic Awareness* 3 (2).

Chapter 21

Gender and technology education

Anne Riggs

The main aim of this chapter is to encourage technology teachers to reflect on their classroom practice. Such reflection challenges teachers to examine their beliefs about gender and about technology for these have major consequences for interactions in the workshop or classroom.

WOMEN ARE UNDER-REPRESENTED IN TECHNOLOGY

Concern has been expressed for many years about the relatively few women in the physical sciences, engineering and technology. Since the 1980s there have been a number of initiatives aimed at understanding and improving participation.

GIST (Girls in Science and Technology)

This action research project, based at Manchester Polytechnic, examined the reasons for the under-representation of girls in science and what was then craft, design and technology (CDT). The findings noted three major factors responsible for the lack of attraction of physical science for girls:

- the girls' lack of self-confidence,
- the masculine image of science, and
- the impersonal approach of science.

(Kelly 1987: 13)

In the light of the findings, practical recommendations for school policy and for individual teachers became available through a variety of publications (Harding 1983; Kelly 1987; Whyte 1986).

WISE (Women in Science and Engineering)

WISE was launched in 1984. Indicative of their findings is the comment on WISE year by Daphne Jackson, Professor of Physics at the University of Surrey:

when we started there was a feeling that these poor unfortunate girls did not know the delights of a scientific [or engineering] career, and if only we gave them the information they would all be converted. What one increasingly discovered is all the other obstacles: peer pressure in schools, parental attitude in some cases, inability to get to the apparatus because the boys grab it. Now I think we need to look at the training of teachers, and the education of boys and men.

(Jackson in Gold 1990: 42)

[handwritten margin note: Why girls were failing]

GATE (Girls and Technology Education)

This small-scale study based at King's College London, indicated that boys and girls have different perceptions of the world (Grant and Harding 1987). It noted the part played by societal attitudes which inculcate 'appropriate' sex-role behaviour and school institutional factors which lend support to gender-stereotyped assumptions. It also argued that girls would welcome greater emphasis on social aspects of technology (GATE Report, Harding and Grant 1984: 2)

SOS (Skills and Opportunities in Science for Girls)

This New Zealand project promotes conferences and workshops involving women engineers and girls aged 13–14 years.

GASAT (Girls and Science and Technology)

GASAT has held five international conferences since 1981 and a wide range of papers has been published.

WHY ARE THERE FEWER FEMALE TECHNOLOGISTS AND ENGINEERS?

A somewhat stereotypical response to this question from a male engineer might be that 'Girls are just not up to it, they do not have the right abilities and need to be re-educated.' A feminist might reply that the way technology is carried out is the main problem: it is not a question of changing the girls but changing technology education. These can be seen as extremes at the ends of a continuum of explanations that depend partly on the framework of meaning or perspectives held by the people asking and answering the questions. These perspectives are determined by the experiences, interests, beliefs, assumptions, prejudices and values of both the individuals and the communities with whom they are associated. Research concerned with the under-representation of women is both influenced by these prior perspectives (Walden and Walkerdine 1985, Walkerdine 1989) and helpful in evaluating them. The research findings are therefore part of the challenge to educators to examine their beliefs about gender and about technology.

Boys are better because of physical reasons

Are girls lacking the necessary abilities?

Some people think that there are innate differences in ability which mean that boys relate more easily to technology and the physical sciences. In *The Missing Half* (Kelly 1981), the only evidence for a biological basis for the differences centred on visuo-spatial ability. More recently Kimura (1992) has noted research indicating men are better at spatial reasoning due to hormonal influences on the brain, and also at target-directed motor skills, (finding a hidden shape in a complex drawing) and mathematical reasoning. Women, on the other hand, are better at tests of perceptual speed, memory, verbal precision tasks and mathematical calculation.

In reviewing the then current findings of psychometric tests Gray acknowledged that boys do better than girls at spatial ability tests but also asks why this should matter (Kelly 1981: 42–53). Jan Harding (1983: 18) partially answers this question when she says: 'no serious study has been reported of the skills required for the pursuit of the physical sciences. It is assumed that competence in mathematics is needed and that some form of spatial ability is involved.' Research has also shown that girls taking technical subjects increase their scores on spatial visualisation tests significantly more than those taking 'domestic' subjects. It is suggested that this shows the importance of experiencing working with materials to make three-dimensional models (Smail 1984).

GIST found that at age 11, girls and boys were achieving equally well in science but girls were not interested in physical science and boys were not interested in nature study. Both girls and boys were interested in human biology. Possible reasons for the differences in interests were given:

> Girls who showed interest in physical science at 11 . . . were more likely to have experienced a lot of tinkering activities (such as using tools, maintaining bicycles and playing with construction toys) and to have read more books and watched more television about science before starting science in school.
>
> (Smail 1984: 13)

Riggs (1992) found that at interview women engineers spoke of such tinkering in their early childhood.

Gold believes lack of ability is not the issue and that this is shown by the greater representation of women in the medical and biological sciences even though descriptive zoology and botany have given way to molecular biology and genetic engineering (Gold 1990: 42). Explanations which see girls as deficient in some way are now generally discredited. This does not mean that differences are not acknowledged, rather the differences are to be respected and valued.

Behavioural and personality differences

Studies of children at play point to differences in behaviour. Boys play in large groups, play competitive games and do not terminate the game if quarrels develop. Girls play in smaller groups and although disagreements occur less frequently than with boys, the game is abandoned when they do occur (Lloyd 1989). Piaget observed that boys make absolute rules for coping with conflict, which are rigidly interpreted. Girls are more tolerant of rules, and are more sensitive to and careful of the feelings of others. The game is less important than the relationships.

Teachers and researchers have noted differences in the way girls and boys approach problem-solving activities in technology (Riggs 1992; Sheffield Biotechnology Project 1987). Girls often take longer discussing and planning an activity and need to be encouraged to make a start. Boys on the other hand are willing to 'have a go' and adopt a 'trial and error' approach. Given time and encouragement girls can succeed equally well if not better than boys. How teachers judge such reluctance in girls will reinforce or will help to overcome lack of confidence many girls feel.

For boys science with its masculine image is an obvious choice for it is not counter to peer norms.

> For girls the decision to specialise in science almost inevitably involves both considerable thought and firm commitment. It is not an easy choice, as it involves running counter to some of the norms of the peer group in studying a subject associated with boys, so that a girl making that choice must have debated the issues and have some sense of purpose. One might expect those girls who opt for science to be mature and confident in their decision, an expectation borne out by the studies.
>
> (Head 1985: 68)

Boys aged 14 who were choosing science were found to have very cut-and-dried views on many issues compared with boys not opting for science. Adolescents who hold beliefs and values adopted from others without question are comfortable with science and technology, for school science and technology make little emotional demand and appears to offer clear, precise answers to problems. In later years

> Male scientists . . . tend to be emotionally reticent, disliking overt emotional expression in others and in themselves. They will also tend to be authoritarian, conservative and controlled in their thinking. . . . Girls choosing science are not particularly emotionally reticent or rigid in their

thinking, although they do seem to have low self-esteem in terms of being socially and sexually attractive.

(Head in Kelly 1987: 19)

Perceptions about gender

The need to prepare girls for domestic roles was the prime motivation for the development of girls' education (Attar 1990: 25–6). This is a clear indication of the influence of society's expectations on education. Now that science and technology education is available to all pupils and boys are taught aspects of home economics, we may think nothing more needs to be done. This is not the case. Science, CDT and home economics, along with the hidden curriculum of schools, have been criticised for transmitting attitudes and values which reinforce sex-role stereotyping: 'teachers have often failed to recognize the influences in society which give rise to the values and assumptions which are transmitted through the formal and informal curricula in schools' (Davies in Tomlinson and Quinton 1986: 87). Such assumptions can be illustrated by the comment from a technology teacher who told me that his department now consciously encourages girls and gave as an example the designing of ironing boards.

In addition to vocational roles there are expectations about attitudes and behaviour. Masculinity is associated with independence, self-reliance, strength and leadership. Femininity is associated with conformity, passivity, nurturing and concern for people. The GIST project found that girls and boys who endorsed sex stereotypes were least keen to learn about a technology commonly associated with the opposite sex. The most 'macho' boys were not interested in 'nature study' and girls who believed they should be 'feminine' were not interested in learning about physical science. This endorses a mainstream view that the under-representation of women in technology is related to socialisation and the influence of sex-roles (Haste 1992). Feminists further note that it is socialisation in a patriarchal society.

Some research has concentrated not on psychological and sociological factors but on educational factors, such as the influence of teacher expectations. 'Many studies in the gender and education literature imply teachers play an important part in the thwarting of girls' potential (Acker 1988: 307). Spear found that work attributed to a boy is rated higher than identical work attributed to a girl (Spear 1984). Cawthorne's research findings show that teachers were more likely to discuss boys than girls (with colleagues and with parents) and had more to say about boys (Cawthorne 1988: 14). Observations of science and CDT lessons have shown that teachers talk more to boys than to girls (Cawthorne 1988; Crossman in Kelly 1987) and that boys talk more in class than do girls. The imbalances are slightly more marked in physics than in biology, and are more characteristic of female teachers than of male teachers (Crossman in Kelly 1987: 64).

Finally a cautionary note about any discussion of perceptions about gender: 'Because hackles are easily raised by generalizations made about girls and boys and stereotyping, the issues is often avoided. This prevents us paying attention to many constructive suggestions for action' (Versey 1990: 10). People label others as chauvinist or feminist, which often means they can be dismissed and the issue ignored.

BELIEFS ABOUT TECHNOLOGY

In the last thirty years many books have been written about the influence and impact of technology on society (Borgmann 1984; Ellul 1965; Niblett 1975; Norberg-Hodge 1991; Pacey 1983). Such writers fear that technology is identified with progress, is seen as value-free and that this interpretation and its associated way of thinking trespasses into all aspects of human activity. The technological milieu with its values and standards such as efficiency, speed and reducibility, has extended until it dominates the global environment (Ellul 1965). This is sometimes described as technical determinism or technicism. It is 'the Technicist game of . . . focusing on the procedures in a technical way which ignores values, implications or consequences of the outcomes and about which there is little or no debate' (Lally 1991: 17). This is a dehumanising picture of technology, yet there is evidence that this is the picture presented in school technology (Riggs 1992).

Feminist writers argue that the impersonal, value-free image of technology is explained to a large extent by the fact that science and technology have been primarily masculine activities as is shown in recognised accounts of the history of science and technology. But writers such as Rothschild (1983), Fee (1983), Franklin (1985), Fox Keller (1985) and others present a history of technology which celebrates women's contributions and perspective. Fox Keller believes that the single most powerful inhibitor confronting women in science and technology is the widespread belief in the intrinsic masculinity of scientific thought. Radical feminists take the discussion further, seeing the masculine, analytic and mechanistic ways of thinking, so valued in science and technology, as controlling, exploitative and ultimately destructive.

CONSEQUENCES FOR TECHNOLOGY EDUCATION

Building self-confidence

As part of the GIST project girls-only science and/or technology clubs were set up in a number of schools. In the technology clubs 'feminine' tasks such as bread-making were first provided to attract girls. Later more 'masculine' projects were introduced. The defining of 'feminine' tasks and the notion of girls-only technology clubs are controversial. There is a danger that girls-only clubs, like other initiatives, may reinforce differences and so produce an effect which is actually opposite to the aims: girls' activities may be seen as separate from 'real technology'. 'The aim is not to produce girl-friendly science [or technology] for girls and to leave the traditional boy-friendly science for boys but to reform the science [and technology] education for all' (Kelly quoted in Moon, Murphy and Raynor 1989: 129).

Nevertheless the clubs indicated three contexts in which 'masculine' technology activities became acceptable to girls and there maybe useful lessons to learn. The contexts were:

1 when girls were asked to fulfil housekeeping functions, e.g. looking after the equipment;
2 when the girls worked in a co-operative group rather than as individuals;
3 when the models they produced were based on objects of concern to women, e.g. children's toys.

Women have traditionally been socialised into housekeeping, organising, supportive roles. While ensuring girls are not restricted to these roles teachers can nevertheless value the organisational skills. This can help counter the lack of confidence many girls have in their abilities.

Challenging assumptions

The first step in any process of change is to examine the attitudes and beliefs of participants. We need to consider whether our assumptions are justified or whether they are in fact prejudices. It has been noted that: 'There is evidence that teachers are reluctant to accept antisexist initiatives' (Whyte 1986: 229–31). There is often resistance and refusal even to consider the arguments. Versey makes a similar point and proposes strategies for staff development such as:

– Take recommendations from experts. Too many teachers, whilst paying lip service to equality of opportunity actively refuse to take recommendations seriously.
– Make gender central to all INSET activities and departmental plans. Appoint someone to monitor gender awareness of teachers in preparation of materials and lessons.
– Anyone who cares about the issue has a responsibility to influence key people. A student or probationary teacher can be a source of influence on an advisor, headteacher or a publisher.
– Look for new ideas and data, monitor their effect on attitudes of all pupils. Explore the influence and work of women in science [and technology] (often in the background), listen to what pupils are saying.
– Scrutinize what they are feeling.

(Versey 1990: 10–12)

Promoting equal opportunities in the workshop/classroom

Studies of play have indicated that boys are conditioned to be competitive and aggressive as in contact sports. So the workshop needs to be deliberately organised to prevent boys commandeering the best tools, material and equipment. The environment of the workshop/classroom is another feature. Female, and indeed many male scientists and engineers, have commented on the drab and unattractive nature of many laboratories and workshops. There have been improvements in recent years but there will always be a need to assess the state of rooms and to maintain an attractive and welcoming environment. 'Many young women think of science and engineering as clinical, cold, unfeminine and difficult. It is vitally important to create an atmosphere that is welcoming, warm and in which they feel comfortable' (Farmer, Godfrey and McCowan 1989). The SOS project suggests that an atmosphere can be created which encourages co-operation over competition. 'Prizes reward originality as well as the most efficient and effective solutions. The presentation of group solutions in a (family) atmosphere means that feelings of inadequacy are minimised and co-operation as well as communication skills are valued' (Farmer and McGowan 1991: 6).

Assessment techniques need to be examined for bias (Burrage 1991; Murphy 1991) and diverse and creative approaches to teaching and learning adopted. This requires teachers to promote active learning strategies (Harding 1987) and to examine content and contexts for relevance (Farmer and McGowan 1991; Kelly 1987; Versey 1990; Whyte 1986). Care should be taken to present a picture of technology which is concerned with people and not things. This is particularly important for womens' interests centre around people and relationships (Gilligan 1982).

THE BENEFITS OF EQUAL REPRESENTATION IN TECHNOLOGY

Without a feminine perspective, technology is limited and diminished. The world of women puts great stock on experience, inventiveness, spontaneity and improvisation. Diversity of skills is valued, as are personal loyalty and a sense of continuity, but these values are often marginalised in a technological process that demands innovation, constant change and personal achievement. Technological order is geared to maximising gain whereas the strategies of the women's world are more often than not aimed at minimising disaster (Franklin 1985). These strategies could be shaping the technological order in a new way.

The idea of a feminist analysis of the social and political impact of technology may be controversial, but it should be remembered that human issues are controversial (Ruddock 1983). Teacher education courses should be nurturing the skills to help student teachers discuss controversial issues and become critically reflective (Sikes 1991).

There must be change in technology education for there is a missing dimension: the perspective of half the world's population. Fox Keller suggests that the implications for science and technology when women are truly represented and add their vision to the male vision, will be a thoroughgoing transformation of the very possibilities of creative vision, for everyone (Fox Keller 1985: 175). This, then, is the challenge; technology teachers have a responsibility to nurture this creative vision.

REFERENCES

Acker, S. (1988) 'Teachers, gender and resistance', *British Journal of Sociology* 9 (3), 307–22.

Attar, L. (1990) *Wasting Girls' Time*, London, Virago.

Borgmann, A. (1984) *Technology and the Character of Contemporary Life: A Philosophical Inquiry*, Chicago, University of Chicago Press.

Burrage, H. (1991) 'Gender, curriculum and assessment issues to 16+', *Gender and Education* 3 (1), 31–43.

Cawthorne, E. (1988) 'Why it is more difficult to be a girl', *School Technology* 21 (3), 14–15.

Ellul, J. (1965) *The Technological Society*, London, Jonathan Cape.

Farmer, B., Godfrey, L. and McGowan, L. (1989) *SOS – Skills and Opportunities in Science for Girls*, Auckland College of Education, New Zealand.

Farmer, B. and McGowan, L. (1991) *SOS – Skills and Opportunities in Science for Girls, An Intervention Programme to Promote the Physical Sciences*, Auckland, GASAT (Girls and Science and Technology).

Fee, E. (1983) 'Woman's nature and scientific objectivity', in M. Lowe and R. Hubbard (eds) *Woman's Nature: Rationalizations of Inequality*, New York, Pergamon Press.

Fox Keller, E. (1985) *Reflections of Gender and Science*, New Haven, Yale University Press.

Franklin, U. (1985) *Will Women Change Technology or Will Technology Change Women?* Canadian Research Institute for the Advancement of Women.

Gilligan, C. (1982) *In a Different Voice*, Harvard University Press.

Gold, K. (1990) 'Get thee to a laboratory', *New Scientist*, 14 April, 42–6.

Grant, M. and Harding, J. (1987) 'Changing the polarity', *International Journal of Science Education* 9 (3), 335–42.

Harding, J. (1983) *Switched Off: The Science Education of Girls*, Schools Council Programme 3, York, Longman.

Harding, J. (1987) 'Tapping into talent', Paper presented to the Centenary Conference of the Royal Melbourne Institute of Technology.

Harding, J. and Grant, M. (1984) *Girls and Technology Education Project Report*, London, Chelsea College.

Haste, H. (1992) 'Splitting images: sex and science', *New Scientist*, 15 February 32–4.

Head, J. (1985) *The Personal Response to Science*, Cambridge, Cambridge University Press.

Kelly, A. (1981) *The Missing Half*, Manchester, Manchester University Press.

Kelly, A. (1987) *Science for Girls*, Milton Keynes, Open University Press.

Kimura, D. (1992) 'Sex differences in the brain', *Scientific American* (Special edition), September 1992, 81–7.

Lally, V. (1991) *Values, Technology and Science – Some issues for the 1990s*, paper no. 4, National Association of Values in Education and Training.

Lloyd, B. (1989) 'Rules of the gender game', *New Scientist*, 2 December, 60–4.

Moon, B., Murphy, P. and Raynor, J. (1989) *Policies for the Curriculum*, London, Hodder & Stoughton.

Murphy, P. (1991) 'Assessment and gender', *Cambridge Journal of Education*, 21 (2).

Niblett, W.R. (1975) *The Sciences, the Humanities and the Technological Threat*, University of London Press.

Norberg-Hodge, H. (1991) *Ancient Futures: Learning from Ladakh*, London, Rider.

Pacey, A. (1983) *The Culture of Technology*, Oxford, Blackwell.

Riggs, A. (1992) Unpublished PhD research.

Rothschild, J. (1983) *Machina ex Dea: Feminist Perspectives on Technology*, New York, Pergamon.

Ruddock, J. (1983) 'In-service courses for pupils as a basis for implementing curricular change', *British Journal for In-service Education* 10 (1), 32–42.

Sheffield Biotechnology Project (1987) University of Sheffield, Division of Education (unpublished).

Sikes, P.J. (1991) ' "Nature took its course?" Student teachers and gender awareness', *Gender and Education* 13 (2), 145–62.

Smail, B. (1984) *Developing the Curriculum for a Changing World. Girl-friendly Science: Avoiding Sex Bias in the Curriculum*, Schools Council Programme 3, Longman.

Spear, M. (1984) 'The biasing influence of pupil sex in a science marking exercise', *Research in Science and Technology Education*, 2, 55–60.

Tomlinson, P. and Quinton, M. (1986) *Values Across the Curriculum*, London, Falmer.

Versey, J. (1990) 'Taking action on gender issues in science education', *School Science Review* 71 (256), 9–13.

Walden, R. and Walkerdine, V. (1985) *Girls and Mathematics: From Primary to Secondary Schooling*, University of London Institute of Education.

Walkerdine, V. (1989) 'Femininity as performance', *Oxford Review of Education* 15 (3), 267–79.

Whyte, J. (1986) *Girls into Science and Technology*, London, Routledge & Kegan Paul.

Chapter 22

Valuing in technology

Ruth Conway and Anne Riggs

This chapter picks up issues related to 'STS' and economic awareness from previous articles and considers the values implicit in technological solutions.

BELIEFS AND PERSPECTIVES

Space technology is a symbol of man's ability. We should invest far more time and money in this type of technology which pushes back the frontiers of our knowledge and control.

What are your reactions to this statement? Your feelings will depend to a large extent on the perspectives, beliefs or constructs you hold. Faced with the same problem or situation, a person with a technocentric perspective may see a technological outcome that is different from that of a person with a humanistic perspective. When addressing the problem of bicycle theft, for example, a technocentric perspective might suggest stronger locks or an alarm mechanism. Consideration of the social aspects of the problem might suggest public use of a fleet of community bikes, active senior citizens staffing bike parks, or perhaps better sports facilities for young people to 'keep them out of mischief'. The most effective action would probably include elements from both perspectives.

People are often unaware they are operating from a particular perspective or that they hold certain values. One way people become aware is by sharing ideas, thoughts, opinions and perspectives with others. In doing this, the beliefs may be reinforced for they are seen to be justifiable and have validity, or beliefs may be changed because they are seen to be unsubstantiated assumptions or prejudices.

There is of course no guarantee that personal or communal beliefs will be examined during discussion and sharing of ideas. People may not wish to share underlying perceptions or they may be unable to access their beliefs. Some psychologists refer to *core or central* constructs/beliefs and *peripheral* constructs/beliefs (Dalton and Dunnett 1990: 31). We can fairly easily access the peripheral constructs necessary to form a judgment such as which machine is most useful for a particular function, but it may be far more difficult to access our core beliefs. These core beliefs are what constitute our personal identity and we become vulnerable to others by revealing who or what we really are. If we take the risk there is a danger that others might not like the person we really are so we pretend to be someone we are not and block any attempts to find the real us (Powell 1969).

During discussion and sharing with others it is our peripheral constructs and beliefs that we are most ready to change: we can be persuaded by the evidence of our senses or by the way others interpret and share their perceptions. Changing core constructs and beliefs is far more difficult; it is usually a life-changing process that can involve a period of self-doubt, sometimes compounded by the fear of rejection.

Closely allied to beliefs and constructs are our values. For example, imagine two people looking at a machine gun. Someone who takes a technocentric perspective may value the engineering precision of the gun and the efficient way it can propel a bullet. Someone within a humanistic perspective may only see the suffering such a piece of technology can produce and see the engineering as a negative attribution. The beliefs we hold influence what we see as important, what we consider to be of value.

In technology, pupils are constantly making decisions: 'What do I want to make?' 'Which material shall I use?' 'How should I design this artefact?' In deciding how to proceed pupils, like all designers and technologists, are making judgments. 'If I make the product out of a cheap material, it may look good, but has it limited life?' Decisions frequently involve conflicting factors, so there has to be compromise. As teachers we have a responsibility to encourage pupils to explain and justify their choices, to say what they consider to be important, to say what they consider to be of value. This will often involve trying to say which values are more important than others. For example, someone who values durability in a product may know that it would last longer if a hard wood such as mahogany was used rather than a soft wood, yet she or he knows that the use of such hardwood is destroying the forests in which the tree grows and causing hardship to the people who inhabit the forest. Perhaps the decision is taken to use a softwood or a plastic substitute because maintenance of the environment and the life of people are considered to be of greater value than appearance or durability. To make such judgments pupils need to be developing a broad base of information and a wide range of criteria.

DOING TECHNOLOGY

There are three basic questions interwoven with technological activities:

1 Which technology and why? Within a chosen group of people or a

particular environment, questions are asked about what is needed and enjoyed and what could be improved or made by technology to meet people's hopes and expectations.

2 How should the technology be carried out? Ideas and plans are developed using imagination and creativity coupled with a knowledge of natural and technical processes, properties of materials and functions of available equipment. Practical skills are then needed to turn the selected idea into a satisfying end-product.

3 How appropriate is the outcome? The effectiveness and appropriateness of both the process and the product are judged, not only from an economic and efficiency standpoint, but also by considering the impact on the various people who are affected and the environment, by addressing the question of who 'wins' and who 'loses'. This evaluation can endorse what has been achieved, or suggest modifications and/or trigger ideas for new technological activities.

These three questions are now examined in detail and examples which relate to classroom practice are included to illustrate the points.

Which technology and why?

Answering this question involves observing, listening, appreciating, researching, analysing, discerning, criticising, empathising, caring, hoping, imagining, prioritising, making and justifying choices.

We live in an environment that has been modified and changed by technology. Observation, analysis and evaluation is about *discerning the meanings, priorities and expectations that people have built into the made environment*. A start can be made in the immediate local area: a market or shopping arcade, a workshop, a playground, a kitchen, a child's bedroom, a railway station, a community centre, a cathedral. Looking around at some of the designs, Ken Baynes and Krysia Brochocka suggest questions that might be asked of those things which have been around for some time, e.g.:

– Who made it?
– Why did they make it?
– What technology did they use? Was it new and innovative at the time or was it readily available?
– Does it tell us anything about how the people who designed, made and used it looked at life? Do we look at things in the same way or have attitudes changed?
– Has it stood the test of time? Is it something we can learn from? Or has it become thoroughly obsolete?

(Baynes and Brochocka 1992: 3)

When embarking on a technology project, there must be *sensitivity to the current needs and expectations of people.* Colin Mulberg issues a prior warning:

> It is tempting to use one's own experience in the hope that this represents the experience of others. Often this may be fine, but there is no way of knowing how near or wide of the mark this type of estimation may be . . . The obvious way of finding out people's views is to ask them.
>
> (Mulberg 1992: 29)

To which must be added a second warning: don't expect the same answers from different people!

Asking is not enough: we have to be honest about *the assumptions and judgments we make when sifting the answers* that have been collected. Colin Mulberg makes this point by suggesting a simple game:

> Ask any group of school students to think of a car they have seen in the last week, but one where they have not seen the driver. They have to imagine who the driver is, what she/he is like and what could be told about her/him from the type of car they drive. . . . They will use such clues as are available to make all sorts of value judgements about the driver: their taste in music, where they go, what they do in their spare time and even what films they like . . .
>
> (Mulberg 1991)

He further illustrates the point from cases where a technology project is being considered in another culture:

> [the students] become aware that technology is used to make judgements about other people; it is easy to assume that a society without 'high' technology is more 'primitive' merely because its level of technology is generally lower than ours. Yet often a lower level of technology may still incorporate a fine balance of needs and available resources. Students soon realise that the assumptions they have made about the needs of other people must be challenged.
>
> (Mulberg 1992: 33)

Explaining our perceptions can be a very useful way to 'check out' the assumptions that have prompted our judgments.

An important part of technology education, therefore, is encouraging awareness of the assumptions that shape our analysis of needs and opportunities. However, if requirements and expectations are genuinely to be met, rather than a new 'want' imposed to increase *our* status or potential profit, then *skills of listening, empathy and caring* are also needed. Techniques for drawing up questionnaires, and visits carefully planned with clip-boards at the ready, are not enough in themselves! Pupils have to be helped to develop an ability to 'stand in another person's shoes' – and technology teachers share this responsibility with colleagues in many other curriculum areas which is one reason for developing cross-curricular work. These same skills also contribute to effective teamwork on which a successful project often depends.

One aspect of our core beliefs that influences the judgments we make is revealed in our response to the question 'How do I want to live in the future?' or more importantly, *'How do we as a group/community want to live in the future?'* There will be many occasions when pupils indicate what it is that they are aiming for and value most. 'People need other people, not machines' was one boy's response to the question whether technology should be taught in schools (Bartlett 1987: 19). Teachers need to create learning opportunities that allow pupils to explore what for them constitutes 'quality of life' and to consider in what way and for what reason other people might have different goals. A critical look at some television commercials, for example, could be one approach. Pupils might be asked what advertisers assume to be most appealing and attractive and how far this corresponds to what people in reality feel is important. Pupils may be challenged to say what excites and interests them most. Perhaps it is friendships, sport, concern for the environment, the latest in information technology or a healthy lifestyle. Anything high on the agenda of pupils will probably be reflected in their chosen projects and how they go about them.

It will also be important for pupils to come to recognise the opposite process, namely that technological innovation influences and alters the choices available to us and subtly revises our vision. For example, when choosing what to eat, technology has made possible both the production and the advertising of fast foods and convenience foods so that quick meals have become part of our everyday experience and expectation, and this can lessen our appreciation of the personally prepared shared meal. Similarly, advertisers use media technology to persuade us that fashion and the sporting of particular brand names contributes more to our status and identity than, for instance, our integrity and concern for other people.

How should the technology be carried out?

The process will involve designing, planning, discussing, imaging, making, balancing conflicting factors and values, co-operating with others, constructing, adapting, monitoring, testing and modifying.

Essential aspects of the process are *using imagination* and *creativity*. 'When a colleague asked "where do ideas come from?" of a group of seven year olds, they gave some revealing replies: "from TV, the shops, books, looking at things, asking my Auntie" ' (Baynes and Brochocka 1992: 6). Teachers of technology and religious education shared the following examples during a seminar:

'The third years started on a project in CDT to make puppets. Interest was aroused in other subject areas and soon plans for a Charity Show were underway . . .'

'Technology is all over any newspaper you open suggesting themes and projects and raising issues that require sensitive handling, cultural awareness, technical know-how, social responsibility and political decisions . . .'

'A group of unmotivated fourth-year non-exam pupils were "converted" by a visit to a school for disabled children and became completely dedicated to designing and constructing a work-table for them . . .'

'Across the third year, work in all subject areas focussed for a week on plans for a nearby Community Centre. The analyses, proposals, designs and models were worked at together in a day off timetable . . .'

'A disruptive 15 year old was wasting everyone's time until it was discovered that he was an authority on the breeding of mice and was encouraged to turn his energies to building a controlled habitat for them. A wide range of resources, knowledge and skills were called into play and coordinated to serve his chosen goal . . .'

(Conway 1990: 1–2)

Part of a technology teacher's job is to provide resources and experiences involving local areas, various cultures and different historical periods which can become sources of inspiration and ideas.

'Making' skills must be learned and practised. If these are properly mastered they not only contribute to the quality of the finished product but, most importantly, to the sense of achievement and pride when it is completed. That is what kept the fourth-year non-exam pupils, mentioned above, working in their dinner hour and after school. Learning the skills was going to make a difference to the delight with which the table would be received and used. One spinoff of design competitions is that they encourage the appreciation of products well-made and provide the incentive to acquire appropriate skills.

Because technology is concerned with the everyday world there are many constraints and often a *variety of conflicting expectations and values* which have to be taken into consideration.

An example might be the design of a new type of passenger seat for large, intercontinental aircraft. Considerations would include ergonomics (the seat must enable passengers both to sit upright and to recline in it); safety (the design must reduce the risk of injury if a crash occurs and also minimise fire hazards); aesthetics (fabrics must be not only fire-resistant but also available in attractive colours and patterns and comfortable to sit on); and economics (the cost of the seat must not be exorbitant, and its shape and size must permit a large number of passengers to be carried). The list could easily be extended by other requirements, such as the adaptability of the seat to the needs of the elderly and the physically disabled.

(Layton 1992: 49)

In many cases pupils can only be helped to judge the appropriate balance between conflicting values if they are given *opportunities to examine the concerns and commitments that give rise to the values*. The weight given to anti-pollution measures will depend on the importance given to conserving natural resources and to providing a healthy environment. Respect and affection for certain people or places will influence the risks that will be tolerated. The joy of making something in a particular material or using a special skill can override more functional considerations. Designs will reflect sensitivity to certain needs – and insensitivity to others. The teacher has a responsibility to explain and justify the choices he or she makes in selecting opportunities and in approving or not approving pupils' designs. This can prompt pupils likewise to try justifying their choices.

There are further questions around *the appropriateness of methods* used in the technological process. Ends do not justify the means!

> Present day environmental concerns such as the greenhouse effect, oil pollution and the destruction of the ozone layer, are due to the inappropriateness of the methods used to answer perceived needs. The discussion of appropriateness of the methods used is one of the main sources of controversy in the area of biotechnology. Few individuals disagree with treating Parkinson's disease or infertility but many disagree with the use of human embryos to do this.
>
> (Riggs 1990: 57)

How appropriate is the outcome?

Evaluation requires matching outcome to intention, and matching both outcome and process to criteria which have been deliberately chosen. It involves critical analysis, the balancing of priorities, and often compromising and modifying.

The selection of criteria is crucial. This is illustrated very powerfully in the following discussion:

> A beautifully constructed knuckle duster, for instance, may meet all the criteria except the fundamental one – that of desirability of the product in the first place! Selection and weighting of criteria are therefore important processes as are the values which are emphasised by the teacher. Our main point is that evaluation in school technology should reflect a wide range of types of values, with appropriate weight being given to ethical, social, political and environmental questions alongside questions about efficacy, efficiency and economics.
>
> (Ditchfield and Stewart 1987: 11)

The following description of the experience of some teachers taking part in a practical activity indicates the danger of setting criteria and then ignoring them!

> At the start of an INSET session a group of primary school teachers were given a mini-project to make a name label for themselves using the rich assortment of materials laid out round the room. Much stress was laid out on the opportunity to present oneself in a dream role; how one longed to be known and identified. After twenty minutes of feverish activity the teachers had concocted elaborate and distinctive head-gear, brooches or bracelets to communicate their name and personality. The artefacts were then evaluated. No mention was made of the original brief to reflect on the impression each hoped to make and there was no assessment of how well personality was portrayed. The criteria were speed of production, quality of material and cost. Not even aesthetic values were considered, let alone the personal values people had struggled to express.
>
> (Conway and Riggs 1992: 29–30)

In any technology project we must question not only the range of criteria being used but we must also ask *from whose standpoint are the criteria being identified and addressed?* Questions have to be asked such as:

- Which people/groups have been consulted and who has been left out?
- Who is going to gain and who will lose, not only financially, but in prestige, or in opportunities for work or for enjoyment?
- What will be the effect on how people relate to each other?
- Does it give to those who already have? Does it take away from those who have not? In other words, does it increase discrimination in the availability of cash, energy, resources and information?
- What is the long-term effect likely to be in the community and on the environment?

Some of these questions may seem to be appropriate only when looking at technology in society. However the design and technology department of the Mount School in York are explicit about *their* basic standpoint when identifying aims for technological activities:

> pupils should be enabled and encouraged:
> - to deepen their concern for the poor and those at the margins of society (both locally and internationally),
> - to deepen their awareness of the need to look after the earth's resources and ecosystem,
> - to challenge racial and gender stereotyping, and to work for genuine equality of opportunity,
> - to develop respect for others, and the skills necessary to work in groups (including the ability to be self-critical and to accept criticism from others) . . .
>
> (Pitt 1991)

ONE STRATEGY FOR MAKING VALUES VISIBLE

The starting point of a technology project will often determine whether the connections between context, technology and value judgments are brought out.

> Martin Grant argued ten years ago that a start can be made within the area of any one of the three inter-locking components of Design and Technology capability: skills, knowledge and values. Most approaches to technology teaching have an initial emphasis on either problem-solving skills (to take an example from *Design and Technology Teaching*, 1992, 24(2): 'design a model boat to travel a 4m. length of guttering') or the application of knowledge (from the same article: 'using knowledge gained from an investigation into the interrelation-ships of light and colour, make a 3D Animal Head Mask'). In both approaches, the values component is likely to receive scant attention. 'In its absence technology can too easily be seen as largely concerned with technical solutions to technical problems . . . and its relevance to people, quality of life, social problems and values become submerged and invisible.'
>
> (Conway and Riggs 1992: 28)

Martin Grant also concluded that starting within the skills or knowledge areas is most likely to alienate girls.

> A third approach – 'Design and Technology from Issues and Situations' – would change the emphasis from objects to people and from the imperso-nal to the personal.
>
> In this approach the 'values' component is highlighted and is used to guide the designing and making activities. . . . Problems connected with the issue are identified by pupils (with the use of resource material such as newspaper cuttings, reports and film) and the appropriateness of techno-logical solutions are examined. This will, of necessity, involve pupils in the making of value judgements about the nature of technology and in some cases could result in the rejection of the 'technical fix' and the proposal of social solutions. However, it is likely that some aspect . . . will be amenable to a technology input. . . . Pupils can then proceed to designing and making activities with the knowledge that *their* work has a social relevance . . . and that *their* moral decisions are controlling the direction of *their* technological activity.
>
> (Grant 1982: 8)

PROGRESSION IN VALUING

As pupils move through the key stages there should be a growing ability to justify the choices they are making with reference to values and beliefs and a growing acceptance of responsibility for the consequences of technological activity.

Levels 1 and 2

Young children start with reactions and tasks in familiar surroundings and they describe and make things on the basis of what they see and like. Later they start to notice difference and variety and are able to say why they like one thing more than another. Young pupils are also able to compare what they have made with their initial ideas and intentions and consider whether they are satisfied with the outcome.

Levels 3 and 4

The next stage is a growing readiness both to listen to what *other* people think they need and want, and to work with others on an identified task. In both cases skills of caring and sharing are encouraged, skills which are developed further as pupils try to identify some of the values which have guided their choices, particularly in relation to the expectations and preferences of other people (Harris and Sampson 1989: 68–9).

Levels 5 and 6

Sensitivity to cultural diversity will be sharpened as pupils use the skills of listening, co-operation and the discernment of values in contexts that are unfamiliar. This will contribute to their ability to evaluate the effect of technological activities (their own and others') on the environment and on peoples' quality of life.

Levels 7–10

Pupils will increasingly recognise a wide range of factors and constraints often within complex human, environmental and physical relationships. They will need to resolve conflicting demands. This will require a conscious choice of criteria and is likely to include discussion about what constitutes quality of life and an appropriate outcome.

Mature technological capability, therefore, will include the person's ability to balance conflicting factors and to justify choices in terms of their own values and beliefs and those that they have learnt to respect and appreciate in others. Finally, it is hoped that pupils will accept responsibility not only for their own well-being but also for the well-being of others and of the environment affected by their activities.

REFERENCES

Bartlett, P. (1987) *Paper 5: Pupils' Perceptions of Technology*, St William's Foundation Technology Education Project, HMSO.

Baynes, K. and Brochoka, K. (1992) 'Past, present and future', *Design and Technology Times*, Summer, 3, 6.

Conway, R. (1990) 'Values in technology? Exploring beliefs underlying its development', *NewsValues* 2 (Winter), National Association of Values in Education and Training.

Conway, R. and Riggs, A. (1992) 'Values and design and technology: exploring an issue', Conference papers IDATER.

Dalton, P. and Dunnett, G. (1990) *A Psychology for Living: Personal Construct Theory for Professionals and Clients*, London, Dunton Publishing.

Ditchfield, C. and Stewart, D. (1987) *Technology and Science in the Curriculum*, Secondary Science Curriculum Review.

Grant, M. (1982) 'Starting points', *Studies in Design Education, Craft and Technology* 15 (1), 6–9.

Harris, D. and Sampson, T. (1989) 'Group projects: issues, practice and monitoring', *Studies in Design Education, Craft and Technology* 21 (2), 68–9.

Layton, D. (1992) 'Values in Design and Technology', in C. Budgett-Meakin (ed.) *Make the Future Work*, Intermediate Technology/Longman.

Mulberg, C. (1991) 'How D & T should be driven', *News Values*, 7 (Winter).

Mulberg, C. (1992) 'Beyond the Looking Glass: Technological Myths in Education', in C. Budgett-Meakin (ed.) *Make the Future Work*, Intermediate Technology/Longman.

Pitt, J. (1991) 'Aims of D & T at the Mount', *News Values*, 7 (Winter).

Powell, J. (1969) *Why I'm Afraid To Tell you Who I Am*, Illinois, Fontane.

Riggs, A. (1990) 'Biotechnology and Religious Education', *British Journal of Religious Education* 13 (1), 56–64.

Chapter 23

Science and technology
Partnership or divorce?

Michael Harrison

At the end of the reader the issue of the relationship between science and technology originally raised by John Naughton is reconsidered. Michael Harrison looks more particularly at the relationship in terms of school subjects.

INTRODUCTION

Few people would deny that science and technology are inextricably entwined in the world. Some would argue that our culture is basically one of 'sci-tech' – in other words it is the combination of science and technology that characterises life in the developed world. But any serious student of culture will recognise that science and technology can be distinguished. Their separate historical development has led to distinctive but interacting communities of practitioners, as has been argued, for example, by Professor David Layton (1993). One useful way in which science and technology can be distinguished is by considering characteristic activities of each. Table 23.1 shows one attempt, by Professor John Sparkes, to illuminate the differences in this way.

It is the ultimate goals of science and technology that are so distinct. Science is about building up knowledge: technology is about getting things made. However, it is in the pursuit of these goals that science and technology get thoroughly mixed up. Most major projects in either area involve both scientists and technologists. The Hubble space telescope is employed in the extension of scientific knowledge – but is the product of a major (and flawed) technological effort. (You may reflect in passing how a successful outcome of such a project is often hailed as a *scientific* triumph, whereas a problem is often classified as *technological,* but that is another story!) Nuclear power is one technological solution to society's energy needs – but is based on an understanding of the nature of matter that is a consequence of scientific enquiry. Now it is quite clear that practitioners involved in such complex projects will see themselves as contributing their own specialisms within a focused context, and may not spend too much time reflecting on the nature of science and technology. But the fact that the two areas of practice exist does mean that they should be carefully distinguished if a curriculum is to include activities that separately represent them.

THE CURRICULAR CONTEXT

Science and technology are inextricably entwined in the world, but if either of them is to be taught effectively, their nature and interaction does need to be explored and understood. When national curriculum technology was being established a very clear statement was made that 'technology is an area of study in its own right, with its own distinctive objectives and content' (DES/WO 1988: 87). This is entirely consistent with the approach of Her Majesty's Inspectors who, in 1985, identified the scientific and the technological as two out of nine discrete 'areas of learning and experience' (DES 1985). Inevitably, however, technology and science consistently refuse to stay contained in the areas of the curriculum specified for them, as the following examples from the world of the classroom suggest.

Science within technology

In school as well as in the wider world, the practice of technology depends at times on applying scientific knowledge (although to classify technology simply as applied science grossly sells it short) and requires at times the carrying out of scientific processes. For example, I was once present in a primary school class where the children were making prototypes of containers in which to grow cress for sale to parents. One group of children decided that they wanted to select, for a particular function in this container, a material that would be waterproof. They organised a little experiment in which they fixed samples of various 'found' materials across the top of jars, then poured water into the cup formed by each piece of material, and timed how rapidly the water went through, if at all. These children were 8 years old, and their teacher was highly impressed. His comment was that 'If I'd asked them to design and carry out an experiment to determine how water-resistant various materials were, they wouldn't have had a clue how to start!' Two important points emerge here. The first is that this was a genuine controlled-variable experiment, carried out on a need-to-know basis: genuine science that needed an experiment to find out the unknown answer to an important question (so often, school science provokes the question from the student 'Was this supposed to happen . . .?'). An unsolicited comment made by another primary school teacher to her 7-year-old pupils was:

> The thing about an experiment is that you don't really know what's going to happen. If you knew what was going to happen then you wouldn't

really need to do an experiment, would you! Not unless you wanted to be absolutely certain of what you thought was so.

So much secondary science is locked in to replications of experiments whose intention is not discovery but confirmation, and that leads not only to the 'Is this what should happen . . .?' syndrome but also to another form of technological encounter that I shall turn to shortly.

The second point about the children testing materials for being water-proof is that this provided a superb opportunity for the teacher to assess the relevant scientific skills of these children – but is there scope for such serendipitous ticking-off of assessment targets even in a primary school where one teacher was aware of most of a given pupil's activities? The possibilities for such co-ordination and co-operation at secondary level, where science and design and technology are taught in different timetable slots by different teachers are vanishingly small in most schools.

Technology within science

I want here to pick up the issue about doing experiments 'to be absolutely certain of what you thought was so'. Some consequences of technology seem determined to make the life of science teachers difficult. For example, I remember well the convenient little circuit boards that were used for series and parallel circuit demonstrations in second year (Y8) Nuffield physics. But with every class I had to confront the issue that two 'identical' bulbs, either in series or in parallel, which were supposed to glow equally brightly as each other to prove a point about current, showed quite different brightnesses. The very reinforcement of the teaching point was subverted by the observed behaviour of the equipment. The reason for the behaviour was, of course, that these were cheap bulbs manufactured to a loose but appropriate toler-ance within the constraints of a profit-making technological production line. The bulbs were not intended to be identical, and certainly not intended to help 'prove' some aspect of electrical current flow. But try explaining that last period on a Friday.

This kind of experience is about using technological artefacts in a scientific context. It illustrates the point that the conceptual models of the kind used in school science tend to be simplified and idealised. The truth is that the real world is far more complicated than simplified models suggest – and children are naturals at asking the difficult questions that give the lie to the simplified models.

Given the existence of this problem about a mismatch between science as taught and the realities of the physical universe, some teachers of science advocate the teaching of much science in a technological context – so that pupils can perceive the science as being relevant and related to their own lives. Some commercially-produced science teaching material has taken just

Table 23.1 Some differences between science and technology

SCIENCE (Goal: the pursuit of knowledge and understanding for its own sake)	TECHNOLOGY (Goal: the creation of successful artefacts and systems to meet people's wants and needs)
Key scientific processes	Corresponding technology processes
Discovery (mainly by controlled experimentation)	Design, invention, production
Analysis, generalisation and the creation of theories	Analysis and synthesis of designs
Reductionism, involving the isolation and definition of distinct concepts	Holism, involving the integration of many competing demands, theories, data and ideas
Making virtually value-free statements	Activities always value-laden
The search for, and theorising about, causes (e.g. gravity, electromagnetism)	The search for, and theorising about, new processes (e.g. control; information; circuit theories)
Pursuit of accuracy in modelling	Pursuit of sufficient accuracy in modelling to achieve success
Drawing correct conclusions based on good theories and accurate data	Taking good decisions based on incomplete date and approximate models
Experimental and logical skills	Design, construction, testing, planning, quality assurance, problem-solving, decision-making, interpersonal and communication skills
Using predictions that turn out to be incorrect to falsify or improve the theories or data on which they were based	Trying to ensure, by subsequent action, that even poor decisions turn out to be successful

Source: Sparkes (1993: 36)

this approach (for example the Association for Science Education's Science and Technology in Society (SATIS) material) – not least because 'pure' science is perceived as being unattractive and somewhat difficult for many pupils. This is a perfectly valid way of finding starting points for science education, but the danger is that it represents technology as applied science, which it is not. Technology certainly does apply scientific knowledge as is appropriate, but it uses other kinds of knowledge and has to take account of a whole range of criteria that determine the nature of 'success', as Table 23.1 indicates. The danger of setting out to teach science through technological contexts is that it sells technology short.

THE RELATIONSHIP WITHIN THE NATIONAL CURRICULUM

The supplementary guidance provided for the chair of the national curriculum design and technology working group set up in 1988 pointed out that

> Science and technology are intimately linked . . . and their teaching needs to be properly coordinated. Scientific concepts and knowledge relating to materials, energy and power are particularly relevant to technology. The working group should where appropriate link its recommendations with those of the science working group so that they complement rather than duplicate one another.
>
> (DES/WO 1988: 91, 92)

This turned out to be an idealistic but impractical suggestion as science and design and technology were separately defined and implemented. However, the review initiated in 1992 was required to focus more closely on specifying scientific knowledge. The 1992 proposals (DFE/WO 1992) identify links between the design and technology programmes of study and those of science (as well as maths and art). So there is now an attempt to achieve some level of co-ordination.

THE REALITIES

The harsh reality is that the needs of science education and the needs of design and technology education do not lend themselves to a neat co-ordination. Some teaching schemes actually set out to produce co-ordinated modules that cover certain subject matter of science and technology in a way that minimises duplication, and that is one way of tackling the job. But in the great majority of schools, science and design and technology are taught in separate timetable slots by separate departments. Each department has its own beliefs and needs about what should be taught when, and this frequently mitigates against co-ordination. It is not just a question of departmental narrowness of mind, either. There are profound questions about whether pupils can transfer and apply knowledge learnt in one context (e.g. science lessons) to another (e.g. the designing of an artefact). The issues involved in the debate over the application of knowledge are too complex to be dealt with successfully here, but they can, perhaps, be indicated by the use of an example taken from a project carried out for a GCSE CDT: technology examination. (For a fuller consideration of the problems of the application of knowledge see Hennessy and McCormick pp. 94–108 in this volume.)

The student in question was year 11 and was continuing at GCSE level the separate study of science and technology which she had pursued throughout secondary education. When faced with the need to identify and carry out a long project as part of her technology assessment, she decided that she wanted to make an anemometer. The reason she gave for this was that she had become interested in the weather through work she had done in an earlier humanities project. So she thought it would be interesting to monitor wind speed. All this happened around the time of several significant wind storms in the UK, so it is interesting to note how sufficient interest to embark on a particular technological project was generated in another subject area, but also prompted by experience from life. Perhaps there is a clue here as to how students in general and girls in particular might find things scientific and technical to be of more interest.

A letter to the BBC weatherman, Ian McAskill, provided some useful clues as to where to find information, but also brought encouragement to select a simpler task, such as rainfall measurement. This was a wise suggestion indeed, because of the relative complexity of windspeed and rainfall measuring devices, but it was windspeed that was the burning issue, so it had to be tackled. Much helpful information was subsequently obtained, and the decision was to build a three-cup rotating anemometer using a digital transducer whose output would be converted to an analogue voltage which would then be used to drive a display. This was an entirely sensible intention but, at that point, although she had studied physics (including electrical circuits) for four years, there appeared to be little knowledge that she was able to bring to bear at even the broadest level of circuit design. The whole instrumentation circuit had to be treated as a unique design problem, with knowledge taught on a need-to-know basis. What she did know about electrical circuits just did not seem transferable. The evidence is that this finding is not uncommon, and it tells us that students compartmentalise and localise knowledge in a way that mitigates against any grand schemes to co-ordinate what is done in different areas of the curriculum. The frustrating thing, from the point of view of coping with an overcrowded curriculum, is that work that relates to one area of the curriculum does occur in other areas. In such cases a primary school teacher (such as the one who noted his children experimenting with waterproof material) has at least the advantage of seeing all that the children do. In the case of the anemometer builder, there was much experimentation that went on in the building of the device that was good and assessable science process, but the science teacher was totally unaware of it and the technology teacher was not looking to assess it.

Looking back over this anemometer project, it is possible to map what was achieved against the science (1991) and design and technology (proposed 1992) attainment targets. The two design and technology attainment targets each contain strands. Within designing the strands are:

- strand a: investigating, clarifying and specifying the design task;
- strand b: modelling, developing and communicating design ideas.

Within making:

- strand a: planning and organising making;
- strand b: using a variety of materials, components, tools, equipment and processes to make products safely;
- strand c: testing, modifying and evaluating.

The evidence is that this student achieved the following levels within these strands:

- Designing (a): 10iii, (b): 7
- Making (a): 9 (b): 7 (c): 8

Within science

- AT1: scientific investigation L6
- AT5: Energy and its effects L5 b (part) c (part) L6 b (part)

The first obvious difference is the level of 'attainment' achieved. However, a closer look at just one detail of this demonstrates the quite different kind of knowledge that science and design and technology courses tend to look for. The primary transducer in the anemometer was a reflective opto-switch that was pointed at a vane rotated by the cups. This opto-switch, therefore, produced a series of pulses whose frequency was determined by the speed of the wind. Science AT5 level 5 requires a student to 'understand the rule governing the reflection of light at plane surfaces'. Now it is quite clear that a reflective opto-switch applies this rule. But the realities of getting it to work were far more complex than just pointing it straight at the reflecting surface, as the physics rule might suggest. The simple rule was just a starting point. It then had to be realised that, purely in optical terms, there was an optimum distance between the switch and the reflecting surface, that the nature of this surface mattered and that the level of ambient light was a problem. So the physics rule was a starting point and the reality of applying it was far more complex.

CONCLUSION

Whilst the message is one of caution and moderation as to what pupils are likely to carry over from one teaching context to another, the profound links between science and technology scream out to be made. At the level of understanding and development of the vast majority of students, and within the secondary system that socialises students into compartmentalised subjects, we have to be highly circumspect in what we can expect to be achieved. But the revised design and technology proposals do offer the possibility of recognising links across the subject boundaries. For me, what is most important is that teachers should take whatever opportunity arises to talk with each other about areas of commonality. There is often reluctance to make such cross-department moves. The truth is that each has a perspective that can enhance the other's understanding, which will be to the ultimate benefit of the pupils.

REFERENCES

DFE/WO (Department for Education and Welsh Office) (1992) *Technology for ages 5 to 16 (1992) Proposals of the Secretary of State for Education and the Secretary of State for Wales*, London, HMSO.

DES (Department of Education and Science) (1985) *The Curriculum from 5 to 16. Curriculum Matters 2: An HMI Series*, London, HMSO.

DES/WO (Department of Education and Science and Welsh Office) (1988) *National Curriculum Design and Technology Working Group: Interim Report*, London, DES/WO.

Layton, D. (1993) 'Science education and praxis: the relationship of school science to practical action', in R. McCormick, C. Newey and J. Sparkes (eds) *Technology for Technology Education*, Addison-Wesley Publishing Company.

Sparkes, J. (1993) 'Some differences between science and technology' in R. McCormick, C. Newey and J. Sparkes (eds) *Technology for Technology Education*, Addison-Wesley Publishing Company.

Acknowledgements

Chapter 1 'What is "technology"?', by John Naughton, from The Open University (1988), T102 Living with Technology, Unit 1, Introduction, reproduced by permission of The Open University.

Chapter 2 'Technological capability', from *In Place of Confusion: Technology and Science in the School Curriculum* (1985), Chapter 2, by Paul Black and Geoffrey Harrison, reproduced by permission of The Nuffield-Chelsea Curriculum Trust.

Chapter 3 'What is design and technology education?', from *Teaching Design and Technology* (1992), Chapter 2, by John Eggleston, reproduced by permission of Open University Press.

Chapter 4 *Technology in the National Curriculum: Getting it Right* (1992), by Alan Smithers and Pamela Robinson, reproduced by permission of The Engineering Council.

Chapter 6 *The Assessment of Performance in Design and Technology* – the final report of the APU design and technology project 1985–1991, by R. Kimbell *et al.*, reproduced by permission of the Schools Examinations and Assessment Council.

Chapter 7 'The importance of graphic modelling in design activity', by S. W. Garner, from *Teaching and Learning Technology* (1993), edited by R. McCormick, P. Murphy and M. Harrison, reproduced by permission of Addison-Wesley Publishers Limited.

Chapter 10 'A critique of the design process', by John Chidgey, from *Design and Technology Teaching* 22 (1), the Journal of the Design and Technology Association, reproduced by permission of DATA.

Chapter 12 'Planning for capability and progression for design and technology in the national curriculum', by Pat Doherty, John Huxtable, Jane Murray and Ed Gillet, from *Design and Technology Teaching* 23 (2), the Journal of the Design and Technology Association, reproduced by permission of DATA.

Chapter 13 'Technology project work', by David Barlex, from *Technology in Schools*, Module 4, Units 5–6 of ET887 (1987). Crown copyright. Reproduced by permission of the Controller of Her Majesty's Stationery Office.

Chapter 15 'Teaching STS: games, simulation and role-play', by Joan Solomon, from *Teaching Science, Technology and Society* (1993), by John Eggleston, reproduced by permission of Open University Press.

Chapter 17 '"One in five": design and technology and pupils with special educational needs', from *Design & Technology – One in Five* (1993), written and published by the Curriculum Council for Wales. Reproduced by permission of the publishers.

Notes on sources

Chapter 1 Open University (1988) *T102 Living with Technology*, Unit 1, Introduction, Milton Keynes, Open University Press.

Chapter 2 P. Black and G. Harrison (1985) *In Place of Confusion: Technology and Science in the School Curriculum*, Chapter 2, London, Nuffield-Chelsea Trust.

Chapter 3 J. Eggleston (1992) *Teaching Design and Technology*, Chapter 2, Buckingham, Open University Press.

Chapter 4 A. Smithers and P. Robinson (1992) *Technology in the National Curriculum: Getting it Right*, London, The Engineering Council.

Chapter 5 Commissioned for this volume.

Chapter 6 Assessment of Performance Unit (eds) (1991) *The Assessment of Performance in Design and Technology*, London, SEAC.

Chapter 7 S.W. Garner (1993) 'The importance of graphic modelling in design activity', in R. McCormick, P. Murphy and M. Harrison (eds) *Teaching and Learning Technology*, London, Addison-Wesley.

Chapter 8 Paper delivered at DATER 91, the Design and Technology Research Conference at Loughborough University, 1991.

Chapter 9 Paper delivered at IDATER 92, the International Design and Technology Conference at Loughborough University, 1992.

Chapter 10 Chidgey, J. (1990) 'A critique of the design process', *Design and Technology Teaching* 22 (1).

Chapter 11 Commissioned for this volume.

Chapter 12 P. Doherty, J. Huxtable, J. Murray and E. Gillett (1991) 'Planning for capability and progression for design and technology in the national curriculum', *Design and Technology Teaching* 23 (2).

Chapter 13 D. Barlex (1987) 'Technology project work', Module 4, Units 5–6 in *ET887 Technology in Schools*, Milton Keynes, Open University Press.

Chapter 14 Paper presented at the Design and Technology Education Research Conference, Loughborough University, 1990.

Chapter 15 J. Solomon (1993) *Teaching Science, Technology and Society*, Chapter 6, Buckingham, Open University Press.

Chapter 16 Based on R.A. Kimbell (in press) 'Assessing technological capability', *Proceedings of INCOTE 92*, Weimar, Germany and 'Progression in learning and the assessment of pupil attainment', in *Innovations in Science and Technology Education*, Paris, UNESCO.

Chapter 17 Curriculum Council Wales (1993) 'Design & Technology – one in five: D & T and pupils with special educational needs', Cardiff, Curriculum Council for Wales.

Chapter 18   Paper presented at the Design and Technology Education Conference at Loughborough University, 1988.

Chapter 19   Commissioned for this volume.

Chapter 20   Based on M. Jephcote and D. Hendley (1991, 1992) 'Developing economic and industrial understanding through design and technology', in J.S. Smith (ed.) *Papers of the Conference in Design and Technology Educational Research and Curriculum Development*, Loughborough, Loughborough University of Technology, and 'Making links between design and technology and economic understanding', *Economics* (Summer).

Chapter 21   Commissioned for this volume.

Chapter 22   Commissioned for this volume.

Chapter 23   Commissioned for this volume.

Index

go/no-go gauges 166,171
graphic modelling 68–72,79
'Great Debate' 199–203,204
grid papers 185
group composition 149,150
group size 149
group work 144–50; assessing 140,149;
   benefits 146–7; negative effects 148;
   planning 136,149–50; problem
   solving 105–6; problems 147–8;
   project work 134–6; qualities
   135–6,145
guides 185
guillotines, rotary 187

hand-drill stand 188
handles, modifying 188–9
hazards, industrial 158–9
holistic judgments 168–9,170–1
holistic 'template' 120,122–3
home economics 45
human activity, technology as 8–12
human capability 14–16
hybrid car 18

imaging 62–4,65,82–3; food 83–5,87–8;
   see also modelling
industry 213–14; decision-making
   156–9; group work 146,147–8; STS
   152–60; see also economic and
   industrial understanding
information technology (IT) 46–7
innovation-driven design and
   technology 78
instrumentalism 201–2
integration 33–4,146
intellectual difficulties 181–2
interaction of mind and hand model
   61–7; assessment of capability 65–7;
   imaging 62–4; modelling 64–5
invention 155
investigation folder 61

Japan 206
judgment in assessment 166–9,170–1

Kenwood food mixer 39
knobs, modifying 188–9
knowledge 7–8,235; problem solving
   97–9, 104–5; scientific 8–9; skills,
   values and 23,24,113–14; subjects as
   forms of 36–7; technological 10–12;
   transferring 97–9,242–4

knowledge bases, project briefs derived
   from 132,133

labels on equipment, tools etc. 187
language of technology 39
large-print rulers 185
lathes 43
learning: benefits of group work 146–7;
   categories of and project work 125–6;
   modelling and 86–7; situated 95–7,
   98–9,101,103; tasks for 16–19
learning difficulties see special
   educational needs
liberal humanism 200–1,204
light-box 188

machinery 7,8,12
making 52,175
market-led design and technology 78
mathematics 96–7
matter, particle model of 76–7
measuring boards/sticks 189
medicine 37
metacognitive strategies 105
modelling 64–5; cognitive development
   85–6; defining 74,82–3; in design and
   technology 79–80; with food 82–8;
   functions of 83–4; graphic 68–72,79;
   as representation 84–5; in science 80;
   teaching and learning 86–7; see also
   imaging
motorway-building 18–19
music 195

nailing, help with 189
national curriculum 42,111–12,200;
   assessment 163–5,167–8; creation of
   for technology 45–53; defining design
   and technology 20–1,22; EIU 211;
   science/technology relationship
   239,242–5; technology 36–41; see also
   attainment targets, programmes of
   study, statements of attainment,
   Statutory Order
National Curriculum Council (NCC)
   consultation report 49–50,50
National Society for Education in Art
   and Design (NSEAD) 43
needs analysis 229–31
norm-referenced assessment 162

Order for technology see Statutory
   Order